First Moments

Newborn Pictures
& Mom Stories

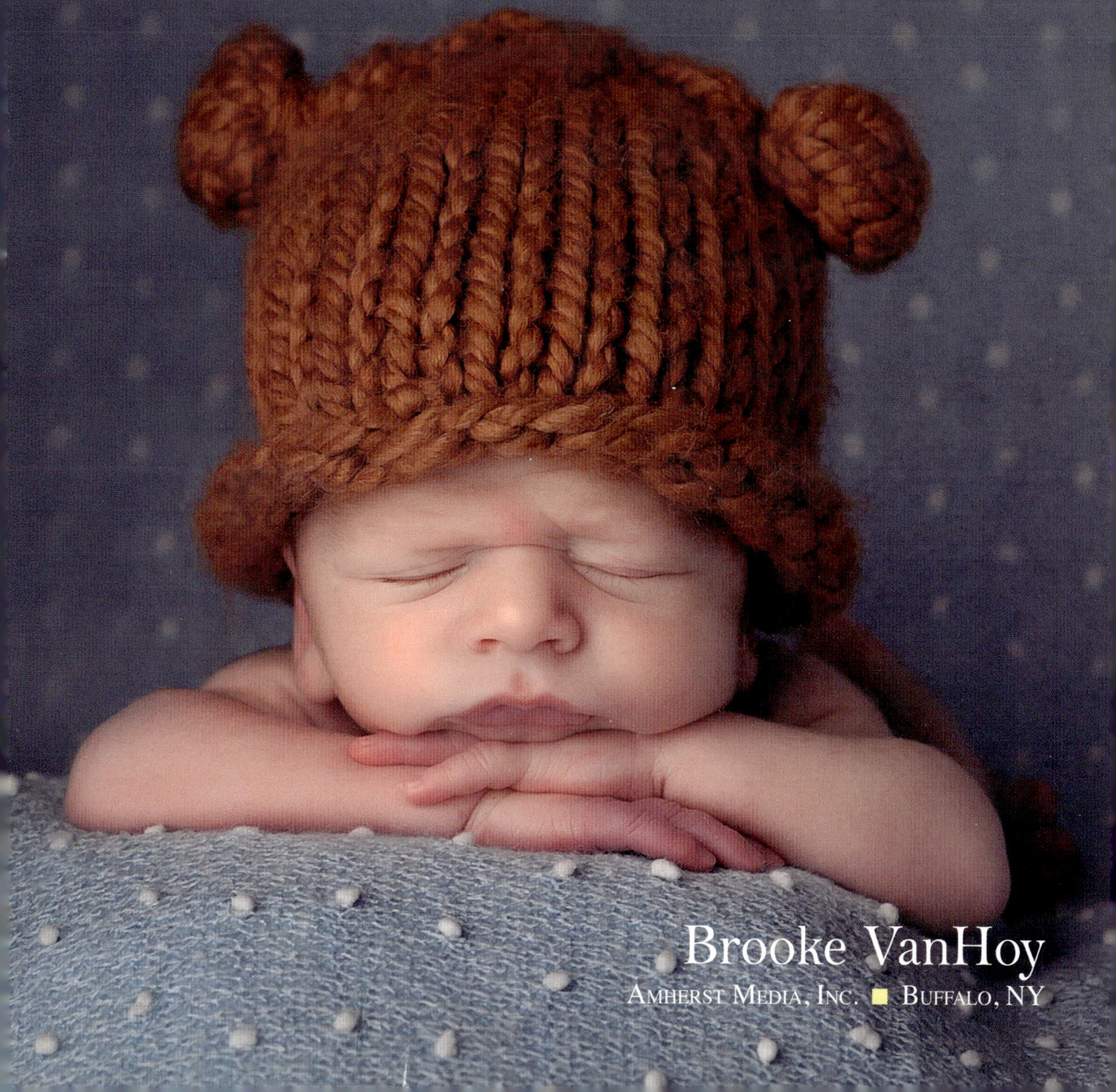

Brooke VanHoy
Amherst Media, Inc. ■ Buffalo, NY

To my children, thank you for being the reason I push myself every day to be the best I can. I love each of you more and more every day. To my family and friends, thank you for all of the help you have been. From watching the kids, proof reading my book or just being there for me to vent. I love you all. To all the moms. I thank each and every one of you for trusting me with your newborn portraits. This book truly would not be possible without you. I'm just glad I am able to help tell your stories. Lastly, to Adam: Thank you for all your support, love, and convincing me to respond to the email that I just knew couldn't be real. This book honestly wouldn't be happening if it wasn't for you.

Published by:
Amherst Media, Inc.
PO BOX 538
Buffalo, NY 14213
www.AmherstMedia.com

Publisher: Craig Alesse
Senior Editor/Production Manager: Michelle Perkins
Editors: Barbara A. Lynch-Johnt, Beth Alesse
Acquisitions Editor: Harvey Goldstein
Associate Publisher: Katie Kiss
Editorial Assistance from: Carey A. Miller, Roy Bakos, Jen Sexton-Riley, Rebecca Rudell
Business Manager: Sarah Loder
Marketing Associate: Tonya Flickinger

ISBN-13: 978-1-68203-364-7
Library of Congress Control Number: 2018936003
Printed in the United States of America
10 9 8 7 6 5 4 3 2 1

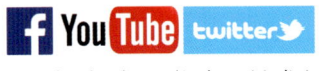

www.facebook.com/AmherstMediaInc
www.youtube.com/AmherstMedia
www.twitter.com/AmherstMedia

Contents

PORTRAITS & STORIES

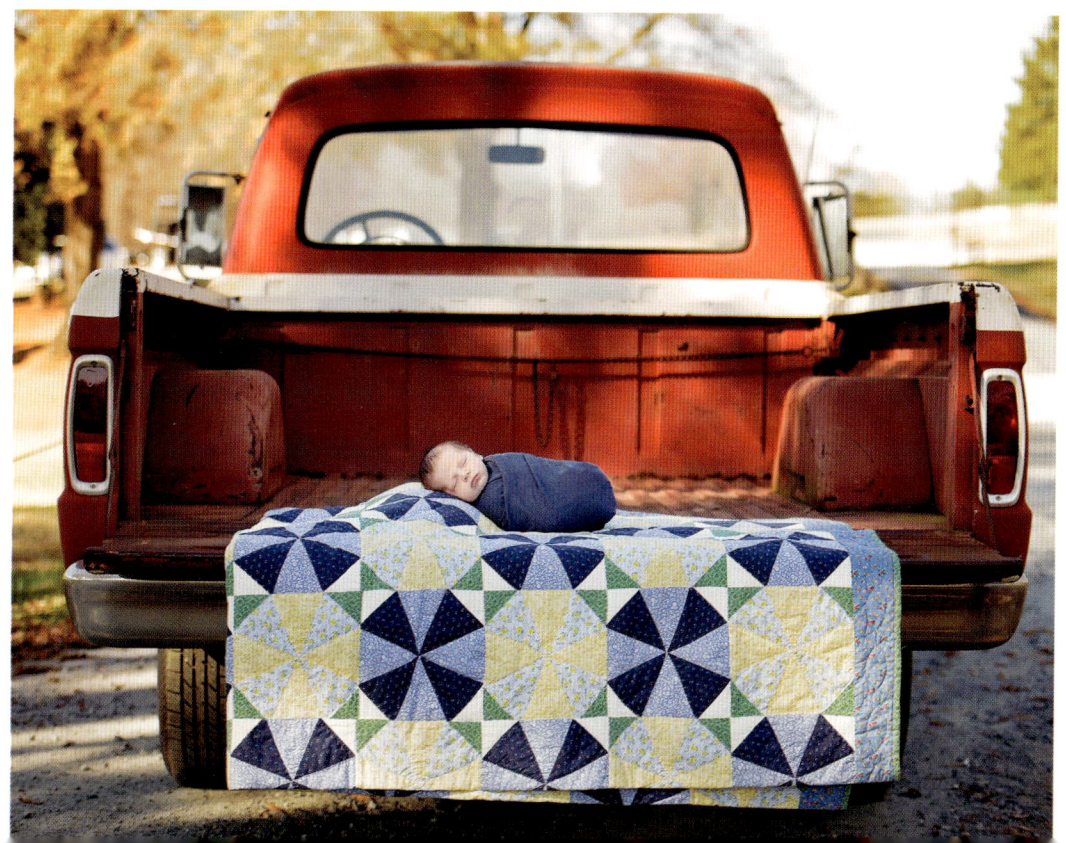

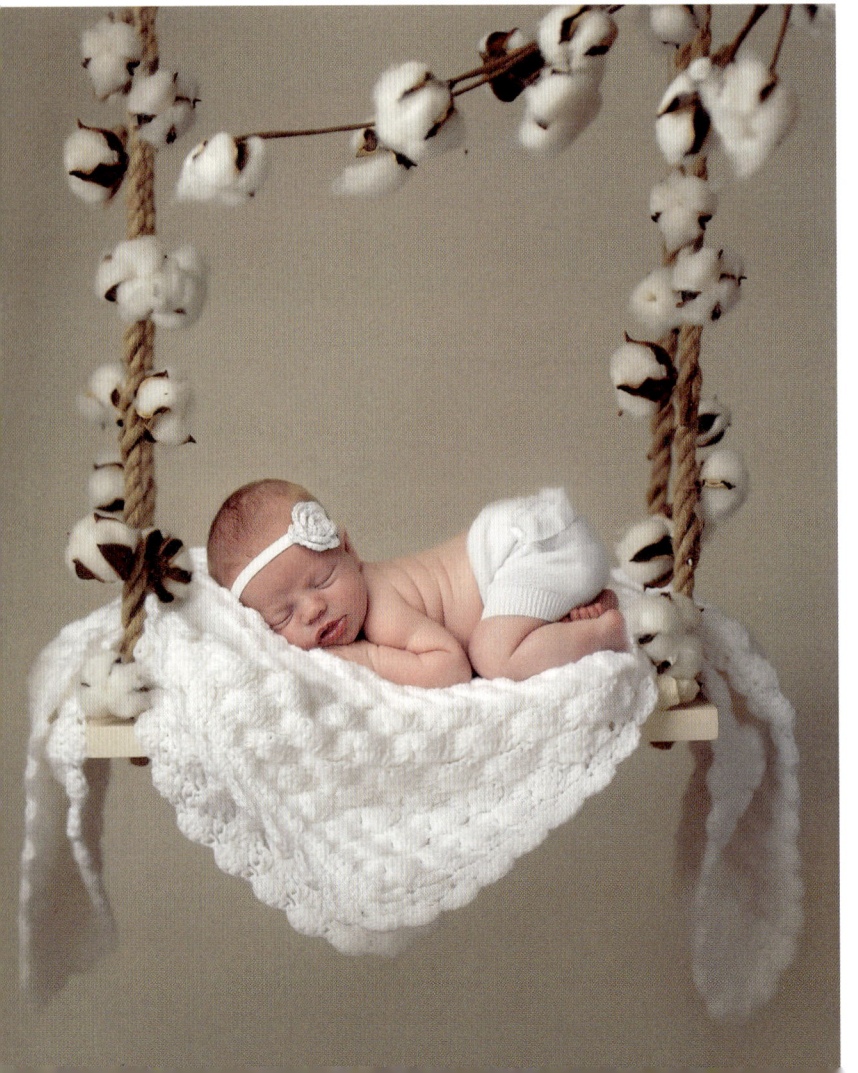

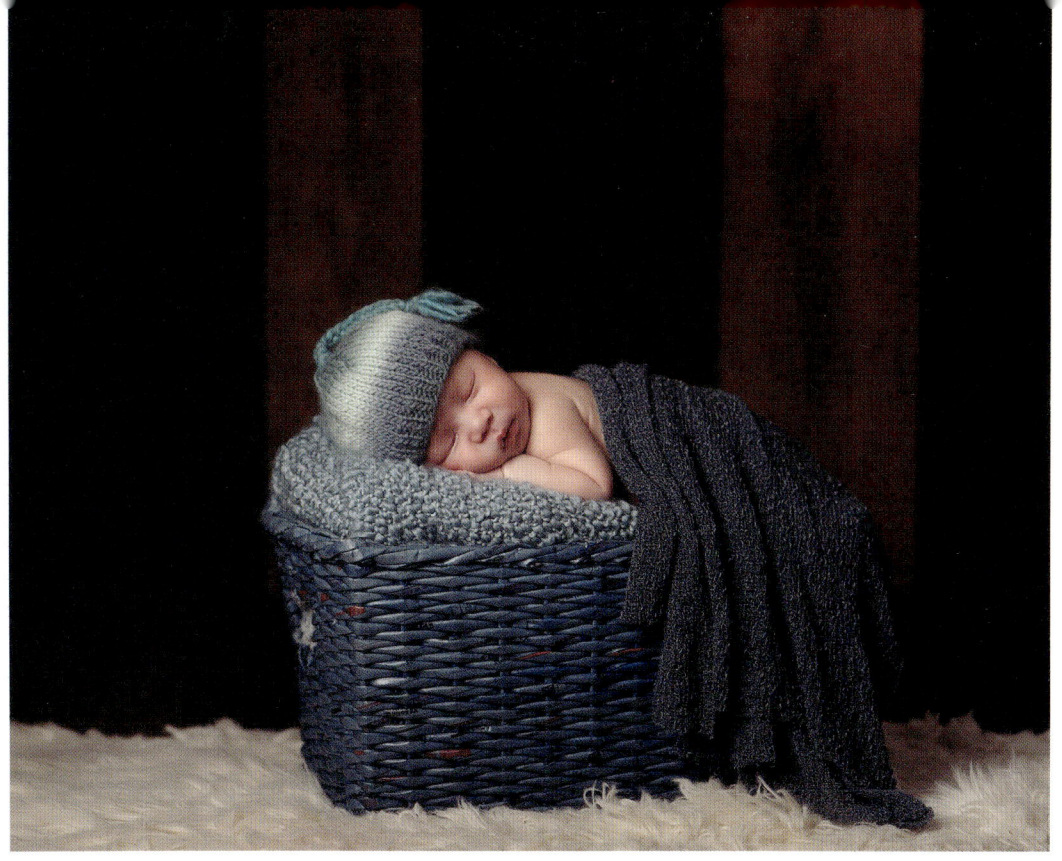

About Brooke

Author Brooke VanHoy is a Photographic Craftsman and a Certified Professional Photographer. She is a member of the Professional Photographers of America and Professional Photographers of North Carolina.

Brooke's passion for photography started at a young age. She was the one with the camera growing up, and has always wanted to work with children. She went to college for elementary education, but when her older son was born, her hobby started to turn into something more. After a few years of learning and growing, she opened a business.

Brooke received the Entrepreneurial Award in her county in 2016, a Loan Image at the International Print Competition in 2015, and has had numerous images entered into the General Collection over the past few years. She also won First Place in the Non-Portrait Wildlife category at the North Carolina print competition in 2017. One of her award-winning images was even published in *Professional Photographer* in 2016.

Brooke lives in Winston Salem, NC, and is the owner of Happy Heart Studio. She specializes in studio portraits of newborns and small children and brings bright and bold colors to the classic studio portraits. Brooke teaches workshops on newborn photography and does speaking engagements on the topic as well.

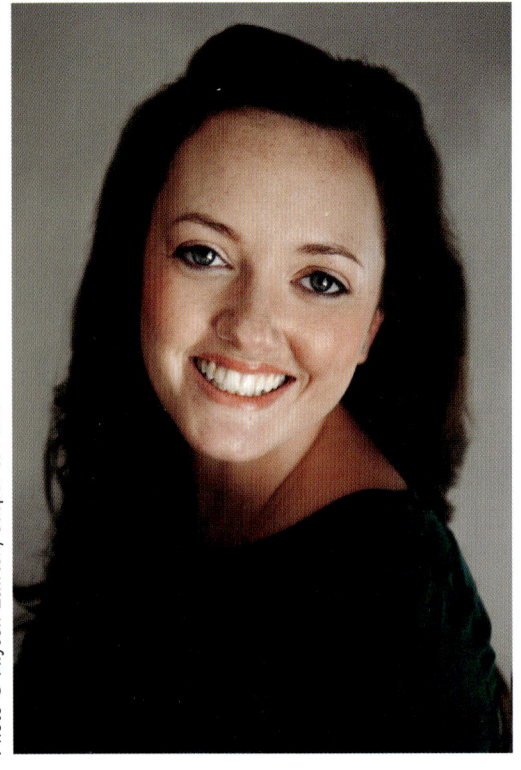

Photo © Alyson Lawton, Jasper & Fern.

Introduction

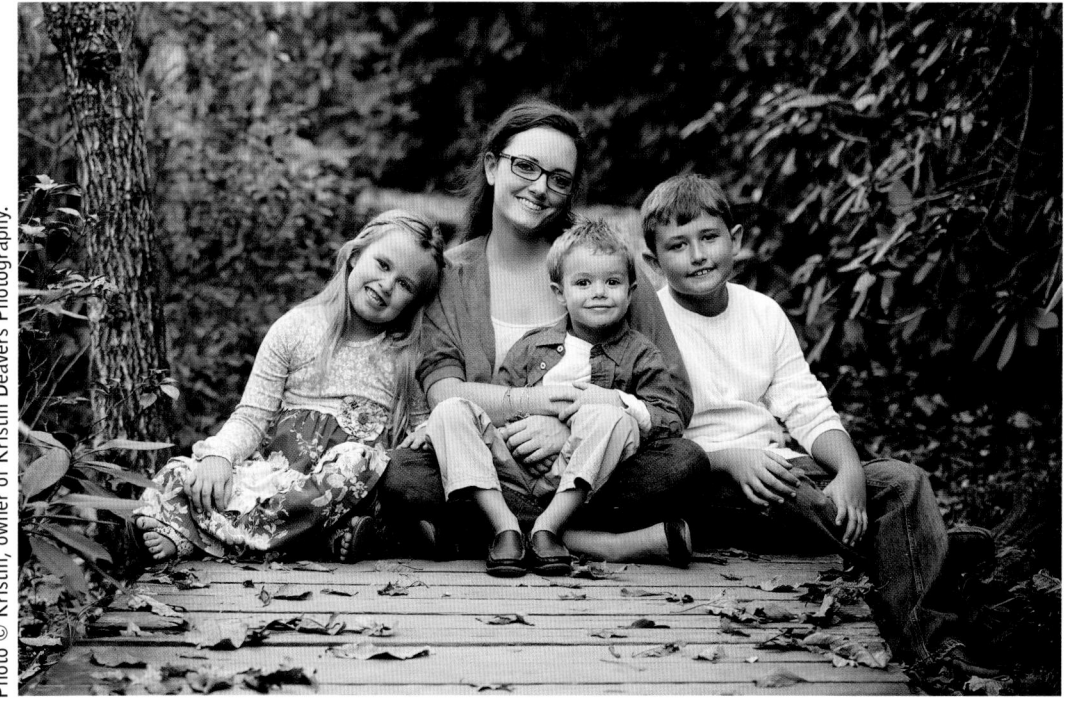

When you first find out you are pregnant, there are so many emotions that run through you. For some, it's excitement after trying for so long, and for others, it's fear after becoming pregnant again after a loss. Some moms have amazing pregnancies, while others are sick every day. There are tons of laughs—like the time you laughed so hard you peed your pants (I was glad to find out I wasn't the only one who had done that!), and tons of tears . . . even if it's just over a Disney movie commercial. Then there's the wonder of who this little person you are growing will end up being. Every pregnancy story in this book is different, but the one thing that remains a constant is the love these moms have for their children!

Portraits & Stories

OLIVE

"Holding Olive for the first time was amazing!
She was absolutely perfect, and I could finally
see all of her and touch her and kiss her. I have
no idea how many times I kissed her little face
in the first few hours!"

—Jessica, mom of Olive,
born December 6th, 2014

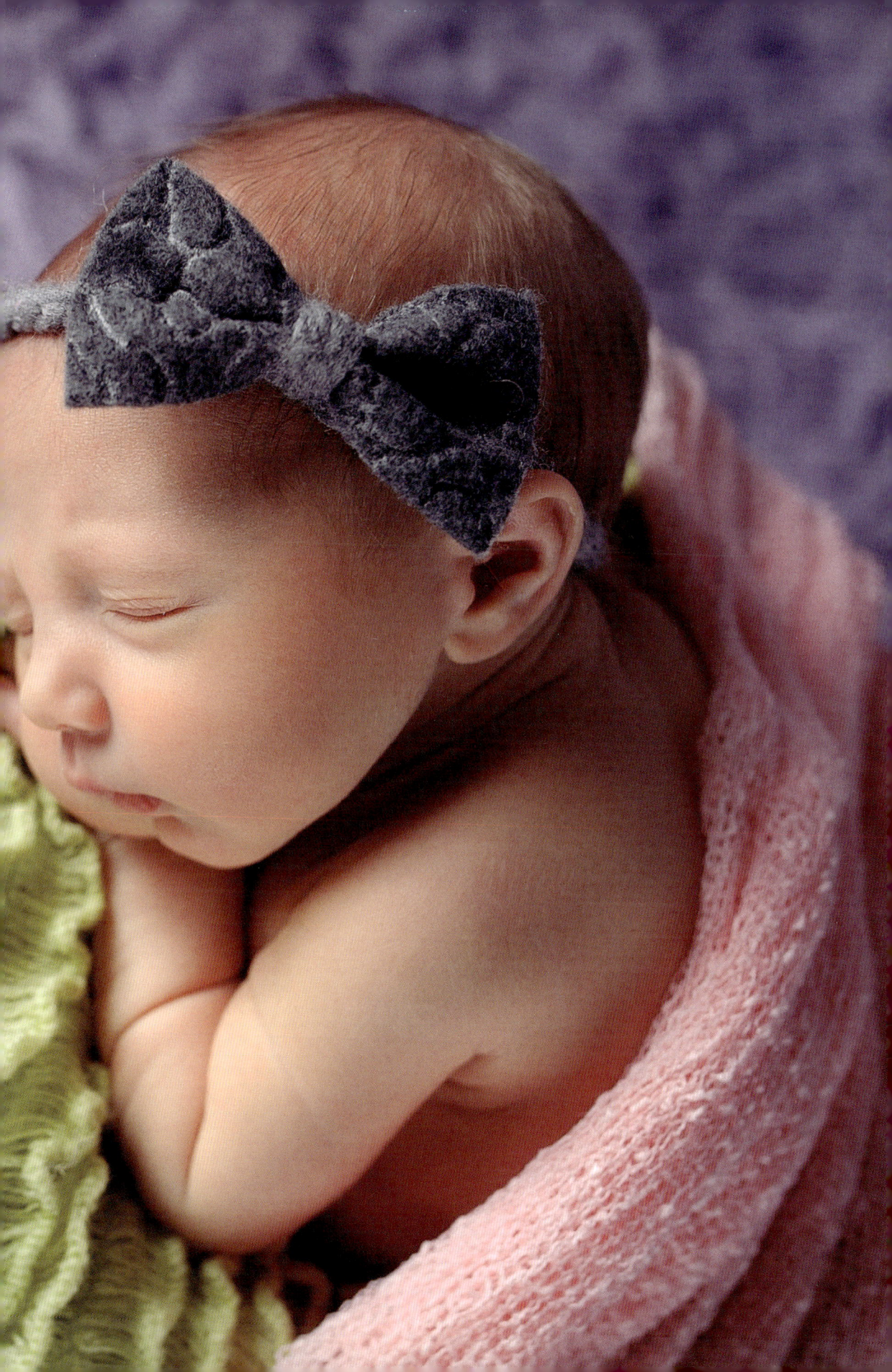

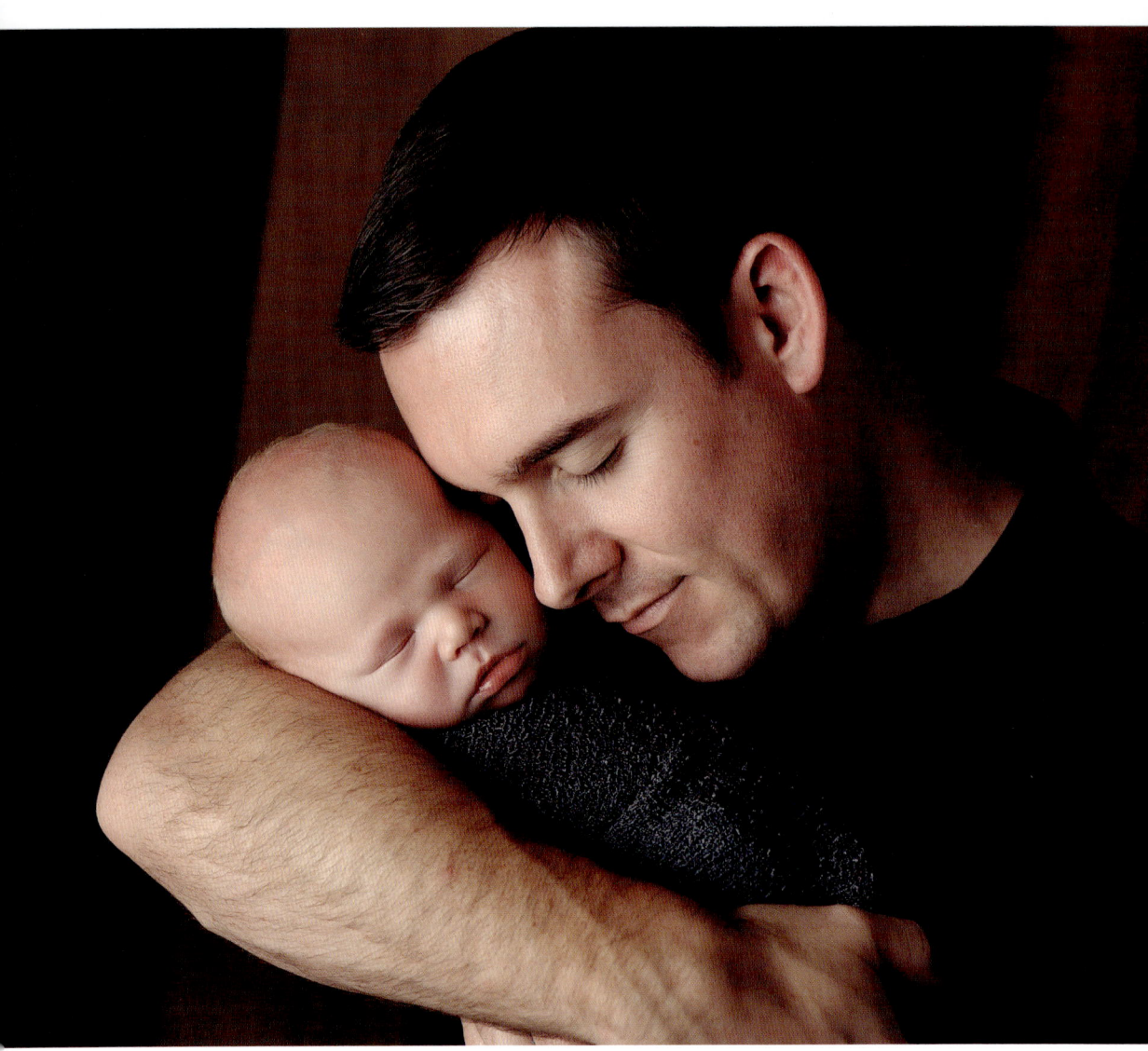

MASON

"I felt nothing but pure joy when I saw my husband with our son for the very first time."

—Beth, mom of Mason, born June 20th, 2015

ADALYNN

"My pregnancy was a complete surprise. When we first decided to have children, we lost an unexpected pregnancy very early. Losing that sweet baby helped us realize we were ready for children. We tried for about six months with no luck, and I had multiple ovarian cysts. We'd just about given up when I took a pregnancy test and it was positive. Nothing compares to the joy I felt running to my husband to tell him we were pregnant."

—Holly, mom of Adalynn, born June 25th, 2013

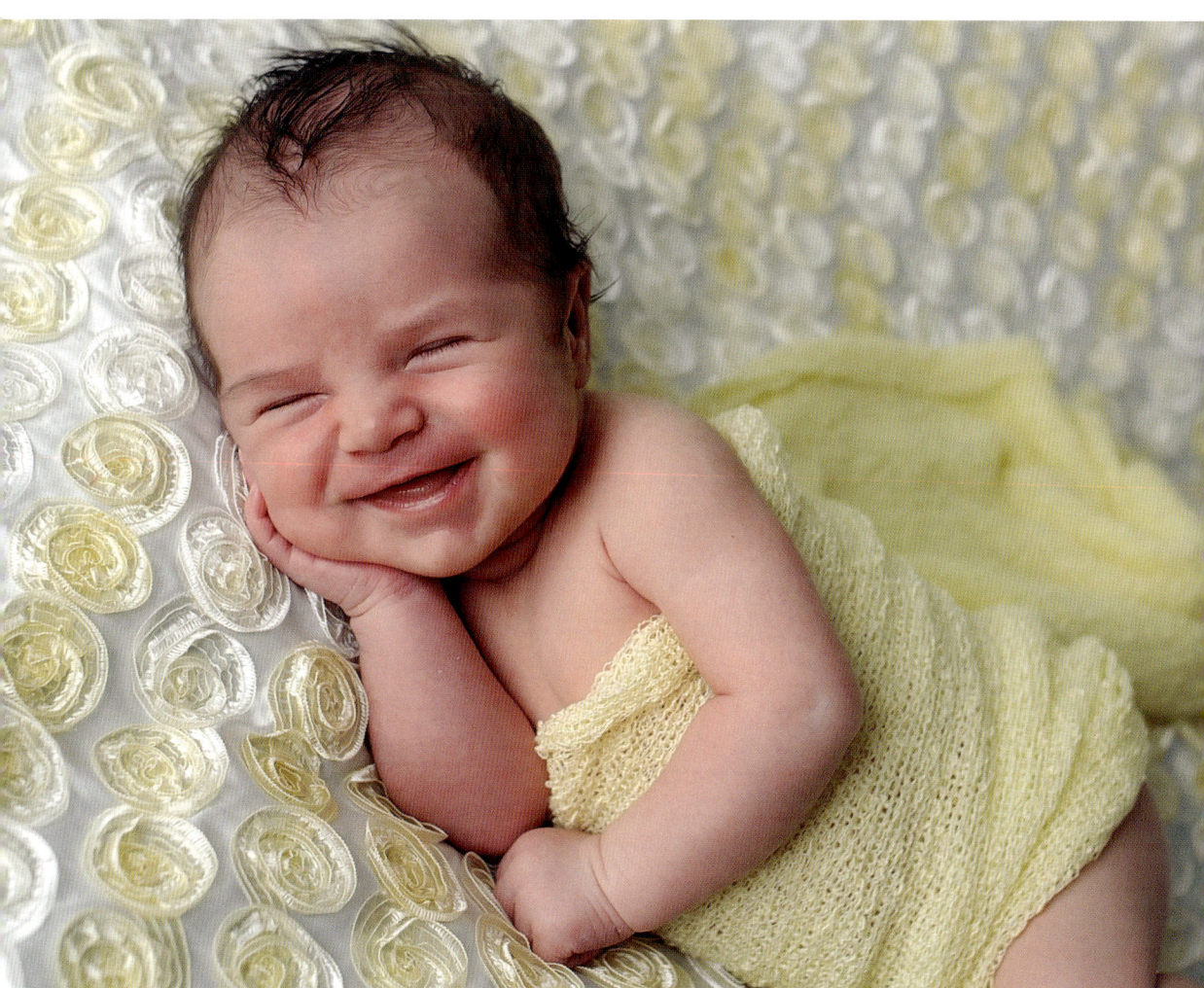

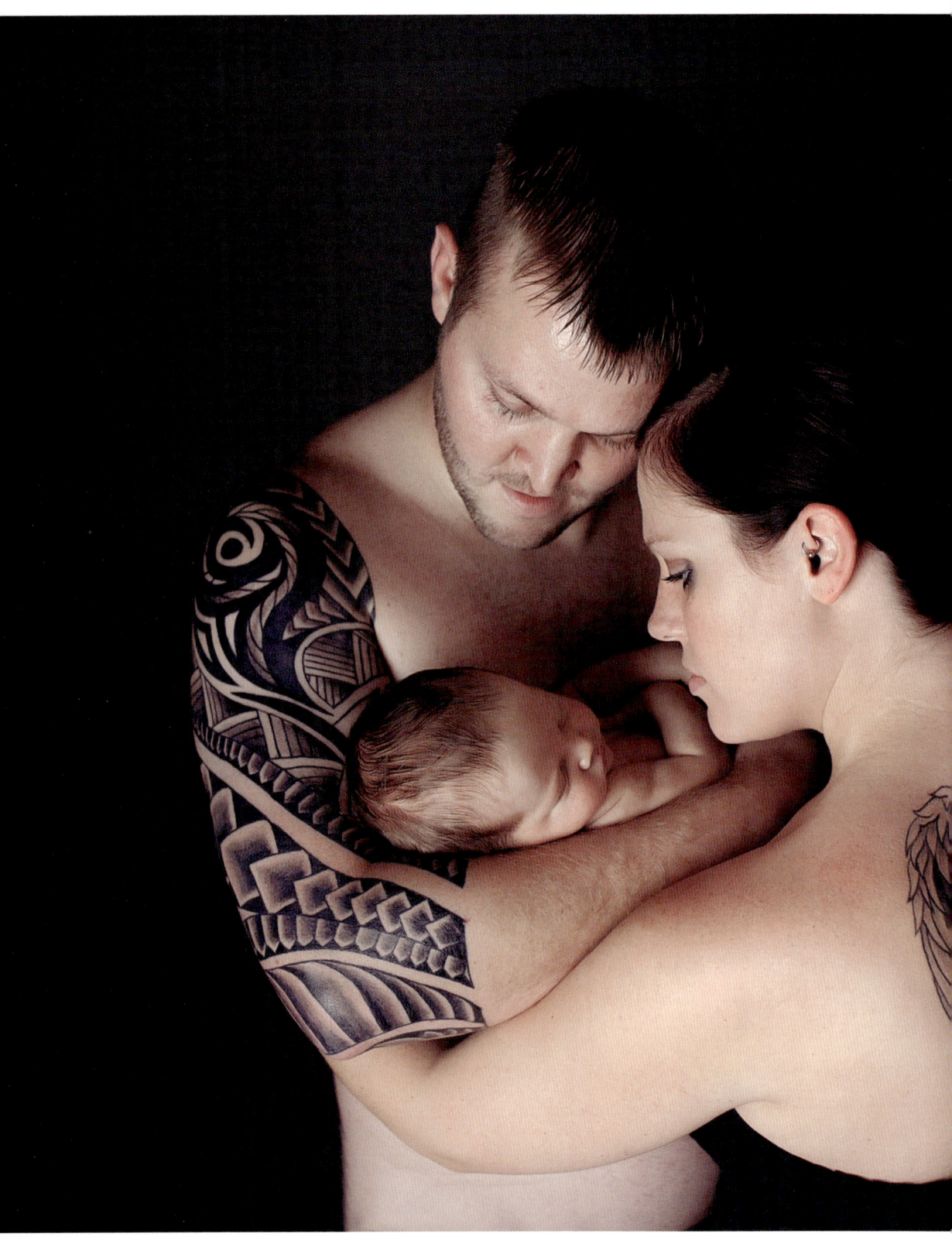

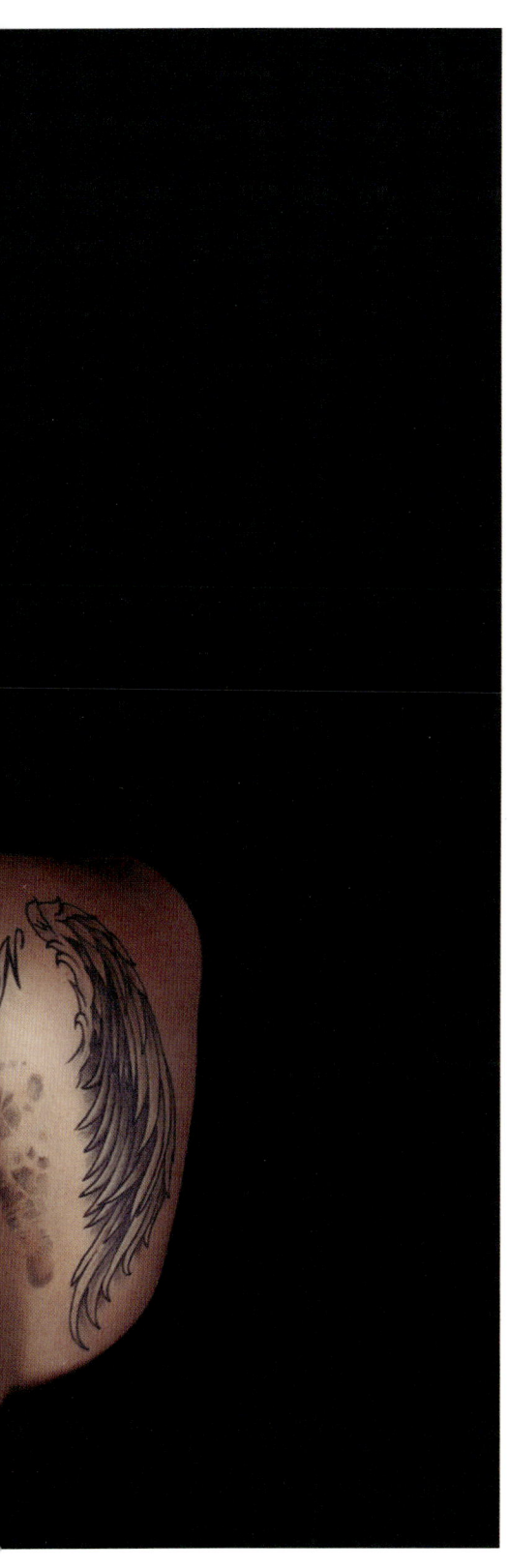

GRADY

"Overall, my pregnancy was very good! We lost our first son shortly after birth, so with this pregnancy, I cherished every moment—every kick and every little hiccup. The first time we saw Grady, my husband and I both cried. We couldn't take our eyes off of him. It was a big relief to hear his cry, since we never got to hear our first son's cry. Our hearts exploded with love."

—Laura, mom of Grady,
born September 23rd, 2014

MALI

"We got pregnant by IVF, so we got to see Mali on the ultrasound at six weeks. It was amazing how tiny she was and how much she moved that early. When I finally felt her move for the first time, it truly hit me that this was for real. I couldn't wait to feel her move more.

Once she was laid on my chest after she was born, I knew that was the moment our lives had changed forever."

—Autumn, mom of Mali, born July 8th, 2017

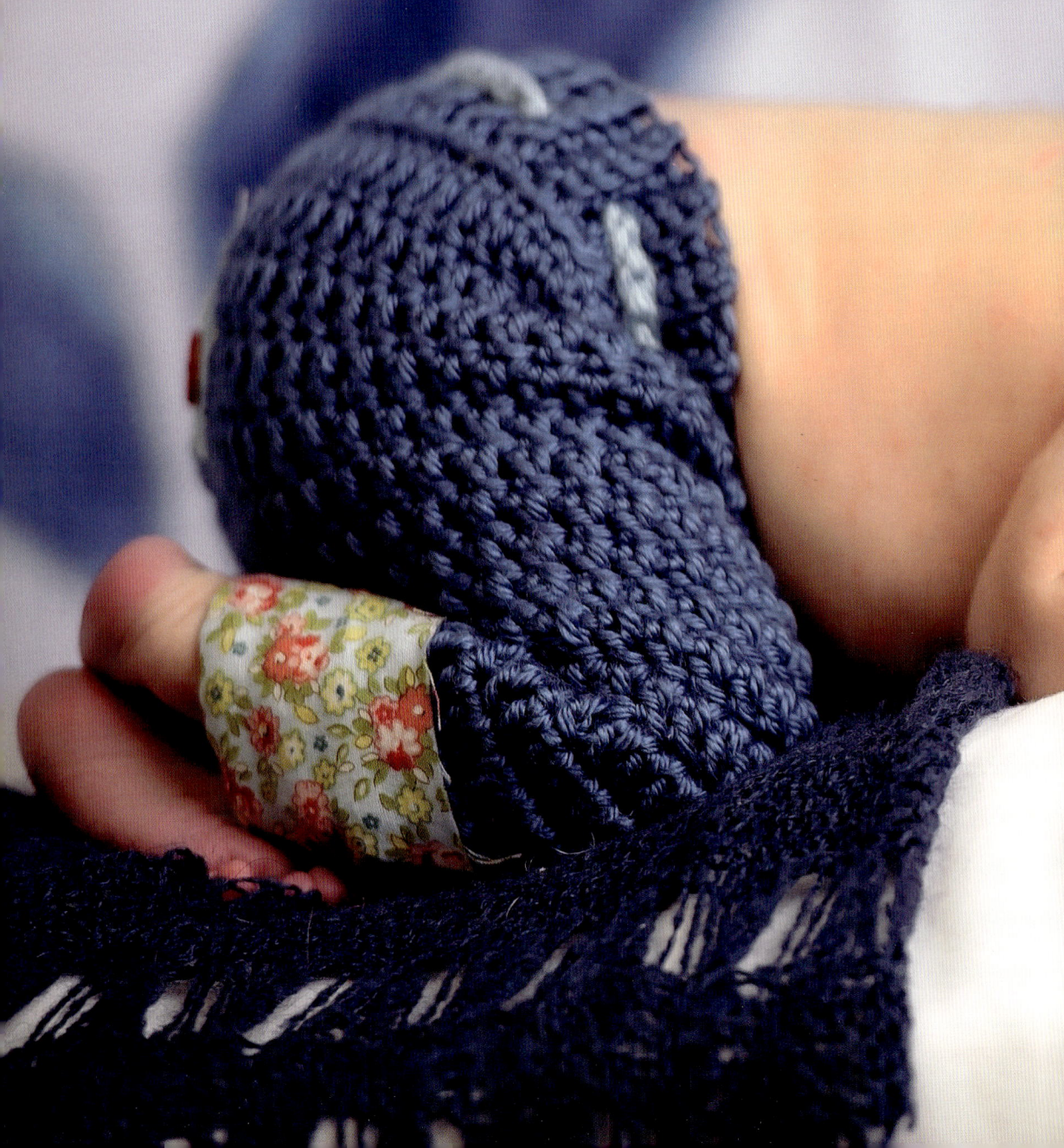

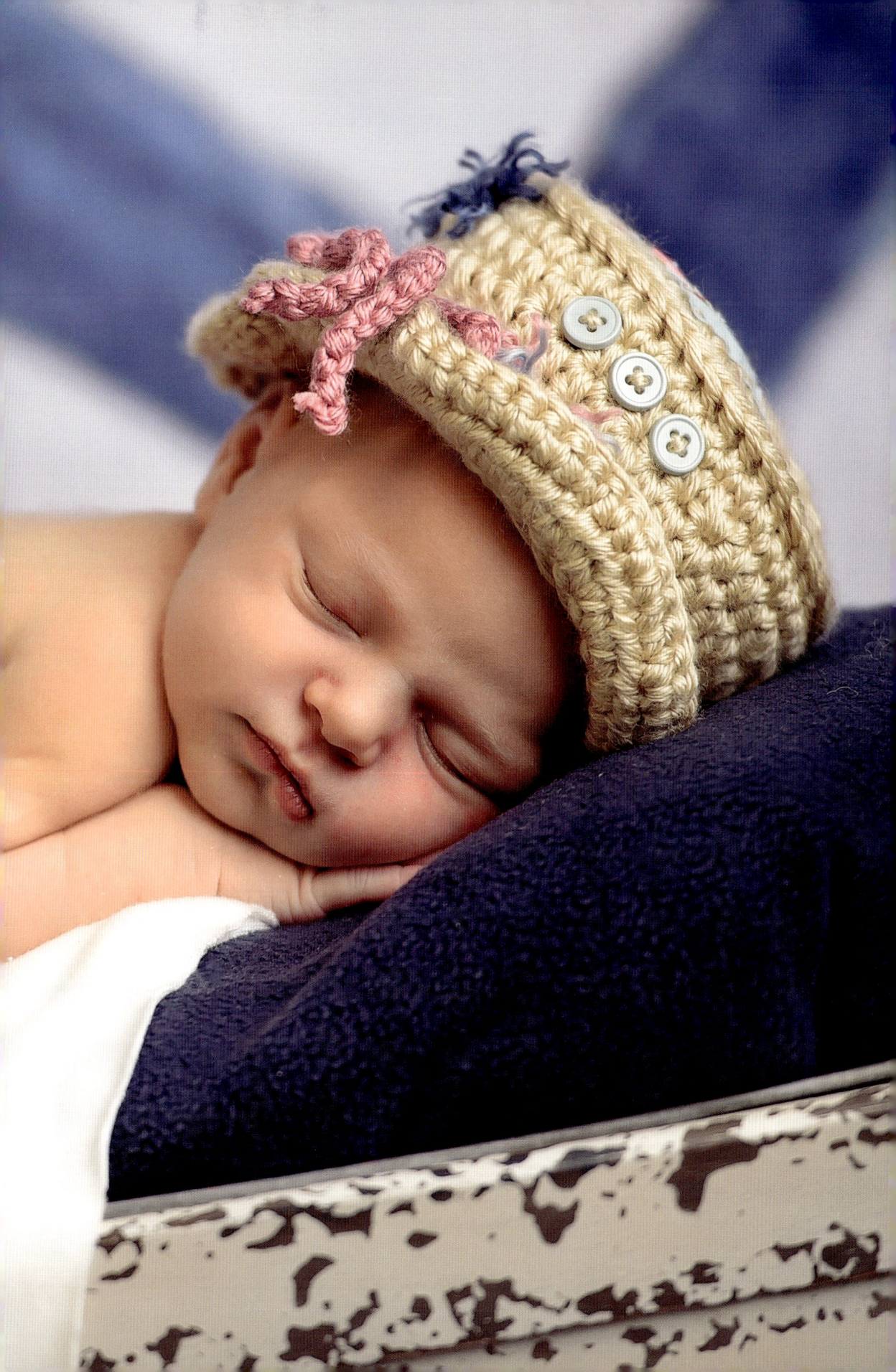

LUKE

"Luke is a sweet and spunky little guy. We hope that he always has the same love of life that he has now. No matter what he chooses to do in life, we know he will do big things."

—Erica, mom of Luke, born October 3rd, 2013

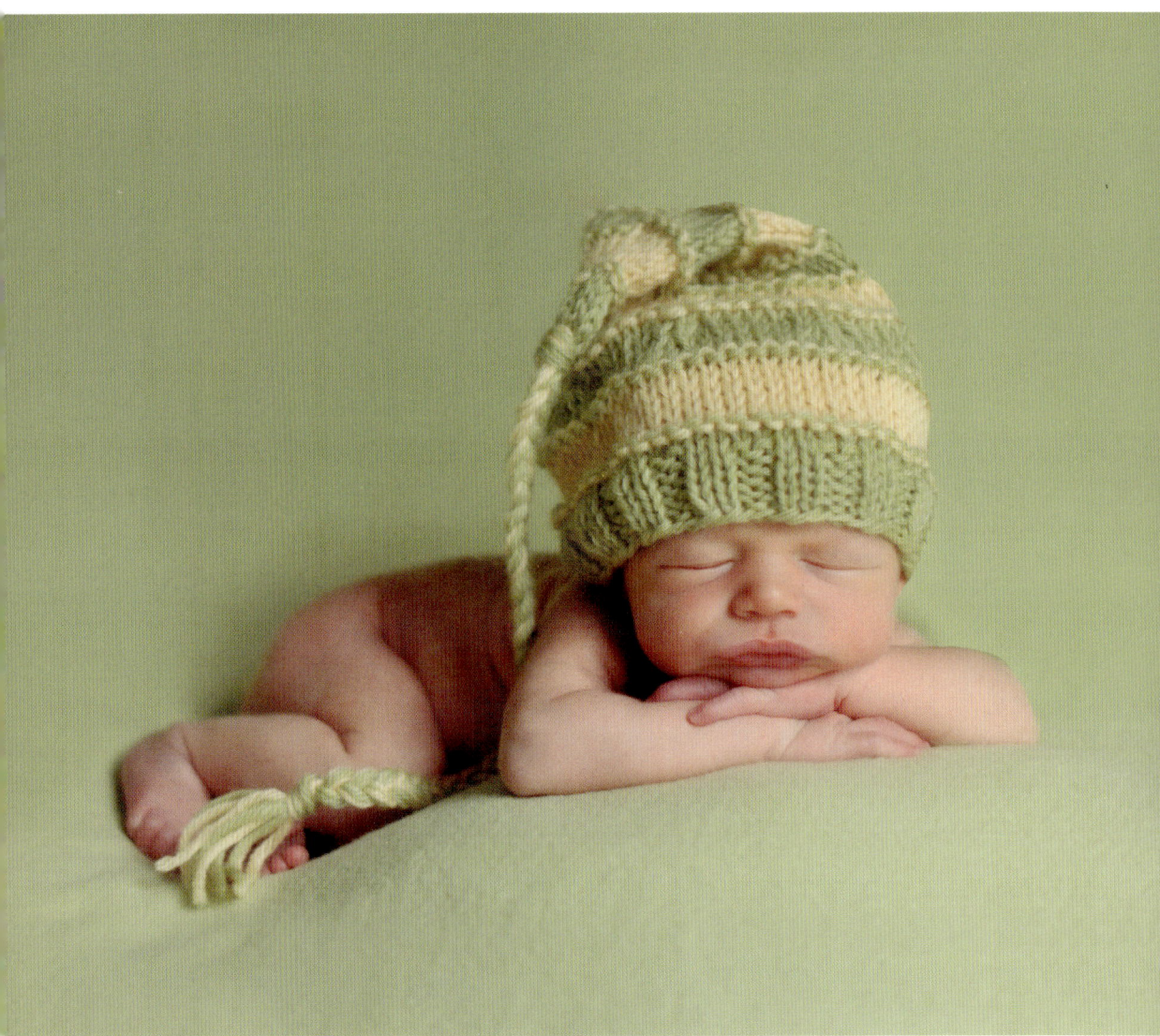

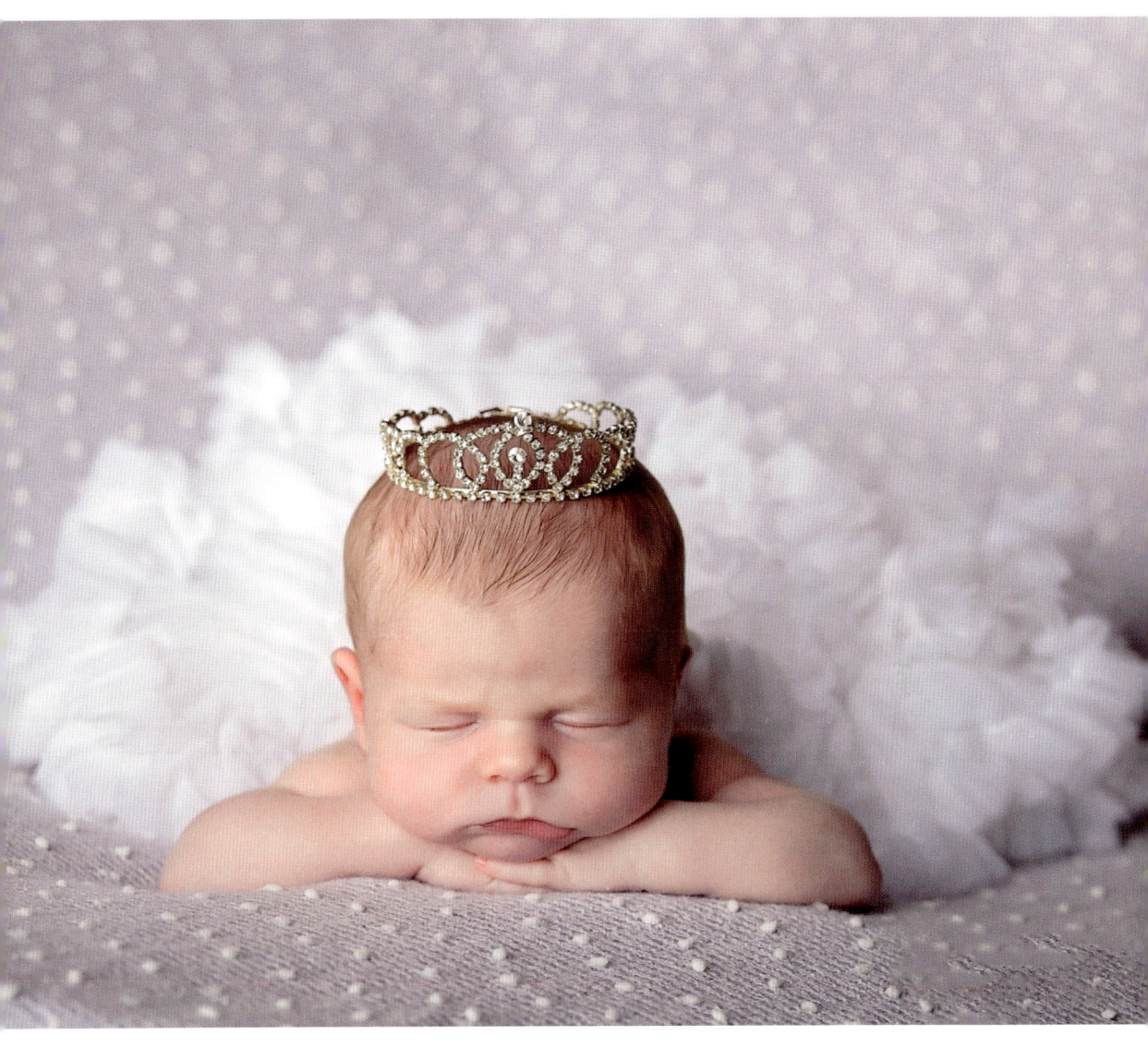

PIPER

"My pregnancy was nothing like I thought. I was sick most of the time. I gained so much weight from fluid, but my baby was happy and healthy. The best part of my pregnancy was feeling Piper move. Once she was here, we were finally a family of four. It was the best feeling in the world."

—Erika, mom of Piper, born April 9th, 2017

EMMA

"The first time I held her, my heart exploded. I couldn't stop looking at her and kissing her sweet cheeks! My favorite part of having a newborn is all the sweet snuggling moments you have!"

—Ellen, mom of Emma, born August 1st, 2017

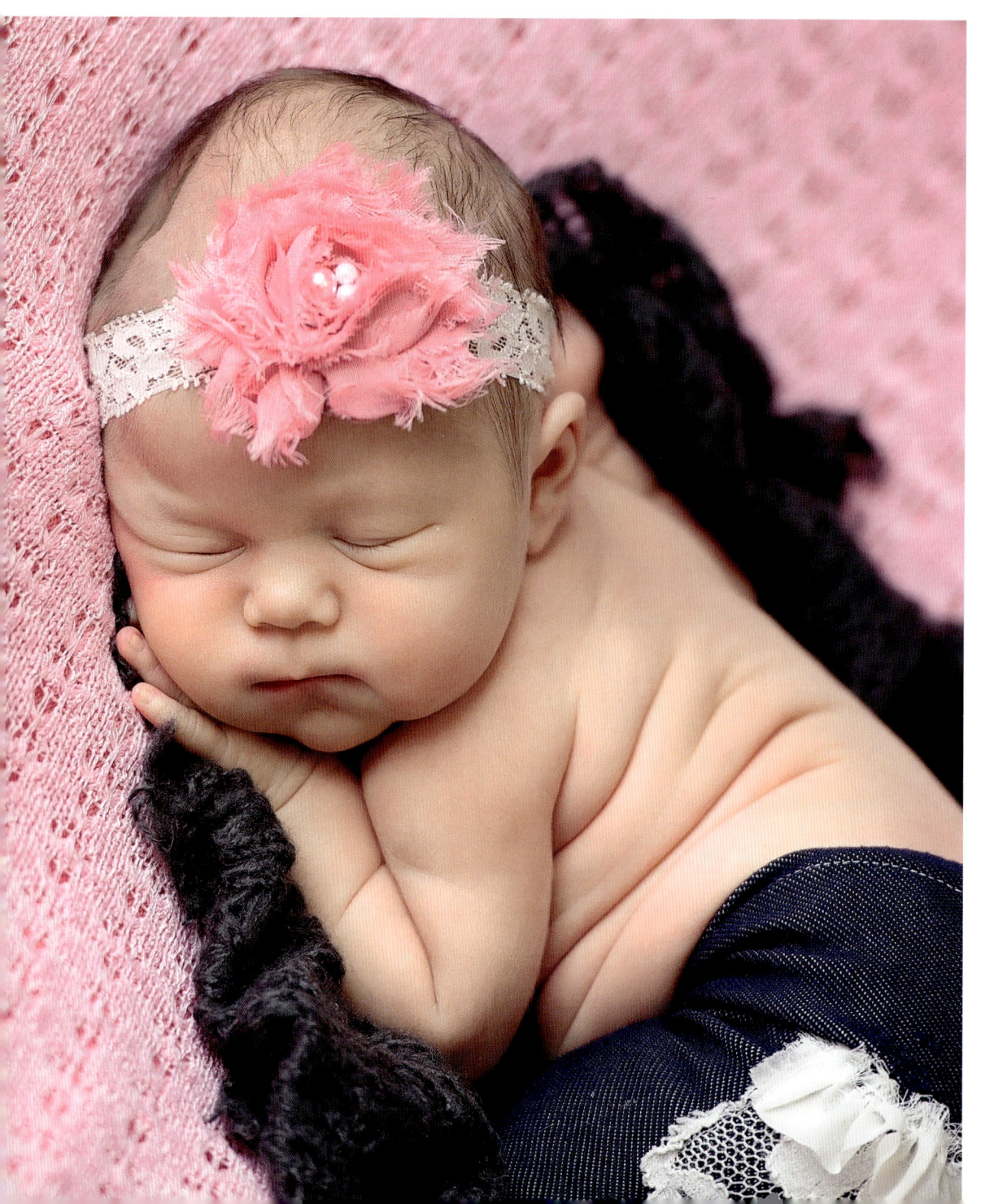

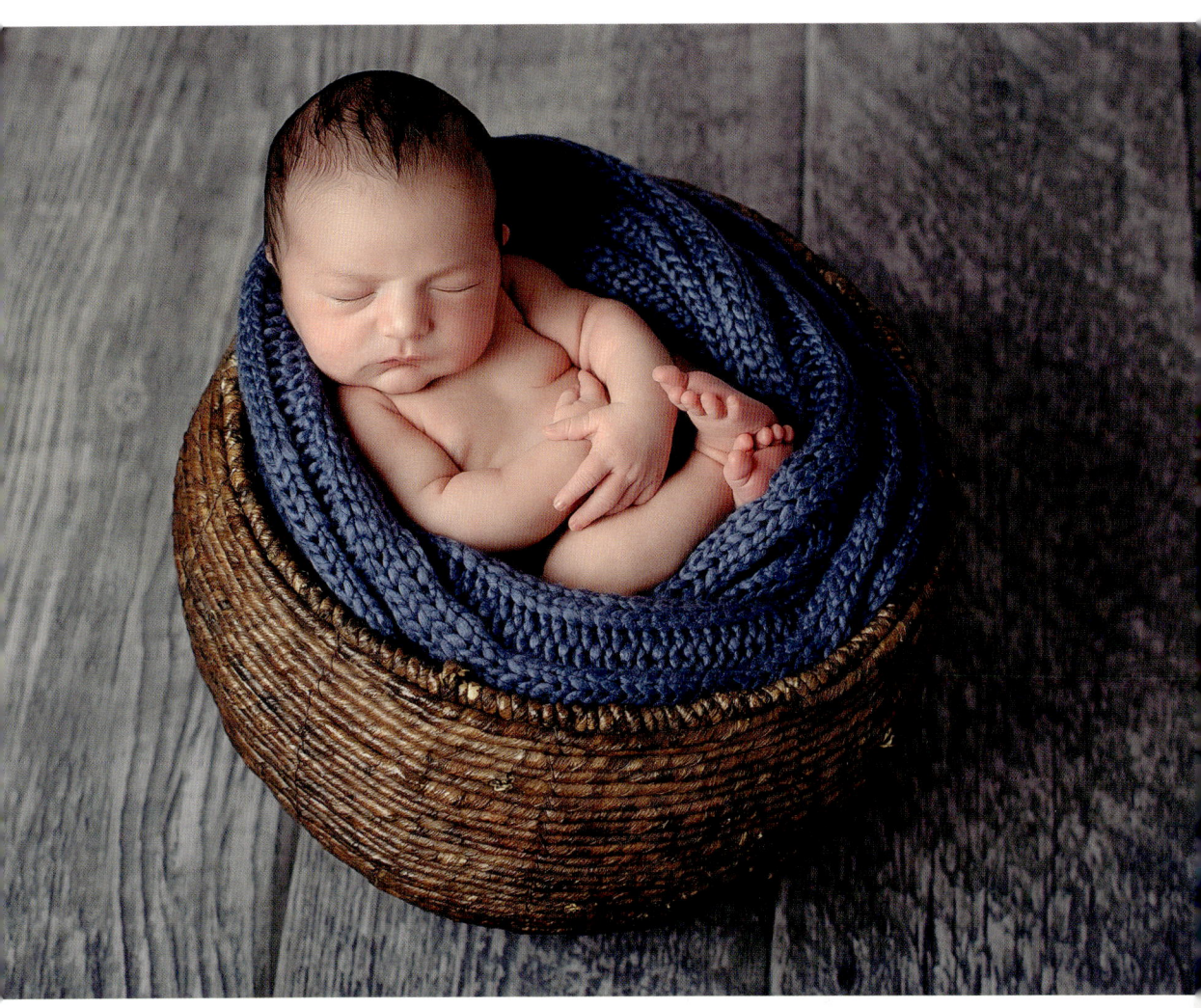

ASHER

"I didn't have an easy first pregnancy, but with Asher, I learned from the first time around, and it was so wonderful. I ate healthy, exercised, took great care of myself, and had such a lovely pregnancy. I truly felt alive and fulfilled. I also tried a birthing method called 'hypnobirthing.' Part of it was listening to relaxation soundtracks at night, and sometimes in the car. I loved how I was able to relax, and truly focus on growing a healthy baby."

—Vanessa, mom of Asher, born May 24th, 2014

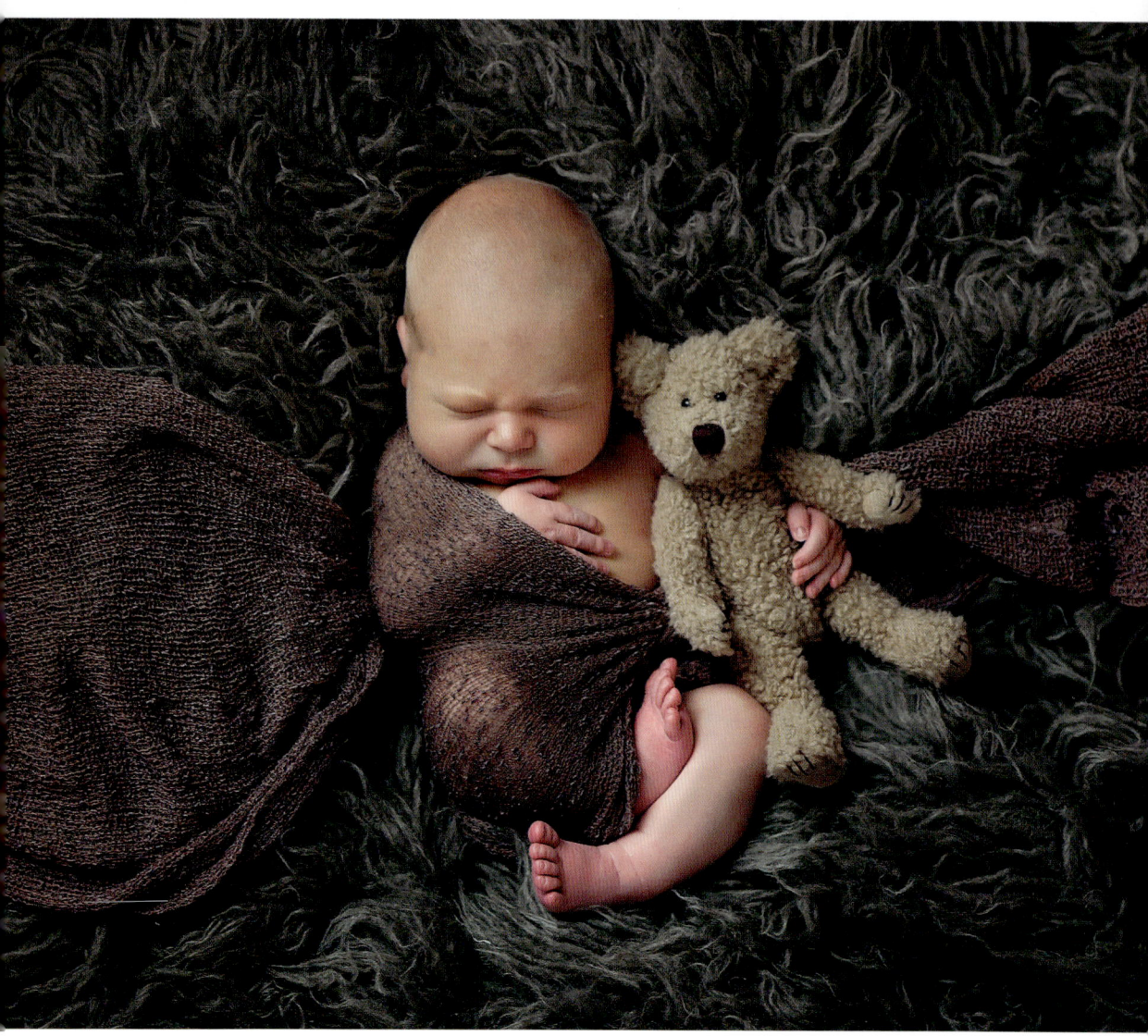

THEODORE

"When I found out I was pregnant, I was super excited, but at the same time a little shocked. We had been trying for some months with no success, so I was caught completely off guard when I saw that the test was positive. I proceeded to take a test every few days until my first appointment, because I was still not completely convinced."

—Brittany, mom of Theodore, born August 5th, 2016

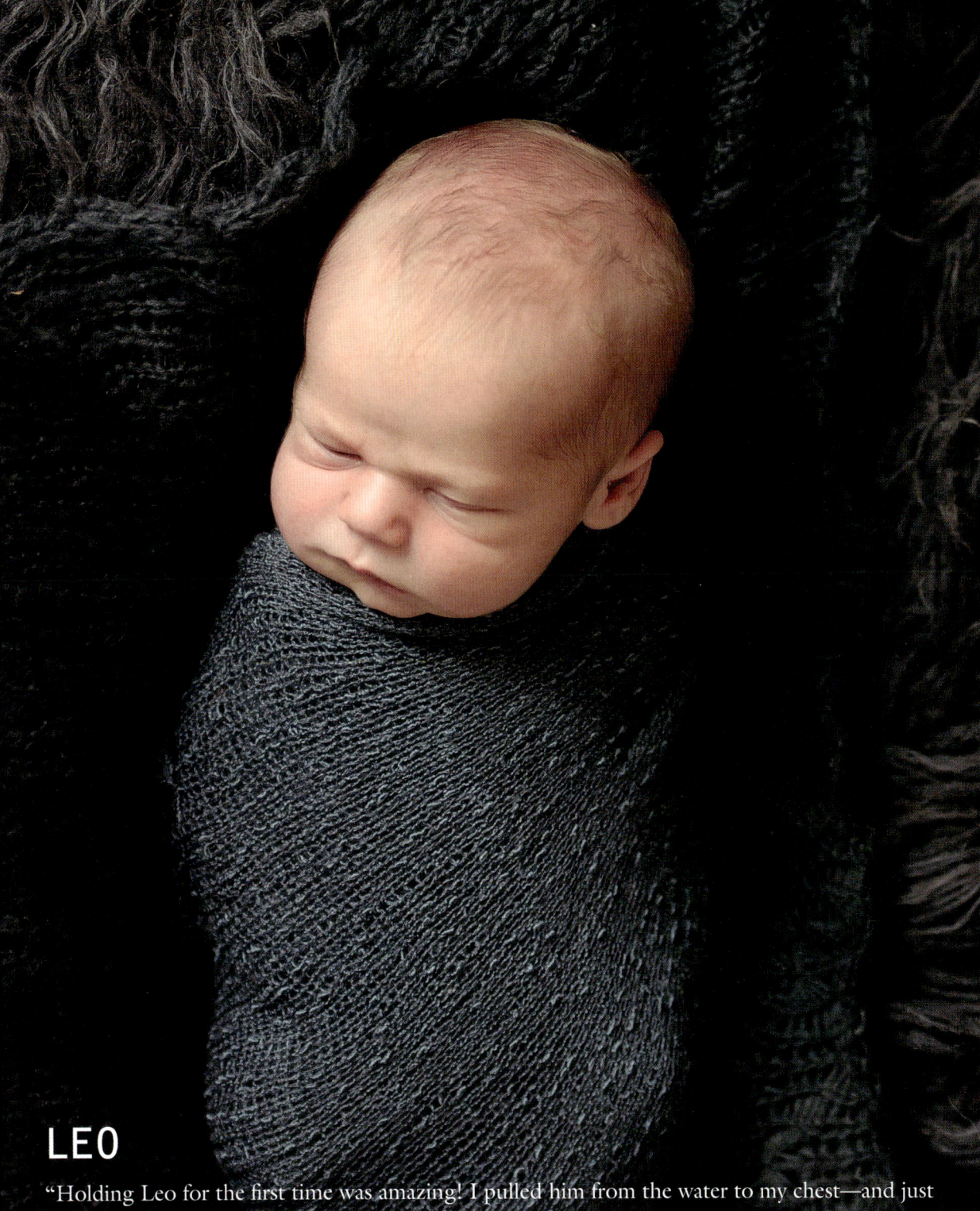

LEO

"Holding Leo for the first time was amazing! I pulled him from the water to my chest—and just being able to do that was so surrreal. I remember saying, 'Hey baby' and thinking, 'Wow! You are here, and you're more beautiful than we'd ever imagined!' It's almost indescribable. The room was filled with so much love and awe when my husband got to hold Leo for the first time. Leo is truly a blessing, and I know right after he was born, we were all thanking God for our little blessing!"

—Maggie, mom of Leo, born June 26th, 2016

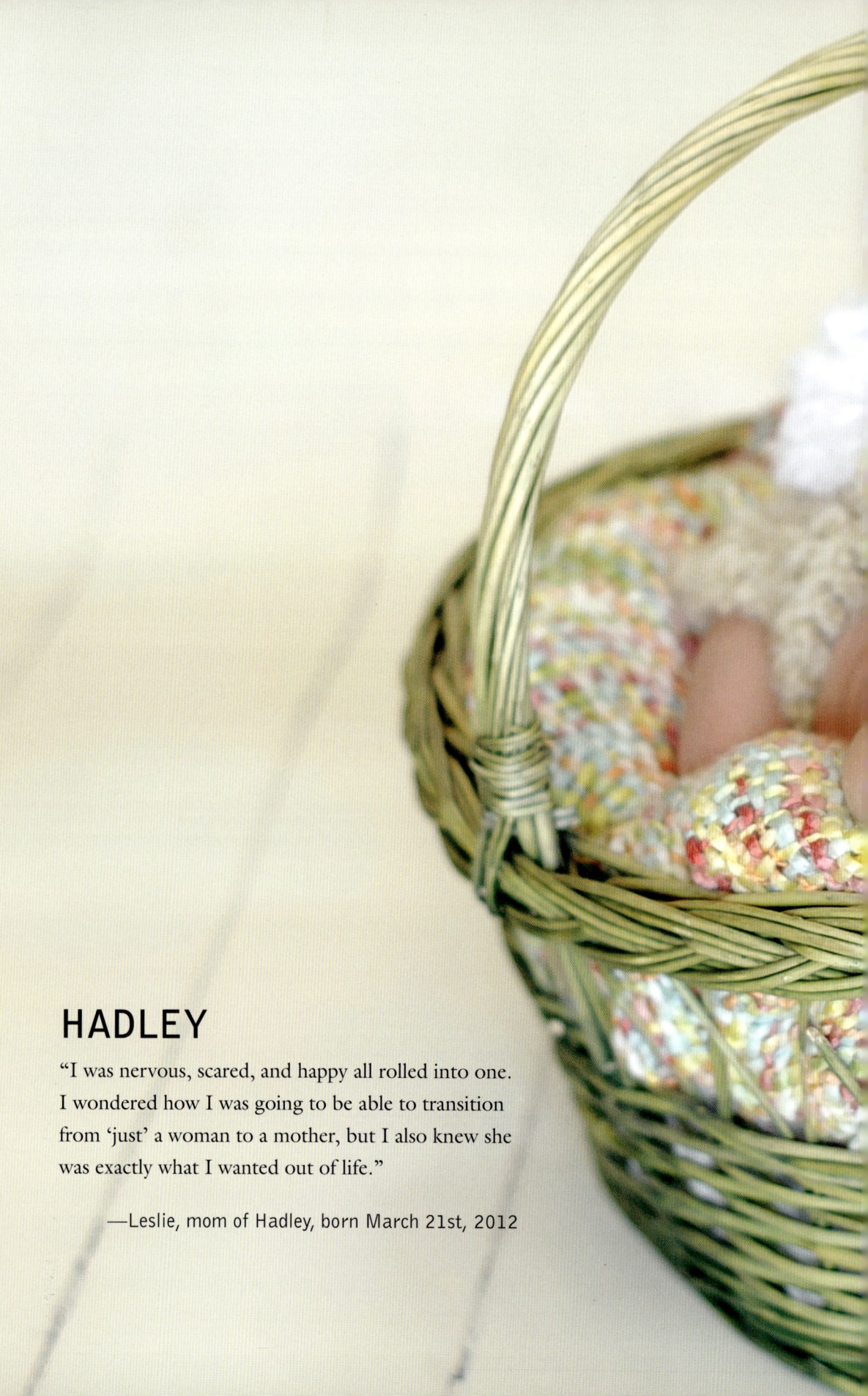

HADLEY

"I was nervous, scared, and happy all rolled into one. I wondered how I was going to be able to transition from 'just' a woman to a mother, but I also knew she was exactly what I wanted out of life."

—Leslie, mom of Hadley, born March 21st, 2012

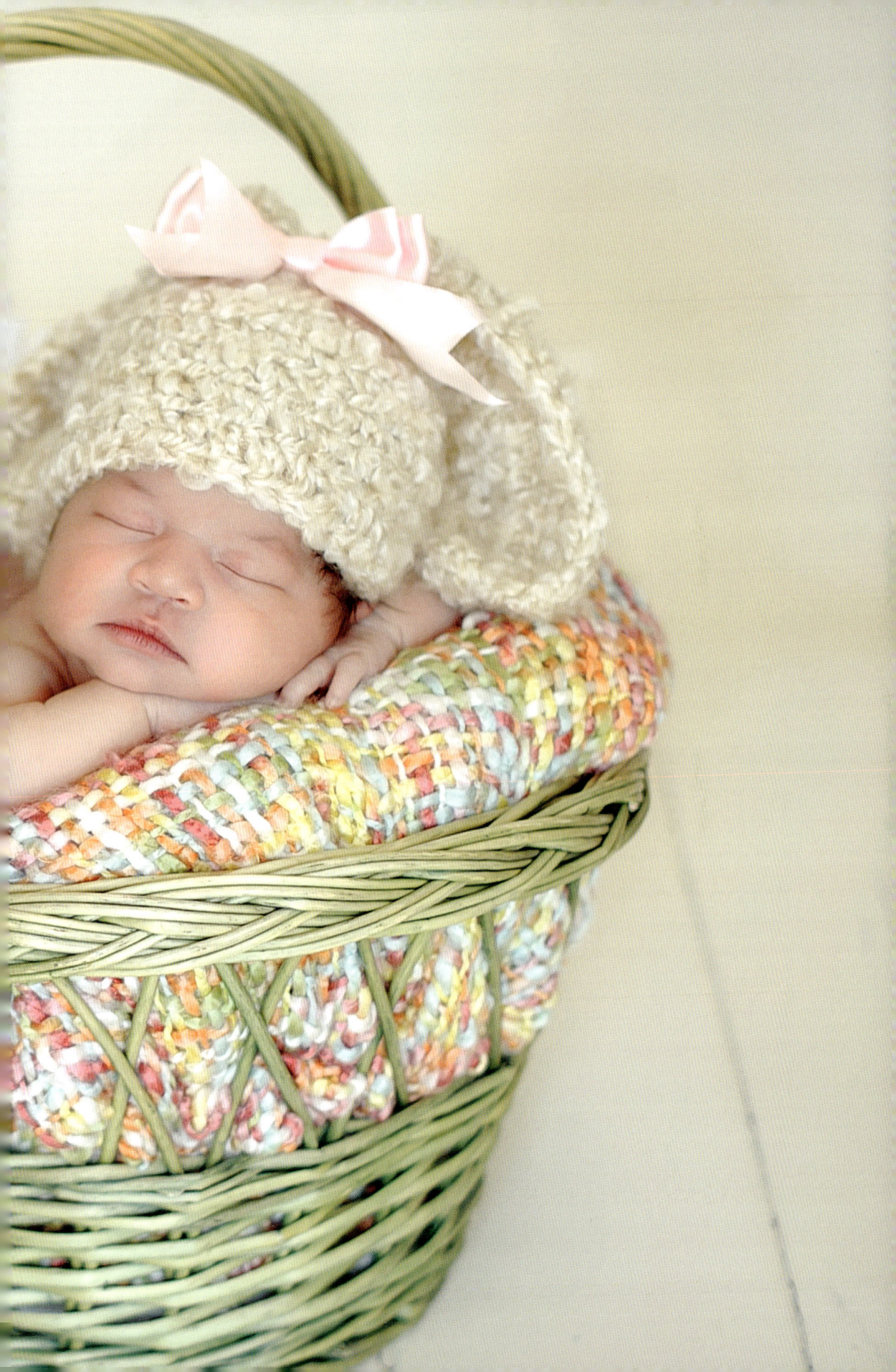

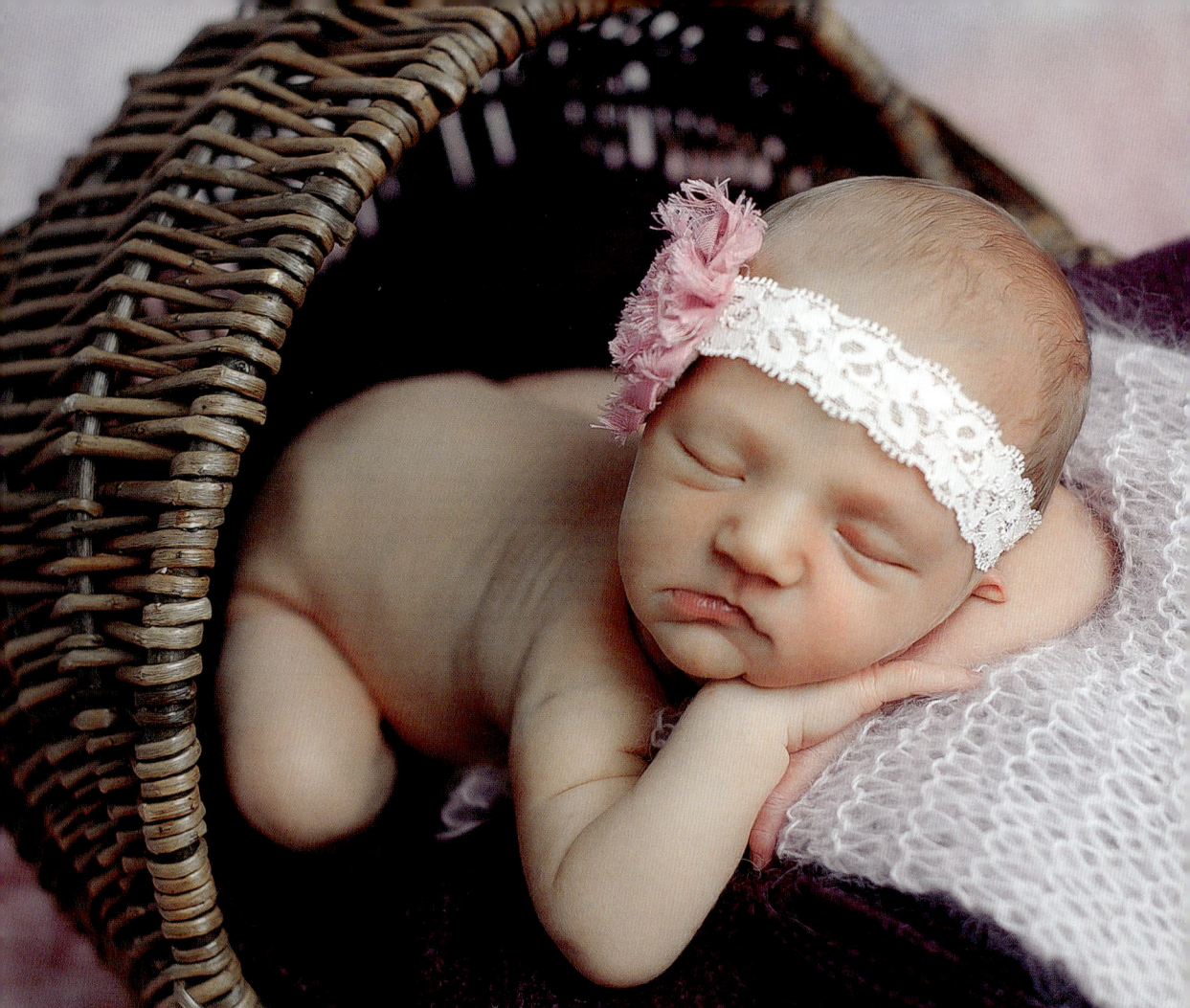

PAISLEY

"My pregnancy was horrible. I was sick the whole nine
months! I developed preeclampsia in the end and had to
be induced. I was at the hospital for three days before she
came, and when I started actual labor, it was so exciting.
I knew I was that much closer to meeting our sweet girl!
The first time I saw her was so amazing. Seeing her beautiful face for the first time was a precious moment!"

—Madeline, mom of Paisley, born August 10th, 2013

MAX

"One thing I loved about my pregnancy was my two-year-old, Jase, talking to my belly. After Max was born, seeing my sons with my husband made my heart explode!"

—Rae, mom of Max, born June 3rd, 2015

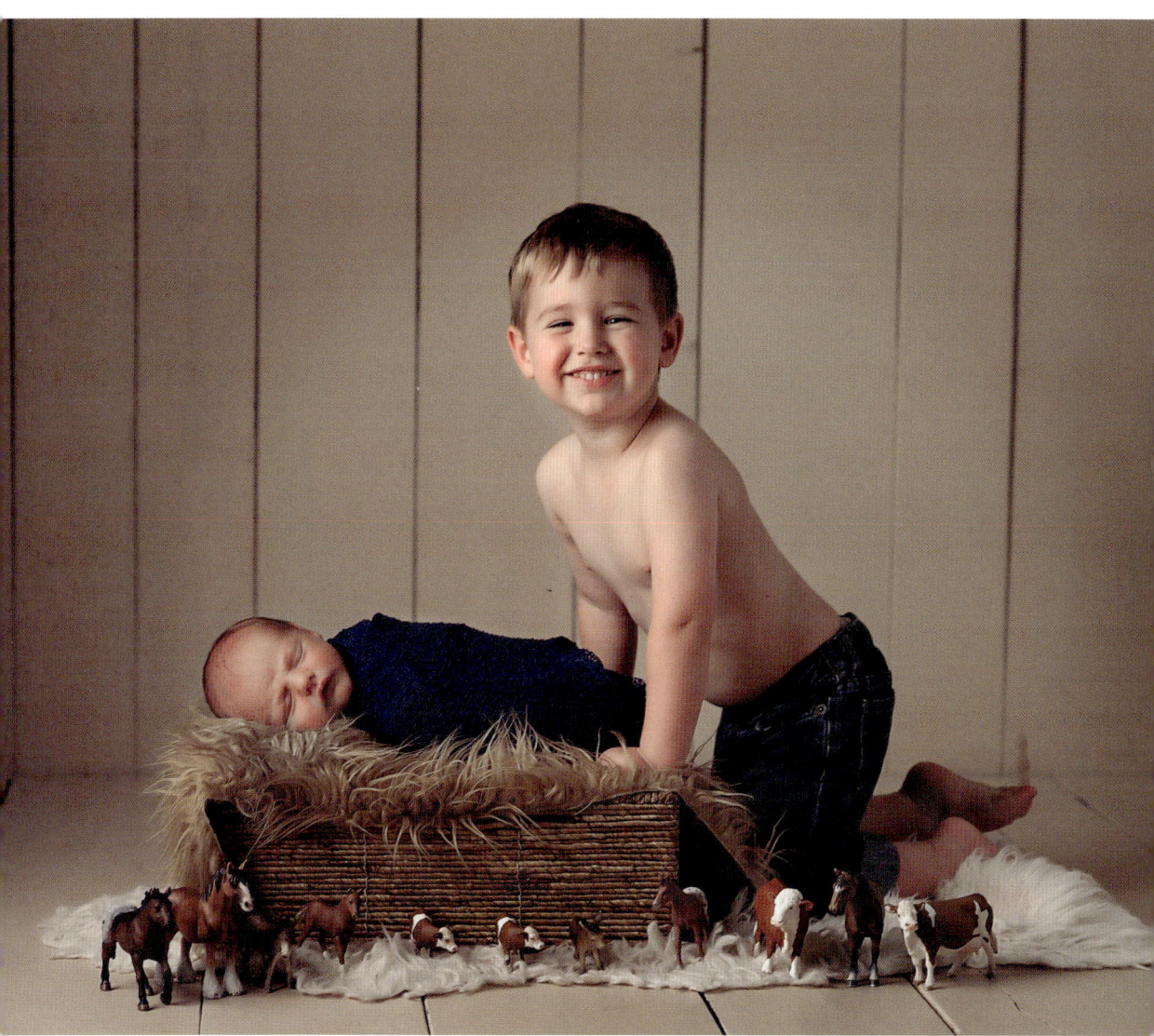

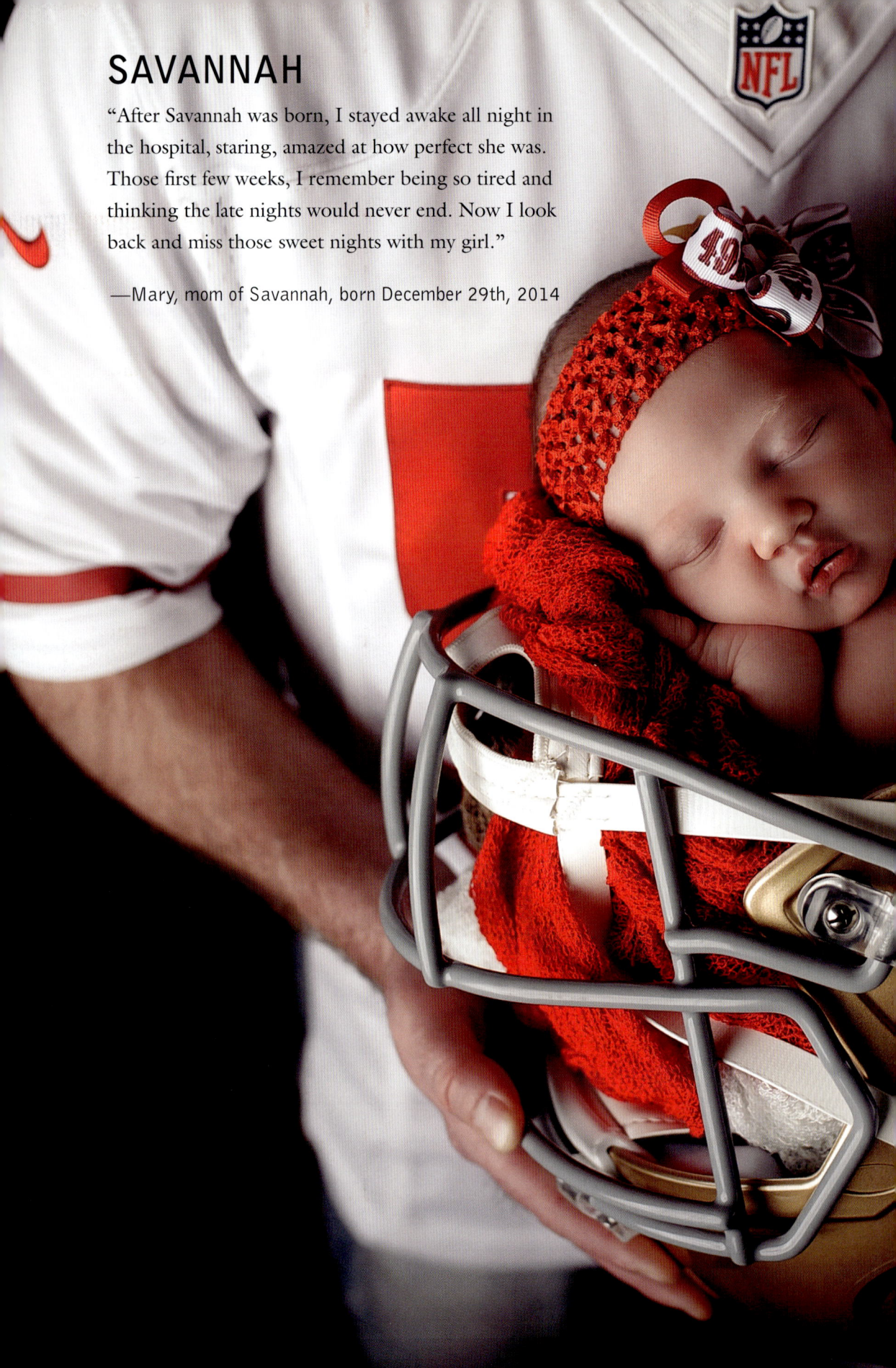

SAVANNAH

"After Savannah was born, I stayed awake all night in the hospital, staring, amazed at how perfect she was. Those first few weeks, I remember being so tired and thinking the late nights would never end. Now I look back and miss those sweet nights with my girl."

—Mary, mom of Savannah, born December 29th, 2014

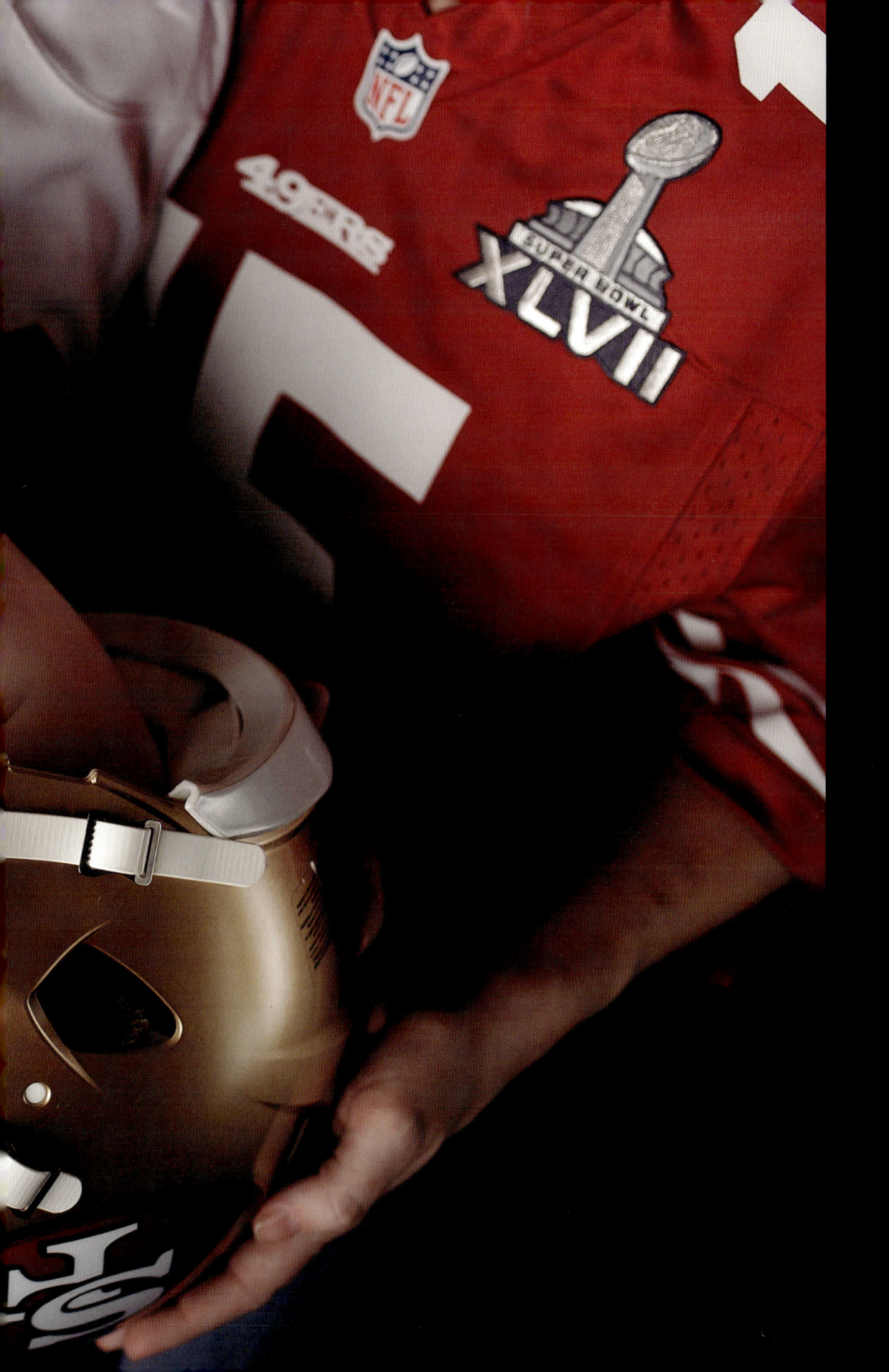

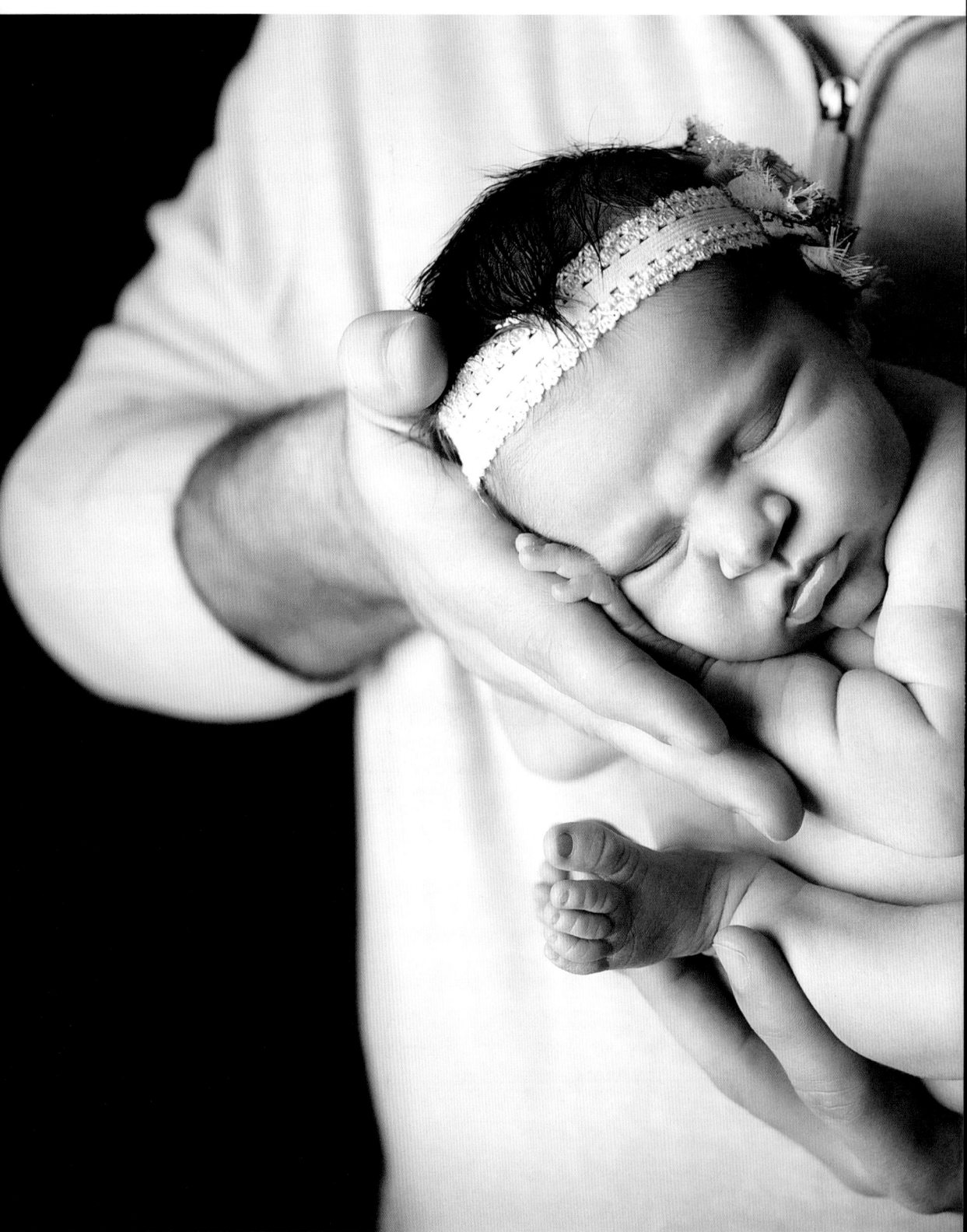

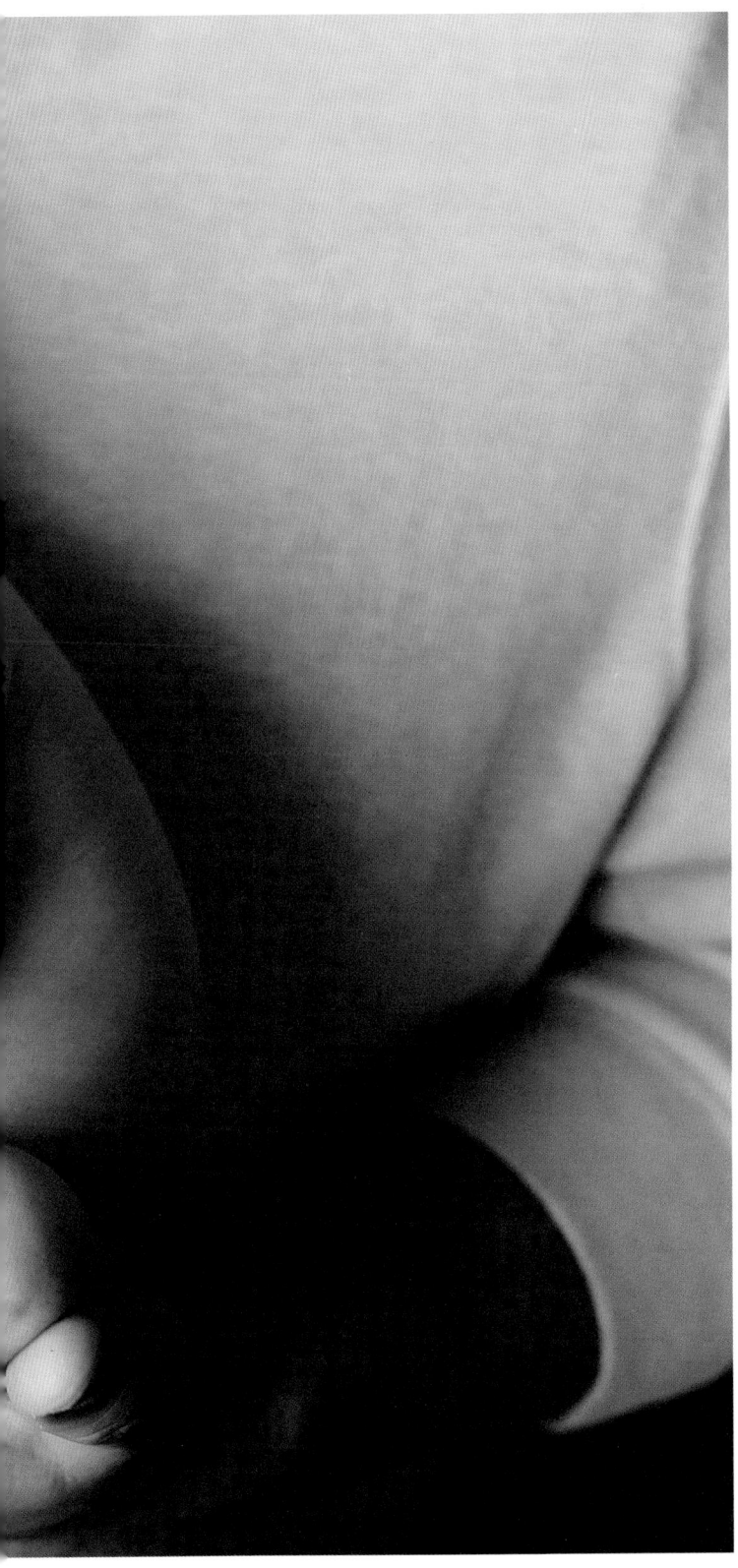

LILLY KAYTE

"I had no idea how much we could love her until the first time I saw her. She was perfect! When she looked at us, we could tell how comforted she was in our arms. Honestly, we could just sit and stare at her—and we did!"

—Courtney, mom of Lilly Kayte, born December 15th, 2014

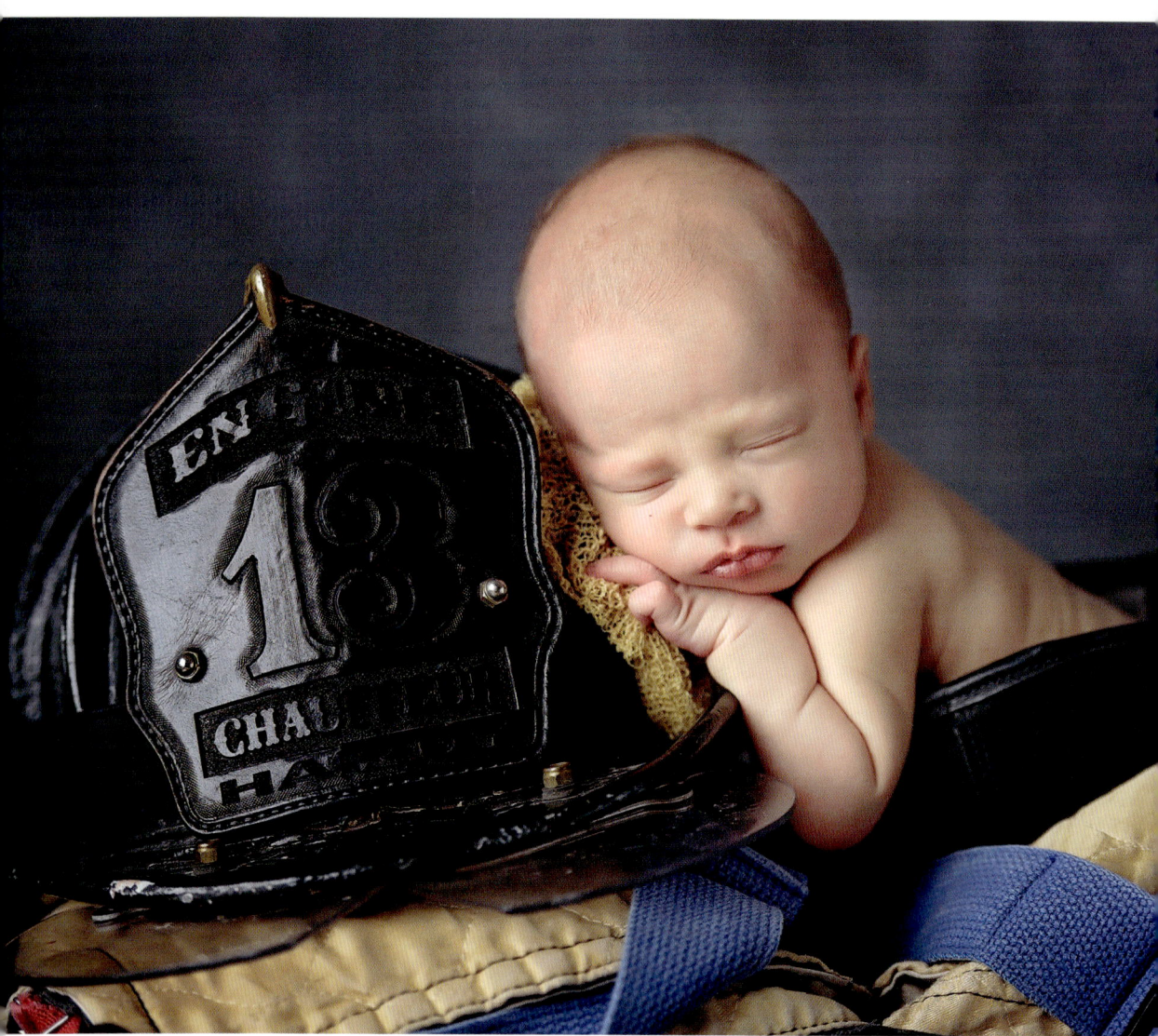

LANE

"When we realized I was in labor, we were excited and ready but also terrified. We knew our lives were about to completely change. When I first saw Lane, all I could think was, 'Thank you, Jesus, for this miracle!'"

—Casey, mom of Lane, born March 11th, 2017

CHARLIE

"I had never been more in love than when I saw Charlie for the first time. I couldn't believe this sweet baby boy was mine. All the worries of the world were obsolete. I felt a sense of total peace. He was perfect, and we were so blessed."

—Julia, mom of Charlie, born March 29th, 2014

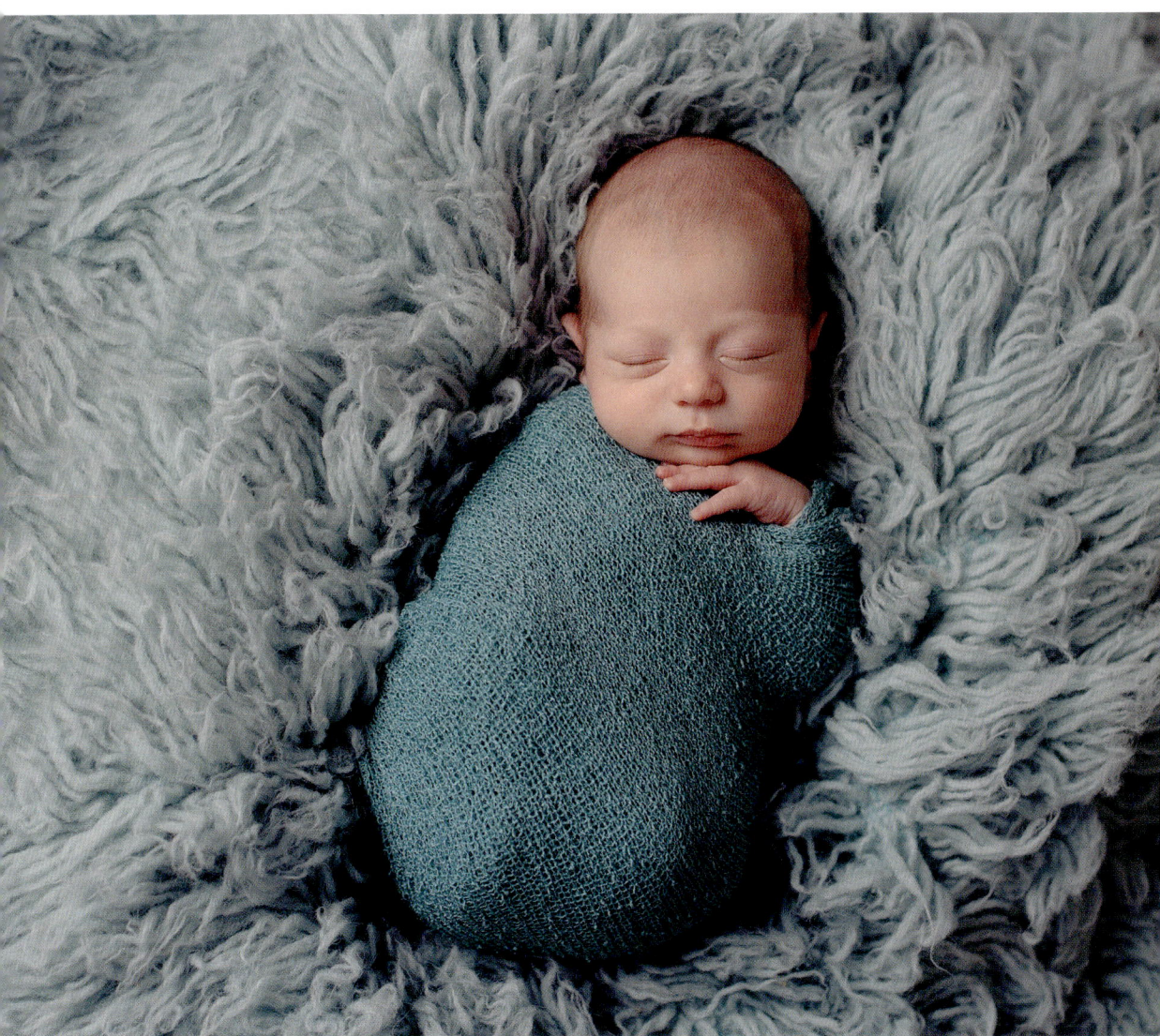

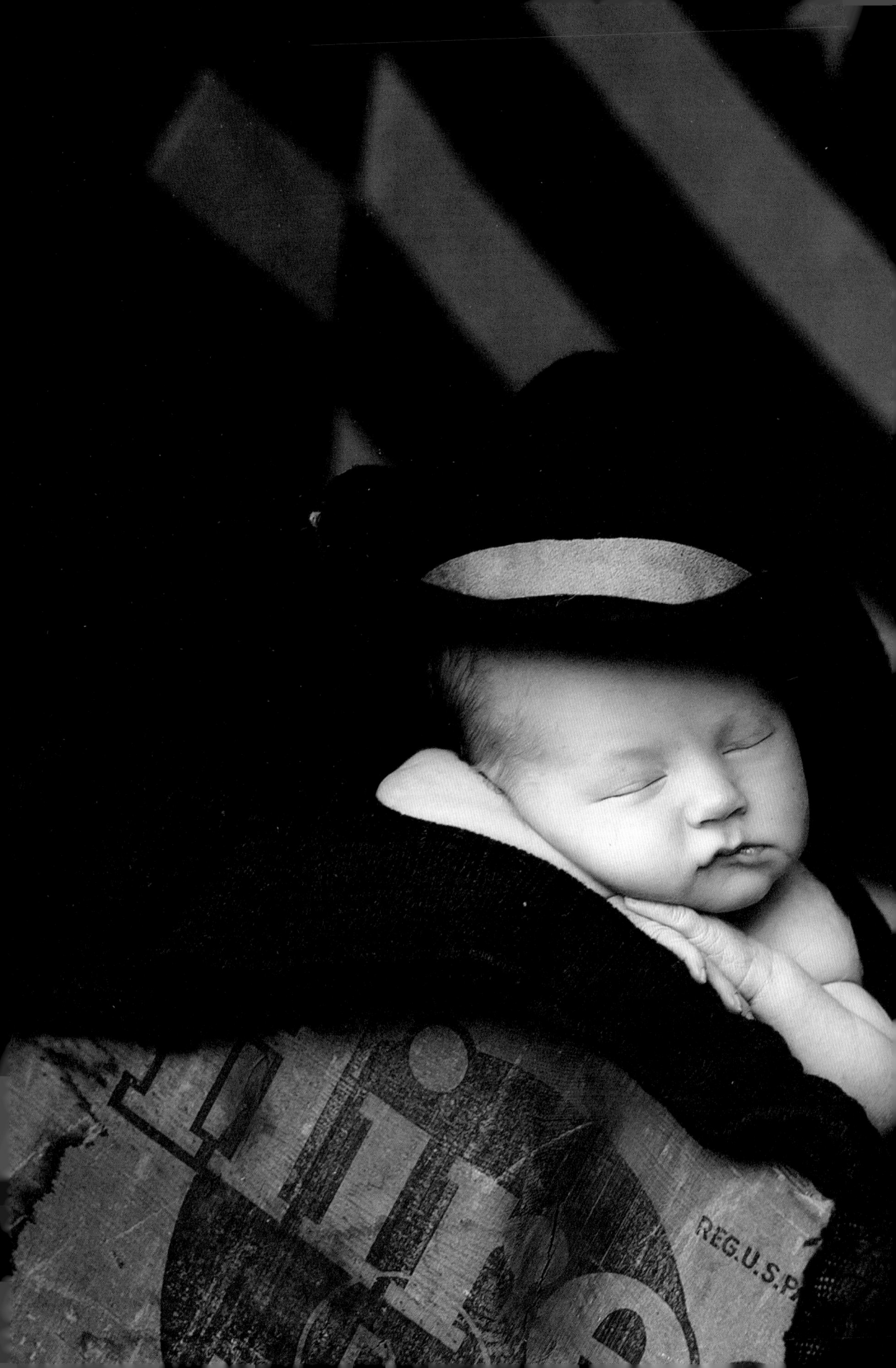

COLE

"The first time I felt the baby move, I was taking a bath and talking to my belly. I was certain that he heard me and was responding."

—Christina, mom of Cole, born September 15th, 2015

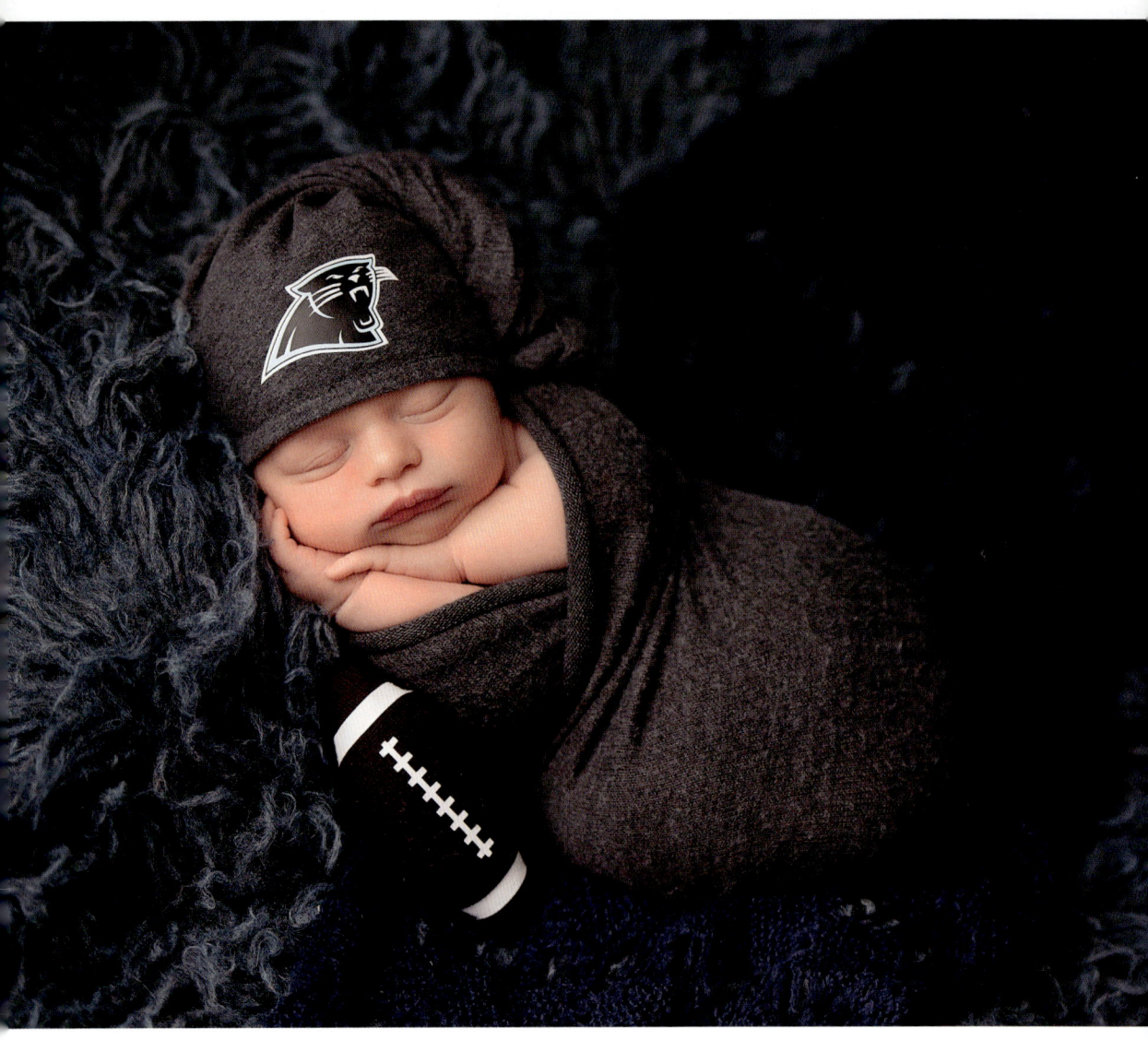

JACK

"My favorite part of being pregnant was rubbing my belly.
I never understood why pregnant ladies did this, until it
was me. I did it all the time, and I loved it!"

—Samantha, mom of Jack, born October 21st, 2017

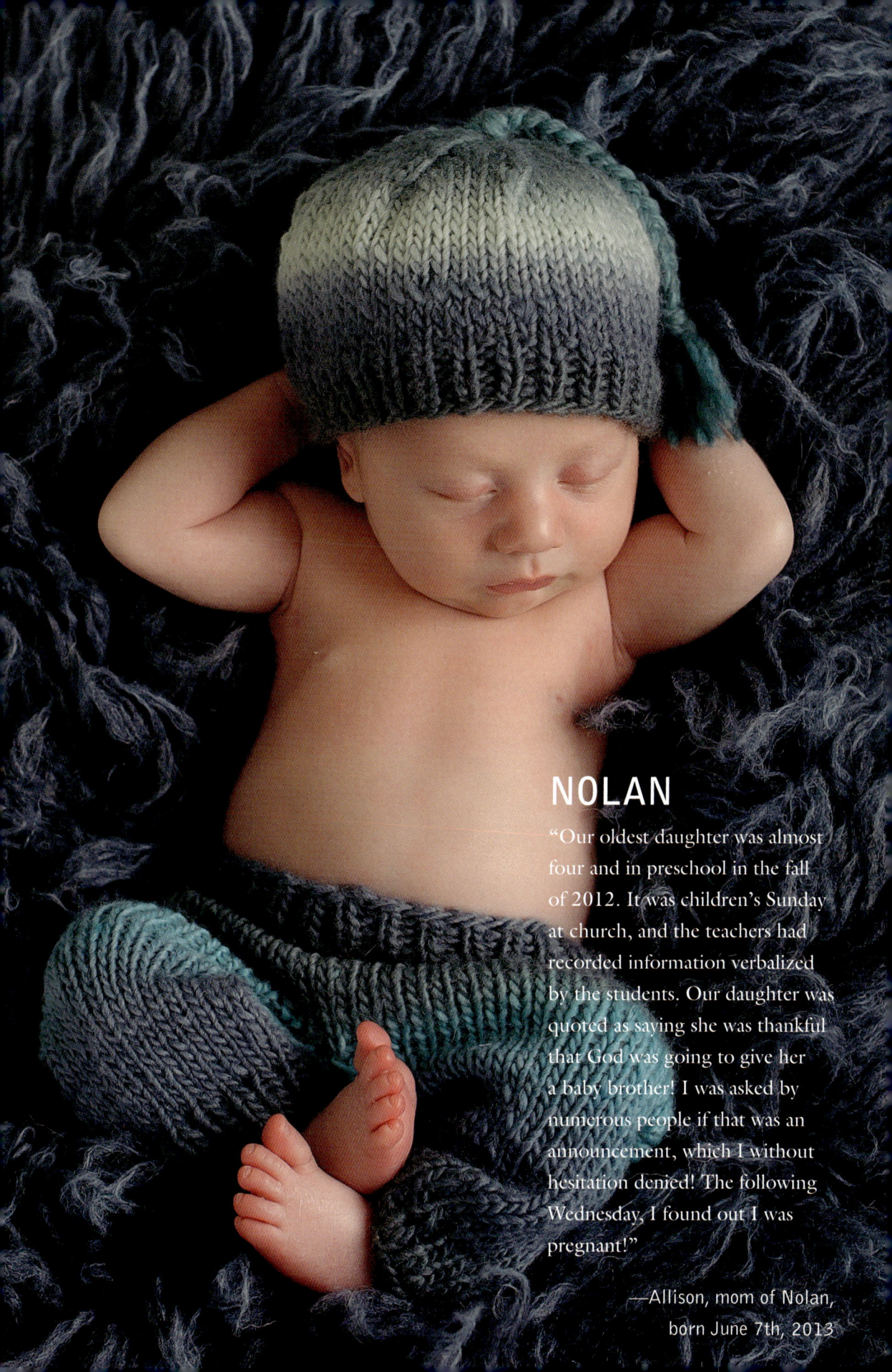

NOLAN

"Our oldest daughter was almost four and in preschool in the fall of 2012. It was children's Sunday at church, and the teachers had recorded information verbalized by the students. Our daughter was quoted as saying she was thankful that God was going to give her a baby brother! I was asked by numerous people if that was an announcement, which I without hesitation denied! The following Wednesday, I found out I was pregnant!"

—Allison, mom of Nolan, born June 7th, 2013

MARLEY

"Marley is my third baby, but feeling her move for the first time was still the most incredible feeling ever. Since I was a little girl, I had dreamed about having a little girl of my own, so when they put her in my arms, it was literally like a dream come true."

—Jennifer, mom of Marley, born December 28th, 2017

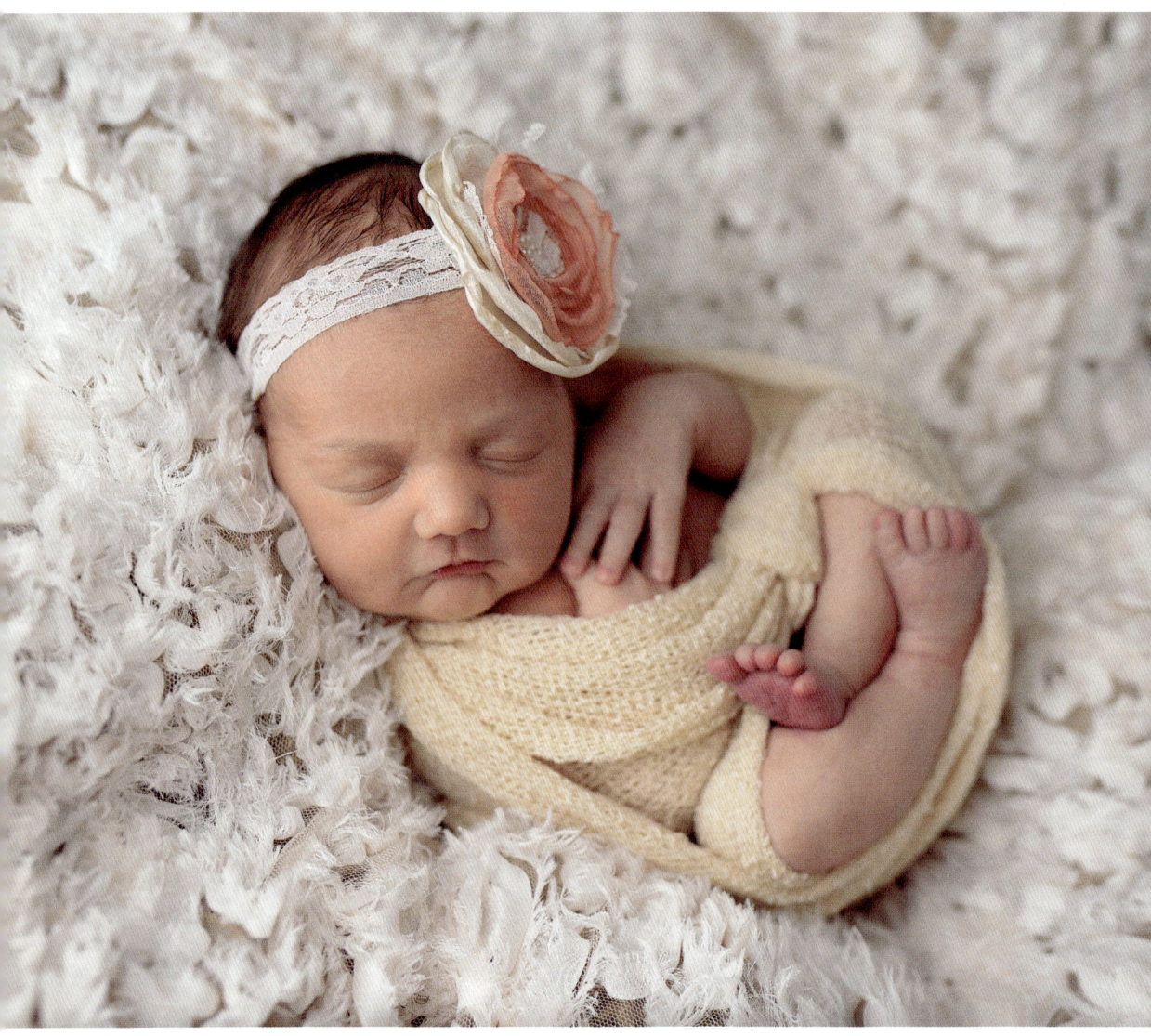

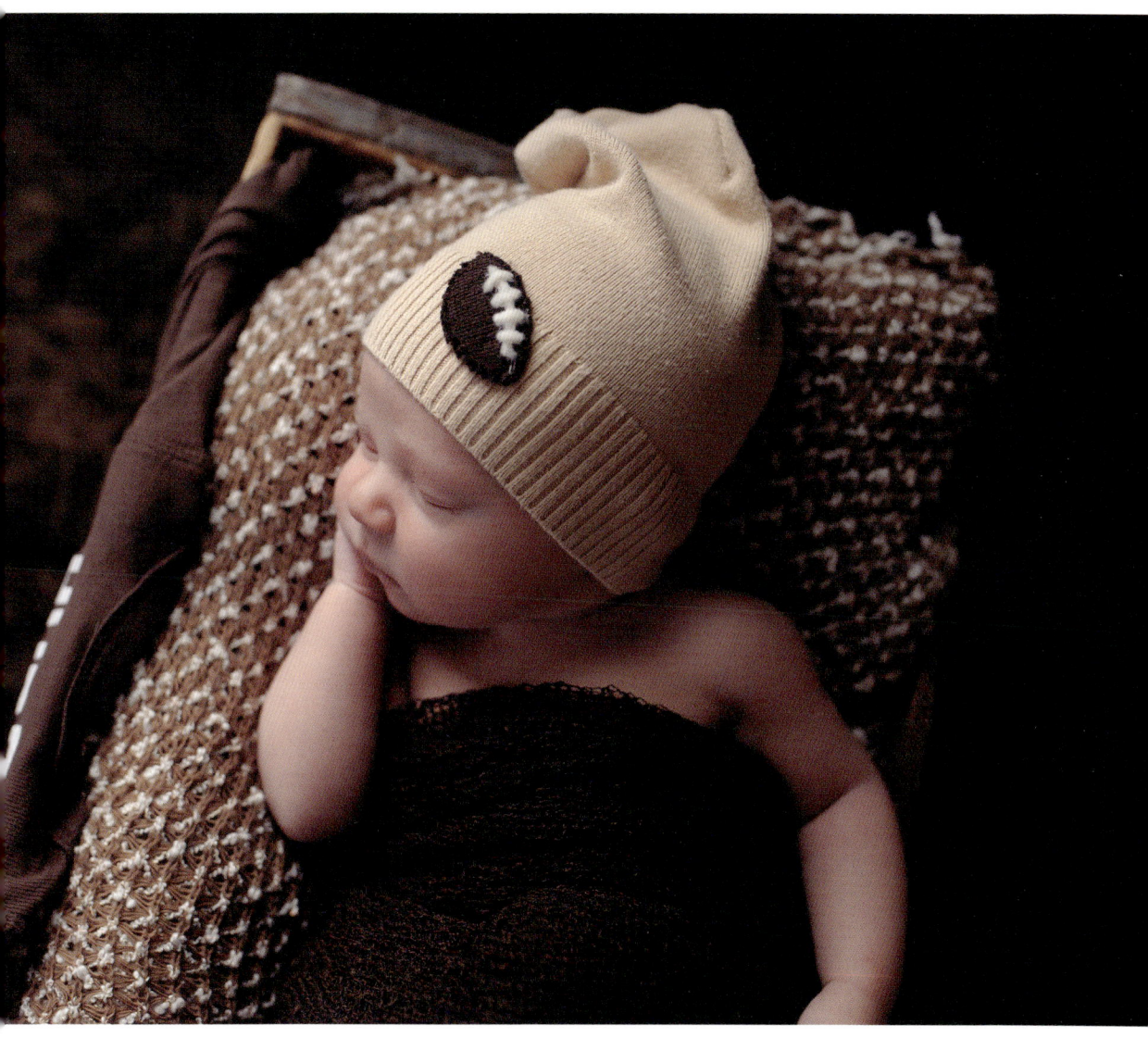

GRAYSON

"When we found out I was pregnant, I felt so blessed, happy, and really in shock, because I just couldn't believe we were finally pregnant. During my pregnancy, everyone thought I was having a girl—including a random woman at the grocery store who came up and told me so! Needless to say, we were so shocked when we found out it was a boy, because so many people insisted that it was a girl."

—Anna, mom of Grayson, born October 21st, 2014

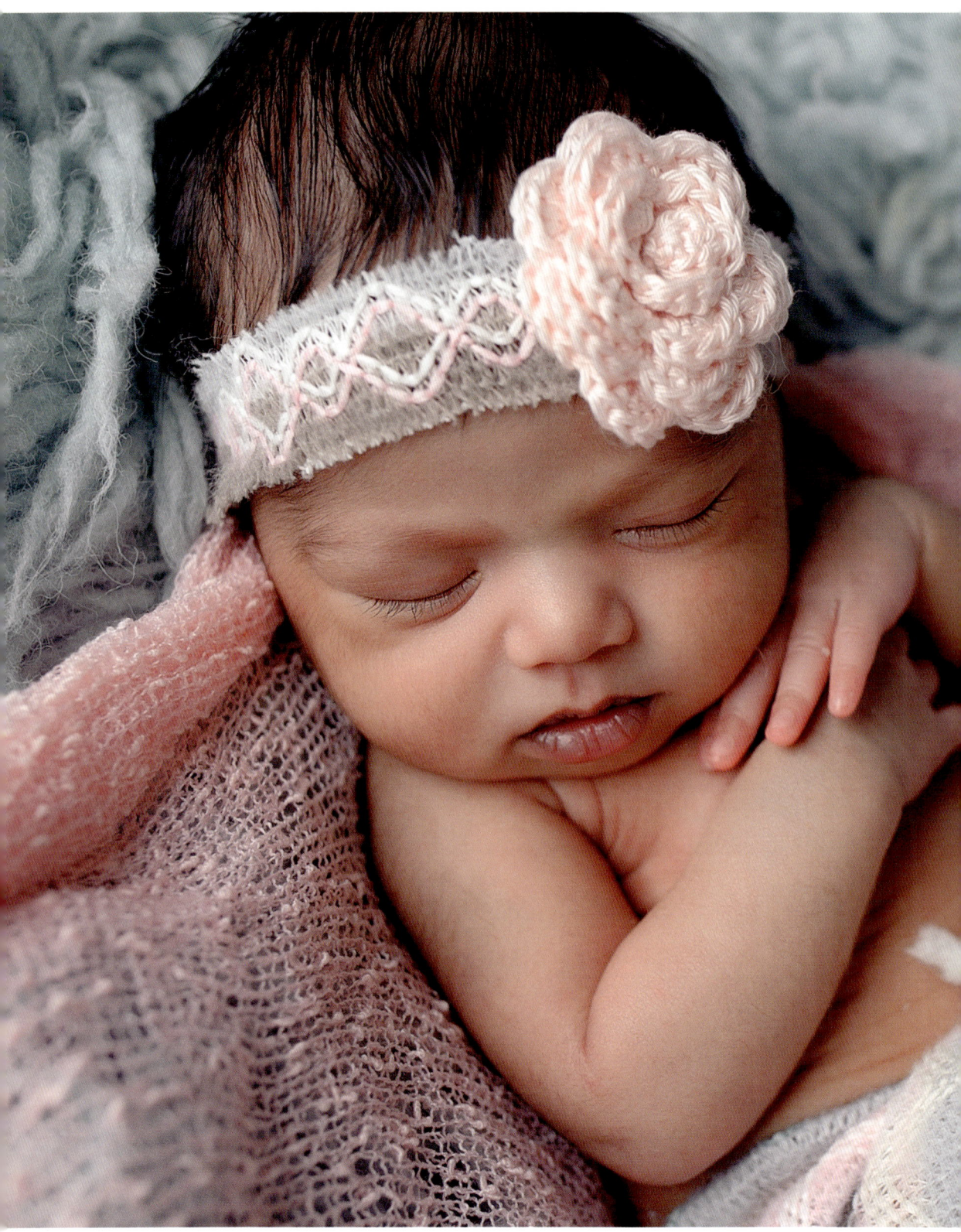

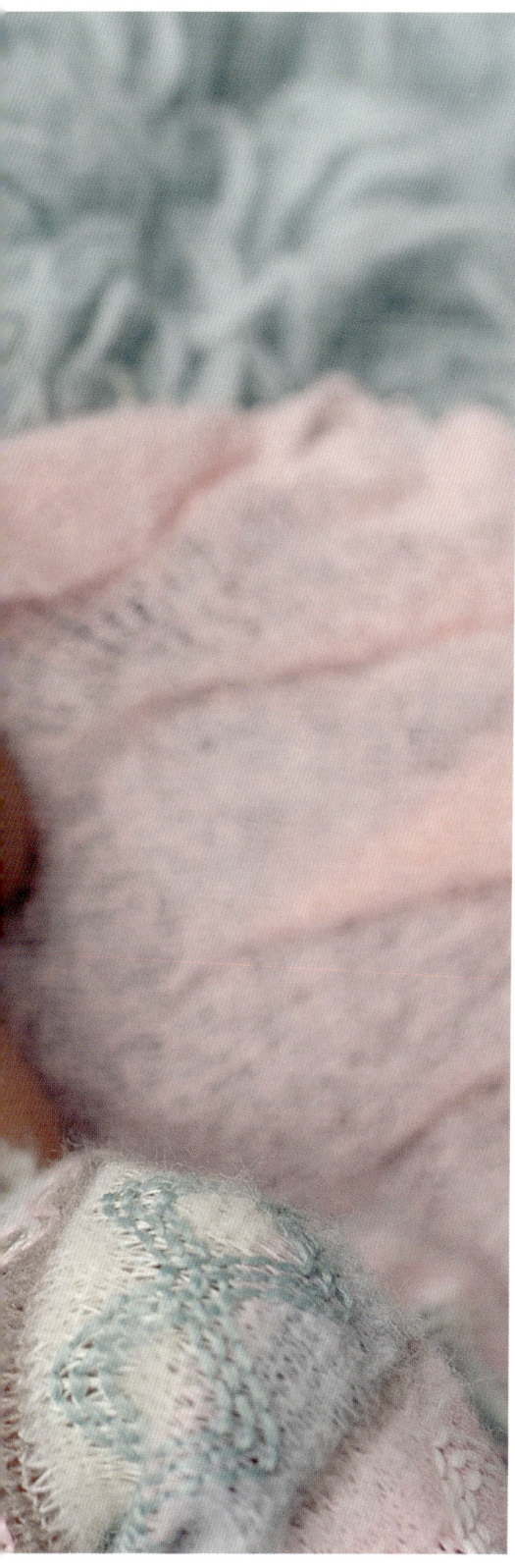

SIYONA

"I fell in love with her right then and there, when I saw the first ultrasound. She was just the size of a blueberry."

—Ratnawali, mom of Siyona,
born November 14th, 2014

PIPER

"Hearing her heartbeat was joyful. It was pure sweetness every time I heard it."

—Jill, mom of Piper, born August 21st, 2015

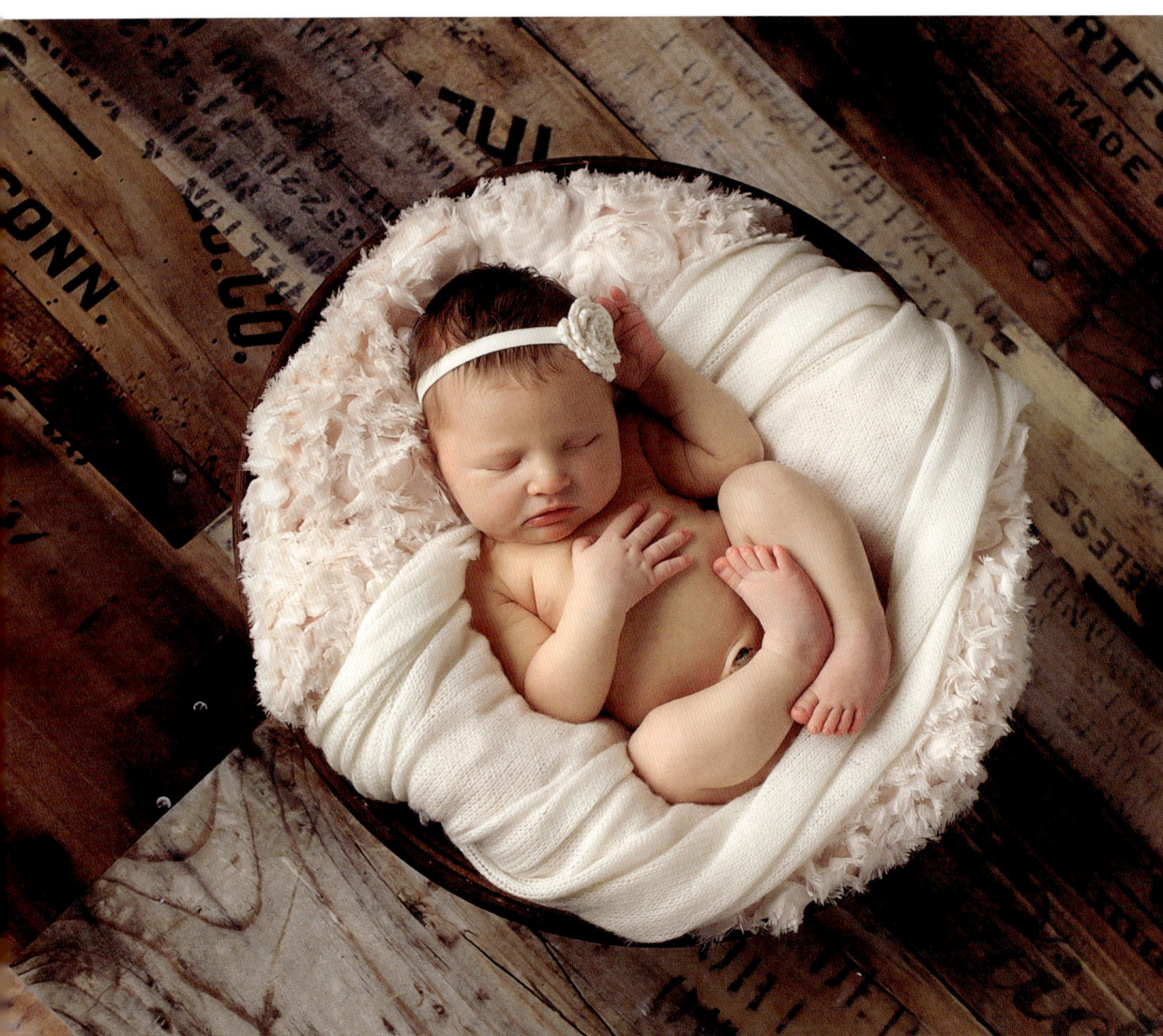

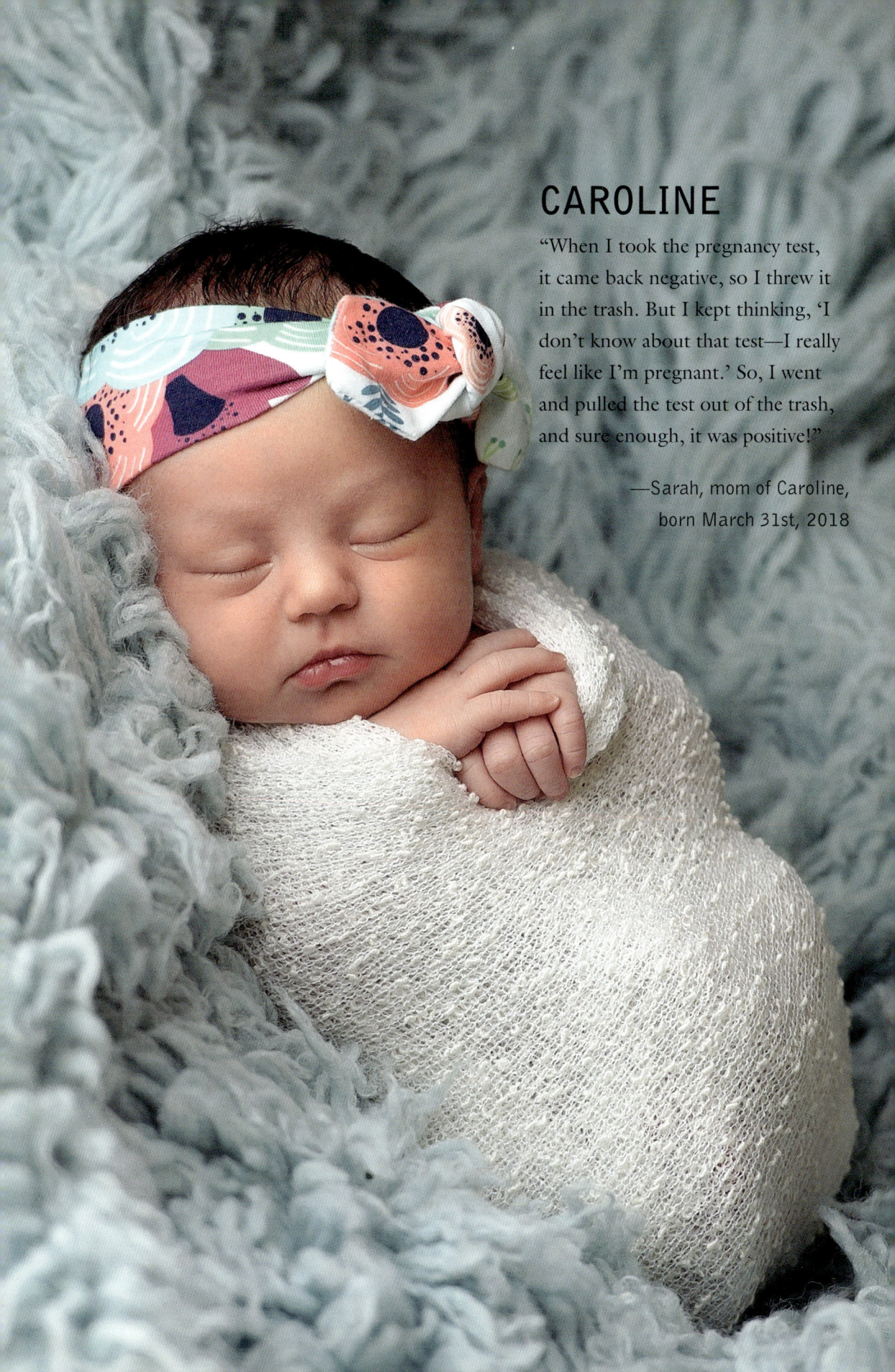

CAROLINE

"When I took the pregnancy test, it came back negative, so I threw it in the trash. But I kept thinking, 'I don't know about that test—I really feel like I'm pregnant.' So, I went and pulled the test out of the trash, and sure enough, it was positive!"

—Sarah, mom of Caroline, born March 31st, 2018

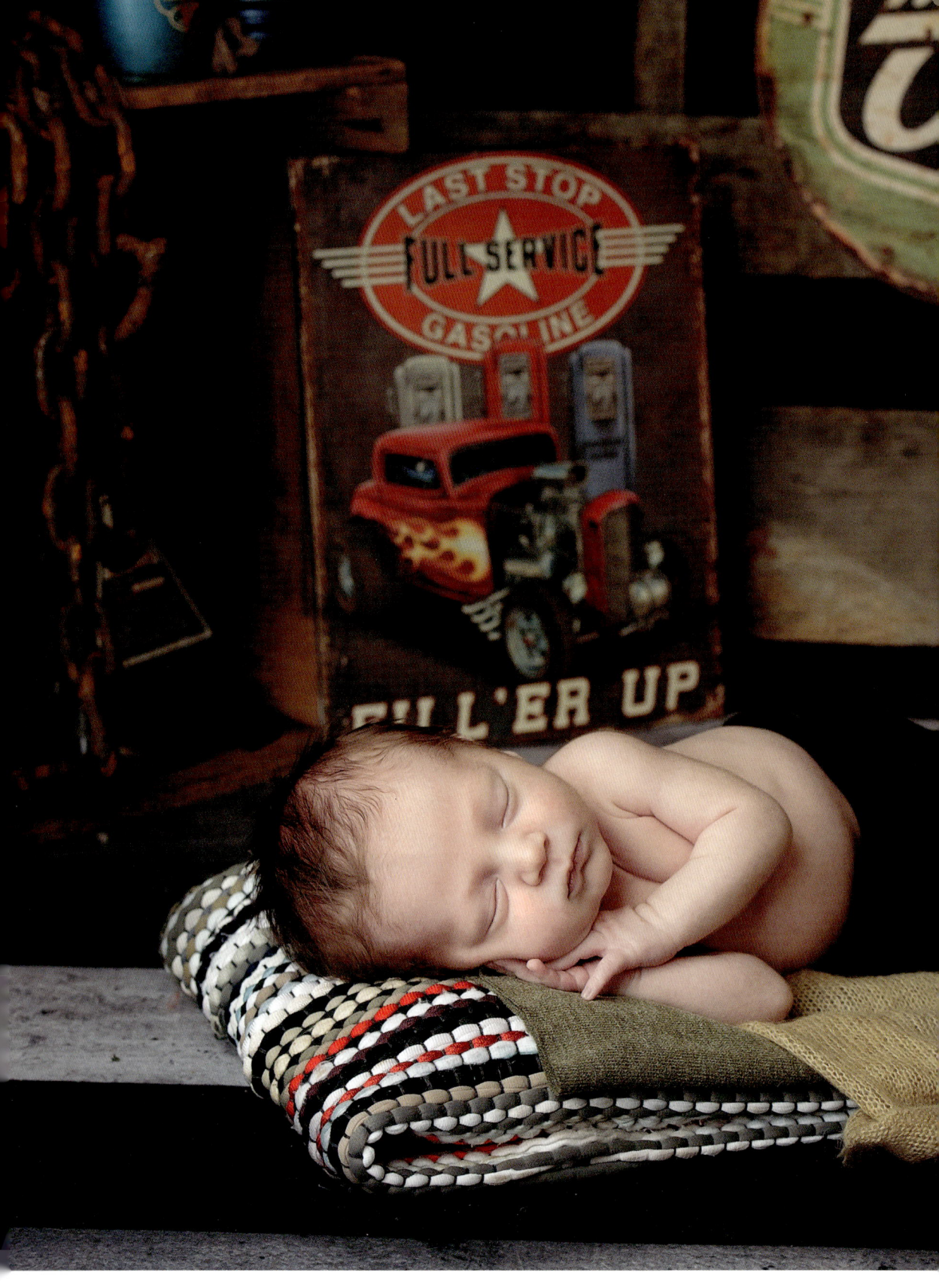

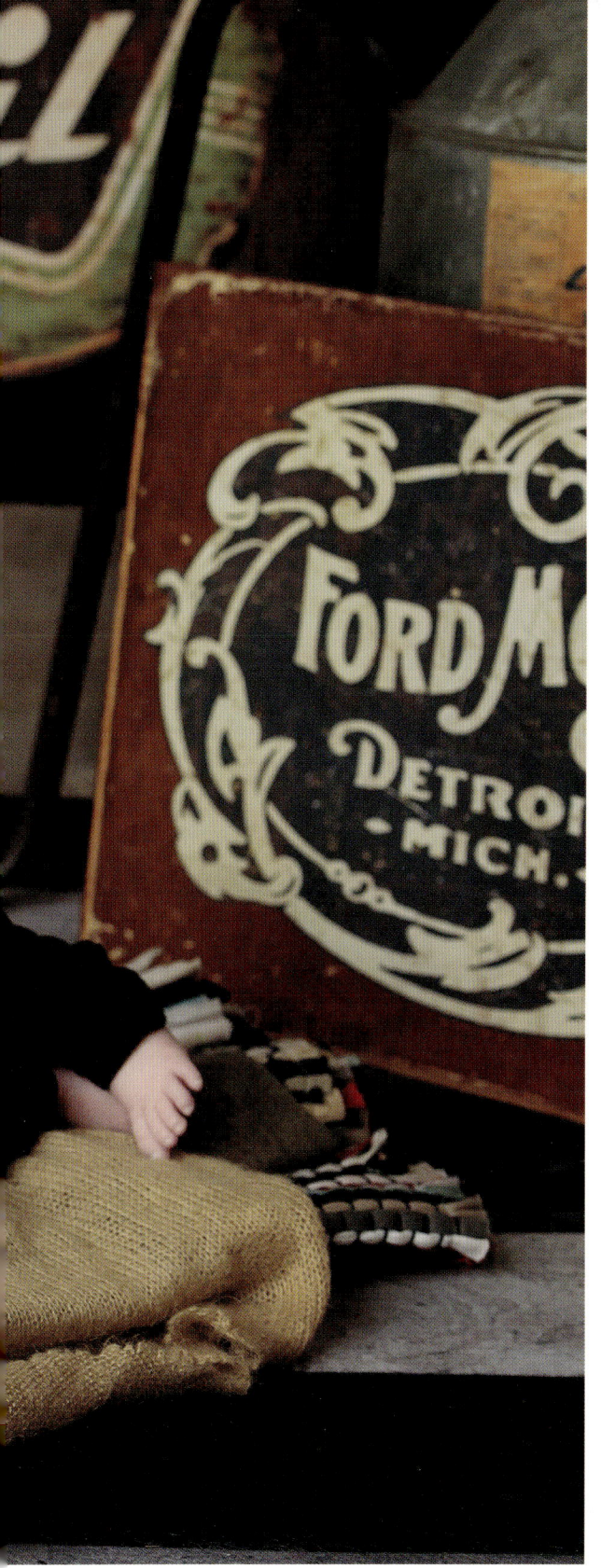

LINCOLN

"Lincoln was laid on my chest while my husband, Brad, cut his umbilical cord. It was as if our lives were finally complete. Lincoln had to be taken to the NICU, so after I recovered, I went into the nursery with Brad to see him. I couldn't even talk; he was beautiful and healthy!"

—Jessica, mom of Lincoln, born November 15th, 2017

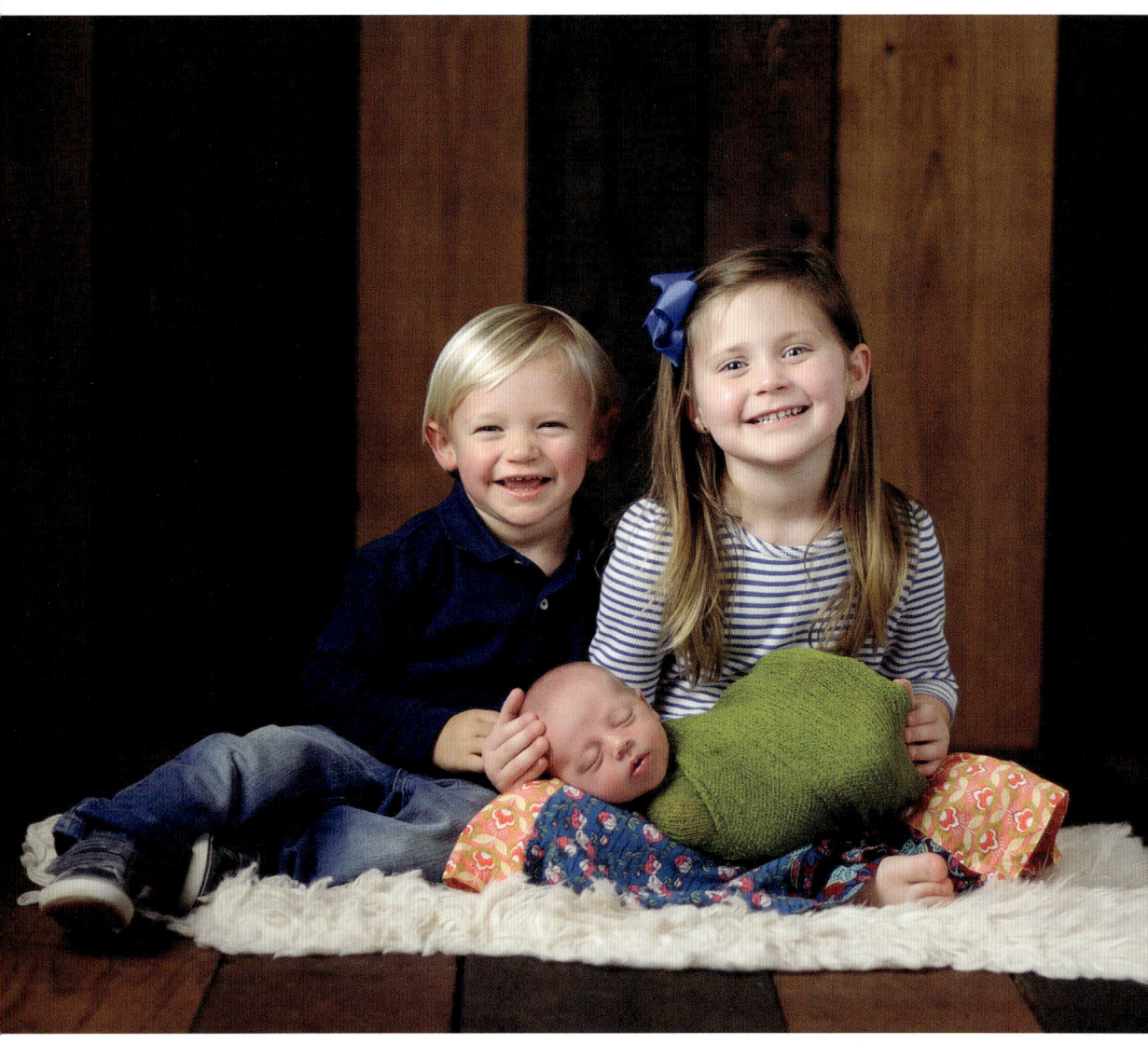

NOAH

"When Ella and Luke came into the hospital room after Noah was born . . . it was a moment I will never forget. They were both so excited to meet their baby brother, and the three had an instant bond. Their love for each other is one of our greatest blessings."

—Erica, mom of Noah, born September 28th, 2015

EMSLEY

"I had an extremely difficult time with our first miscarriage. When I held Emsley for the first time, I finally felt at peace about losing our first baby, because I understood I was meant to be Emsley's mama."

—Leslie, mom of Emsley, born October 10th, 2012

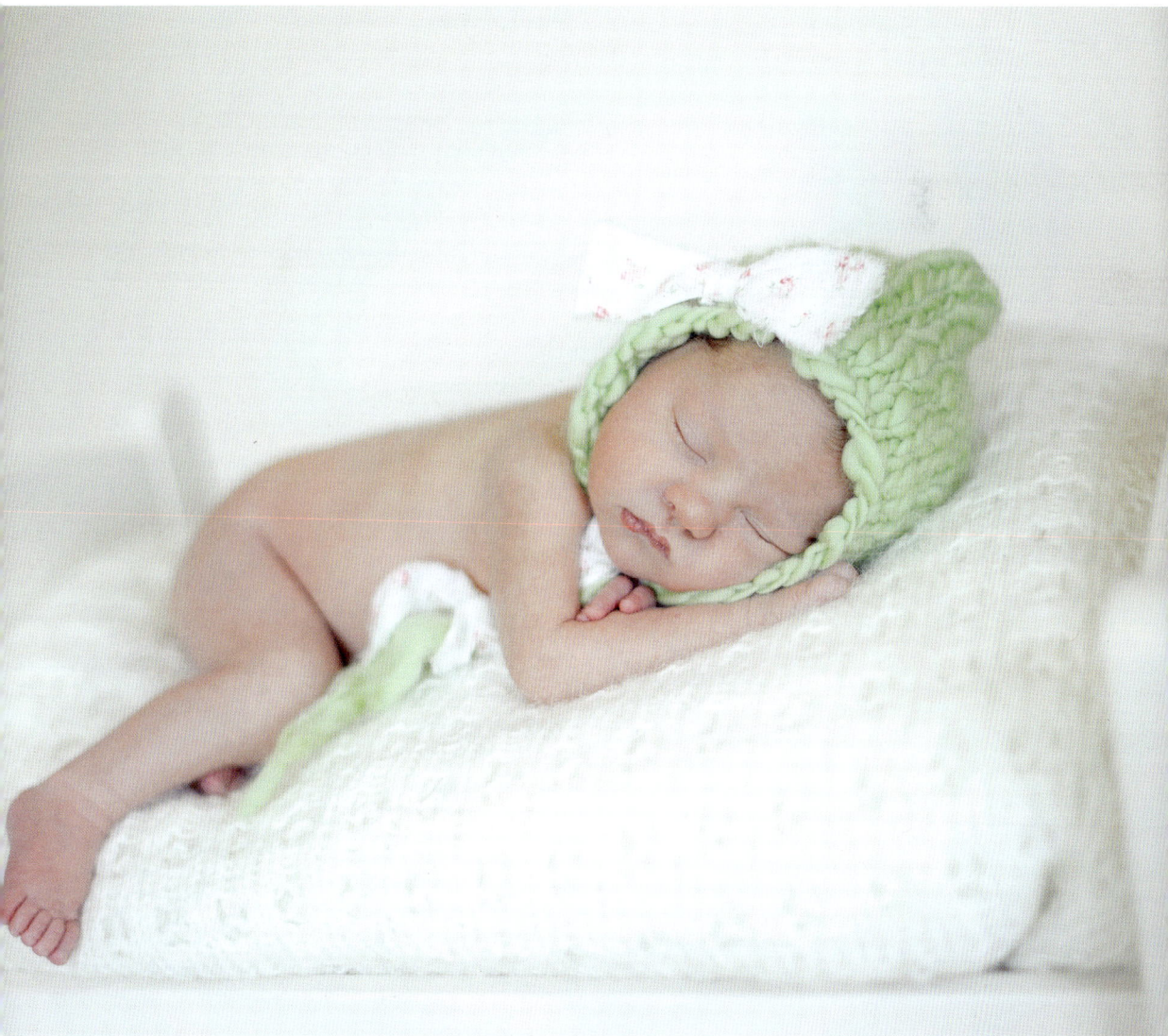

LUKE

"When I found out I was pregnant with Luke, I was so excited, but nervous at the same time!"

—Lindsay, mom of Luke, born April 7th, 2016

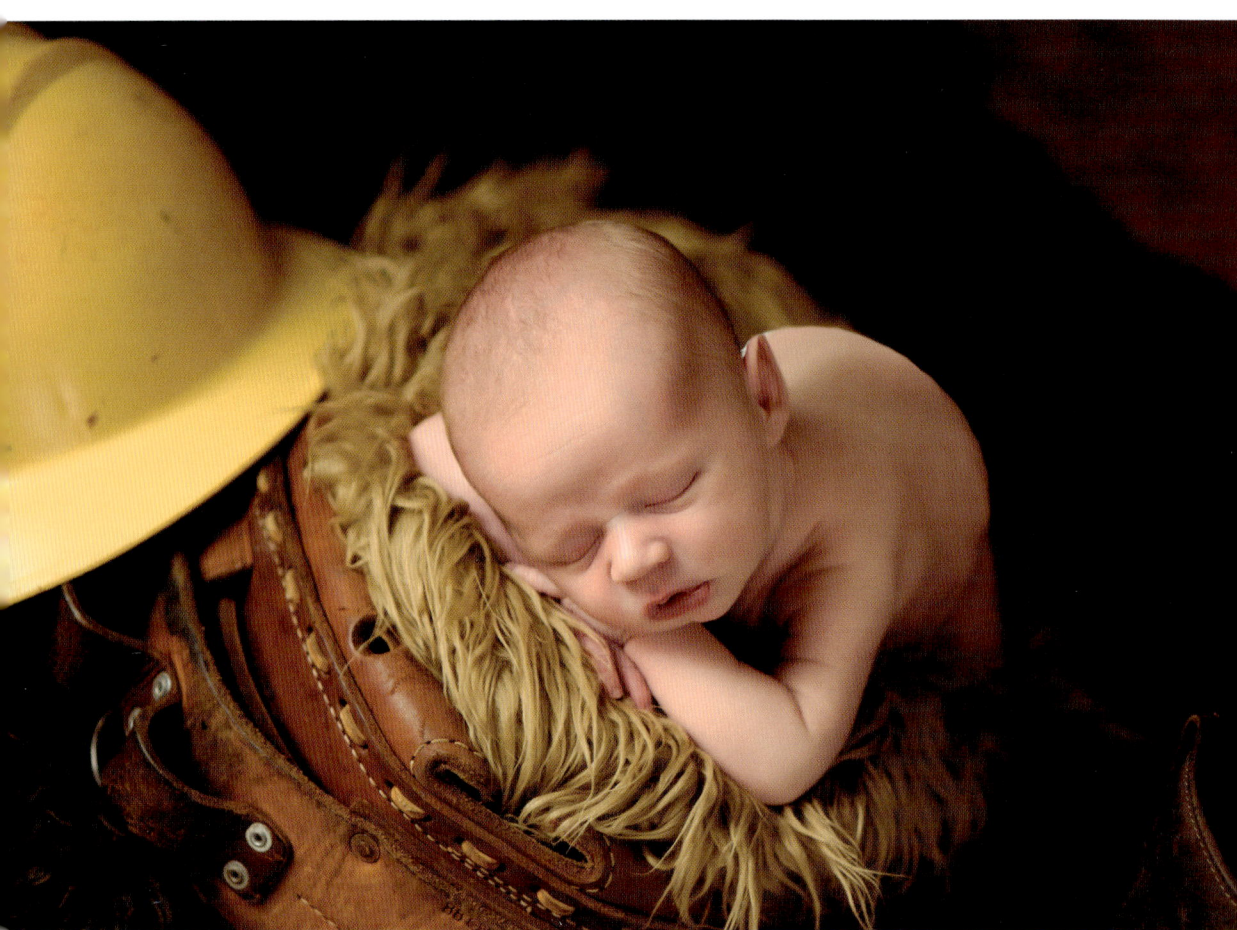

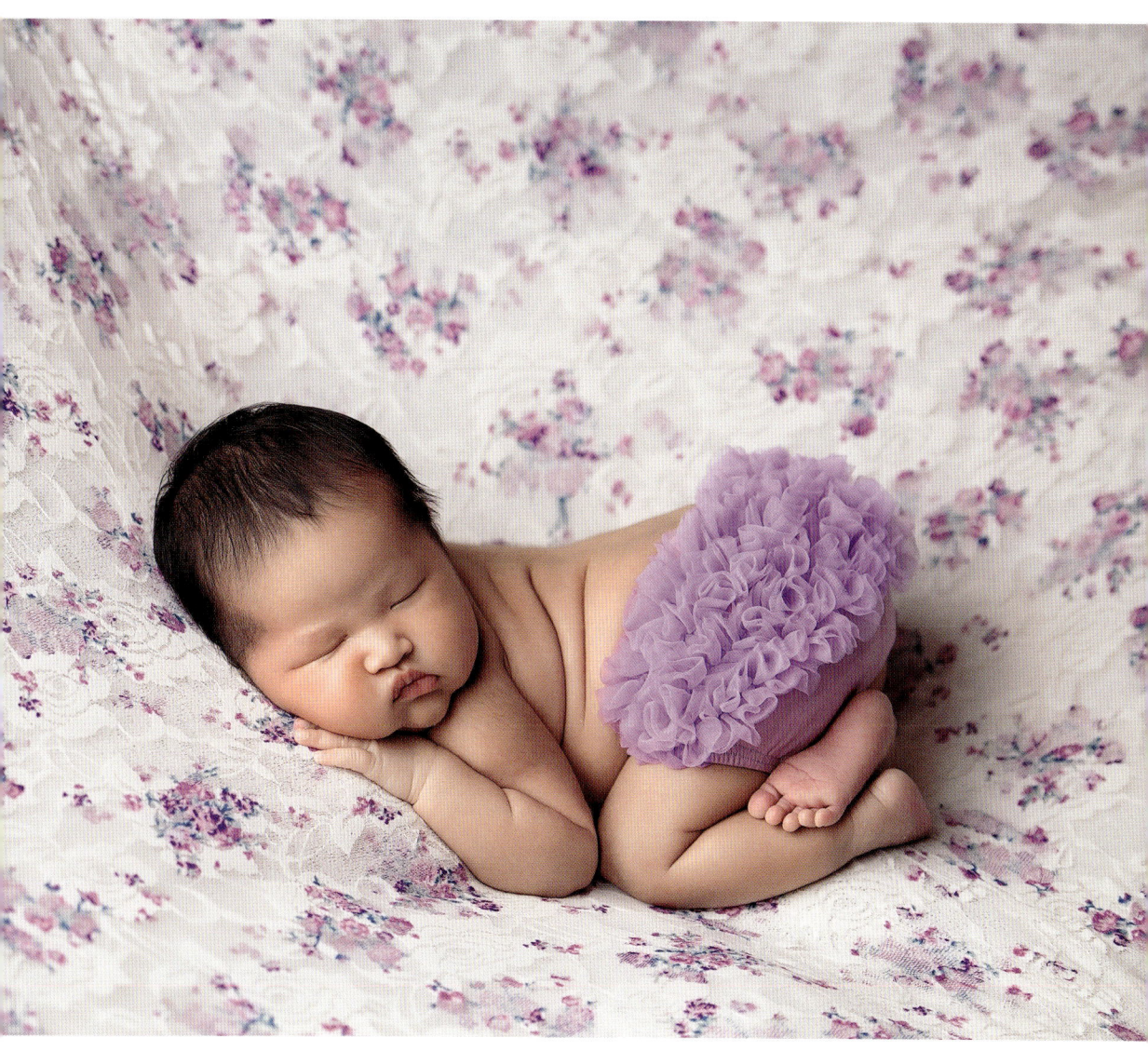

LIANNA

"The first time I laid my eyes on her, I felt so blessed to have such a beautiful and healthy baby!"

—Susan, mom of Lianna, born April 20th, 2017

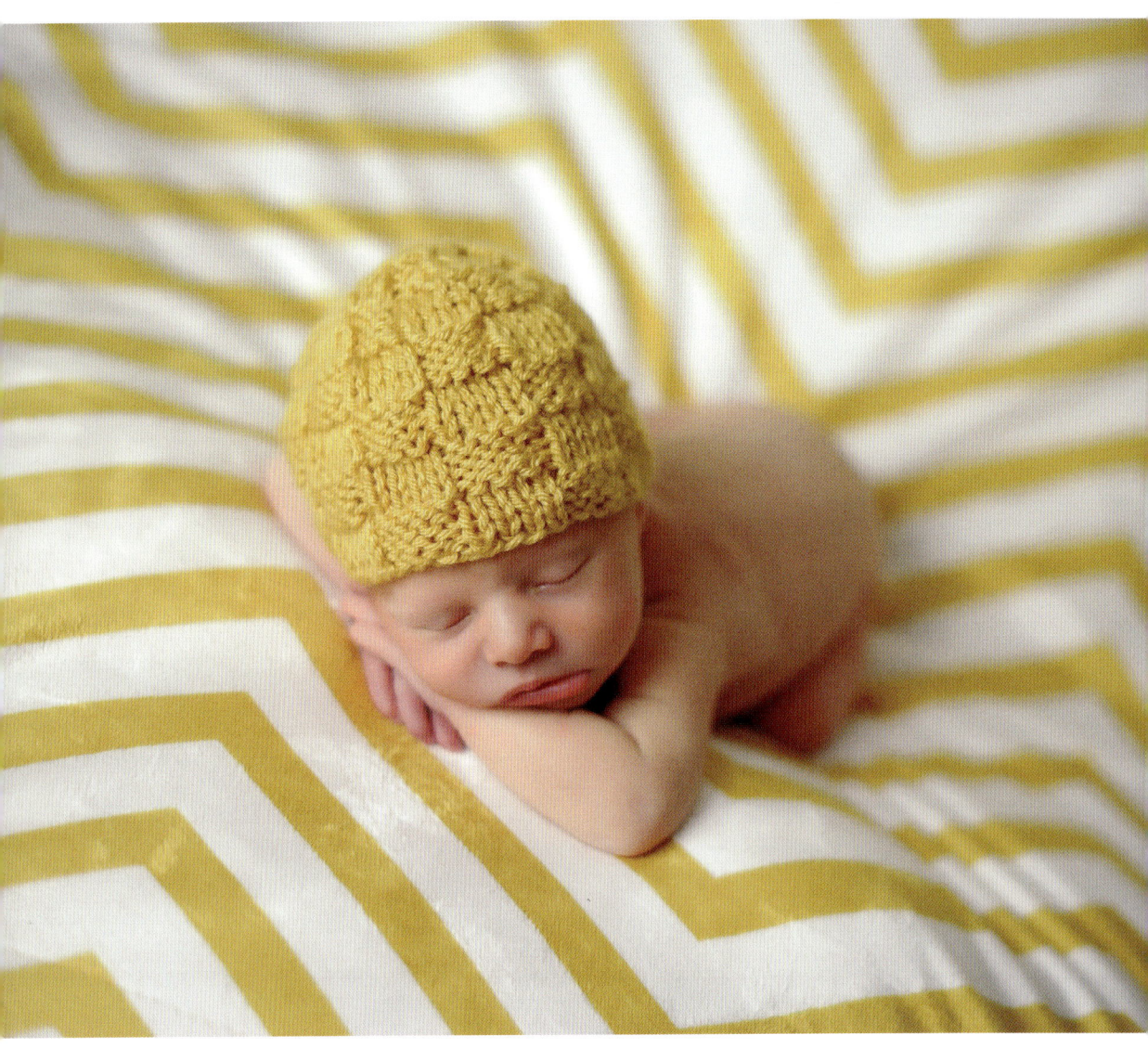

MYLES

"The first time I saw him, I felt a love that I never knew
I could feel."

—Kristin, mom of Myles, born March 10th, 2013

LYNDON

"We tried for nine years to get pregnant. Through numerous failed infertility cycles, multiple procedures, and a miscarriage, to finally get pregnant was nothing short of a miracle. We thank God every day for our little miracle, and for keeping him safe throughout the pregnancy."

—Lindsey, mom of Lyndon, born November 29th, 2017

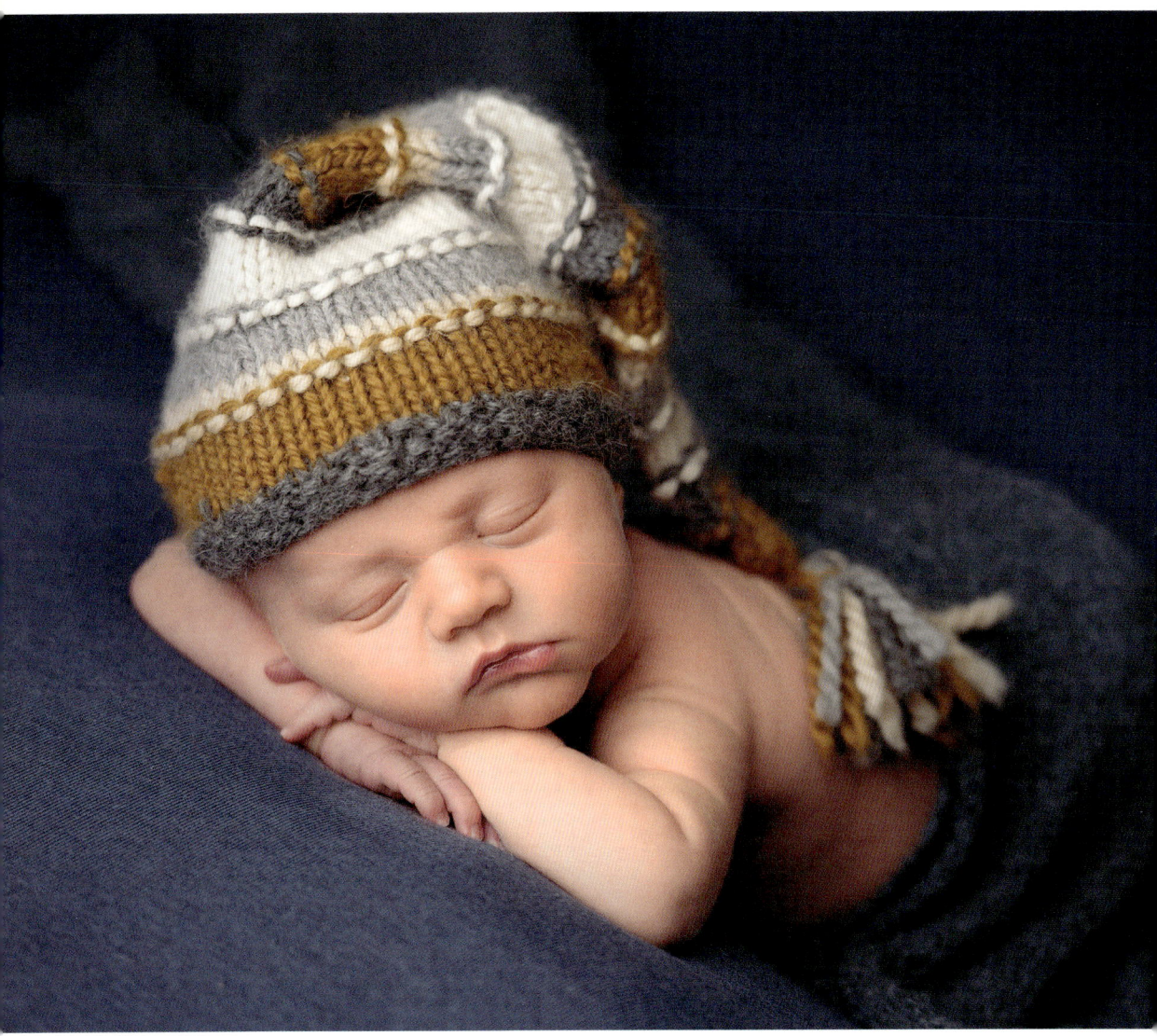

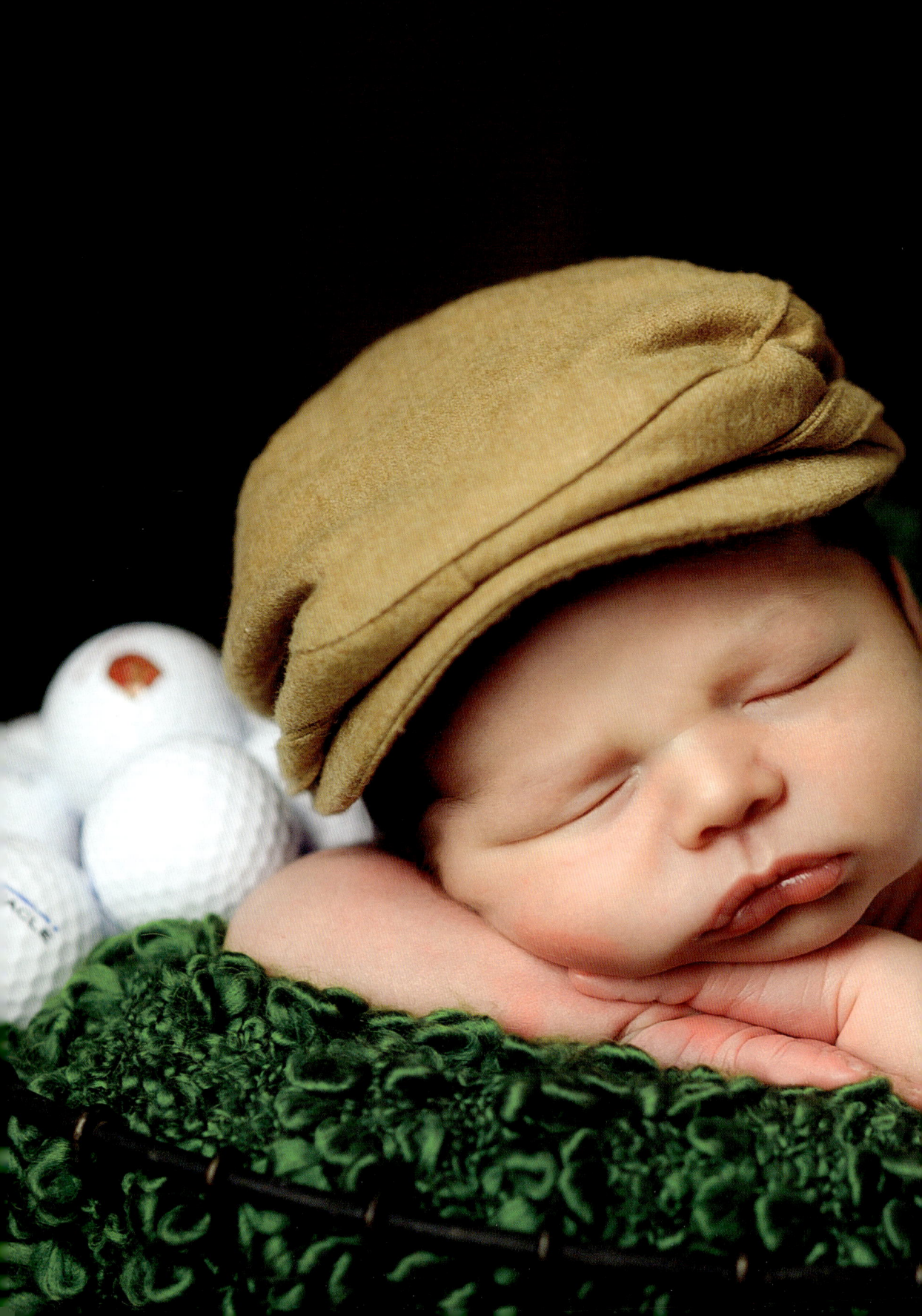

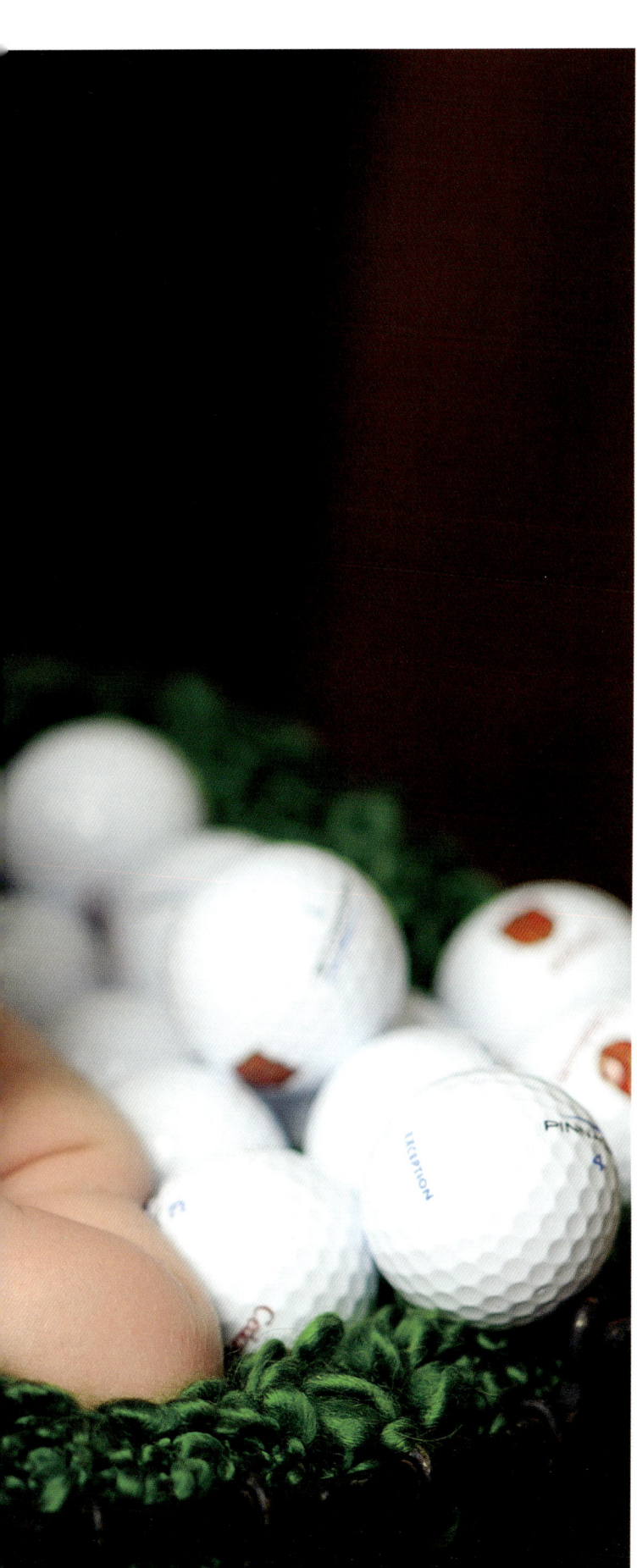

HUDSON

"Seeing my husband, Matt, with Hudson for the first time was so special. I remember looking over as the nurse was getting Hudson cleaned up, and seeing the love Matt had for his son. He bent down and said, 'Hey, big guy, Daddy loves you.' That's a moment I will never forget."

—Kara, mom of Hudson, born October 29th, 2015

HARPYR

"It's funny; we always joked when we were pregnant that we would have a bald-headed, chunky girl, since my husband and I were both big babies and I was bald as a baby. We ended up with a tiny baby girl with a head full of blond hair!"

—Megan, mom of Harpyr, born June 26th, 2014

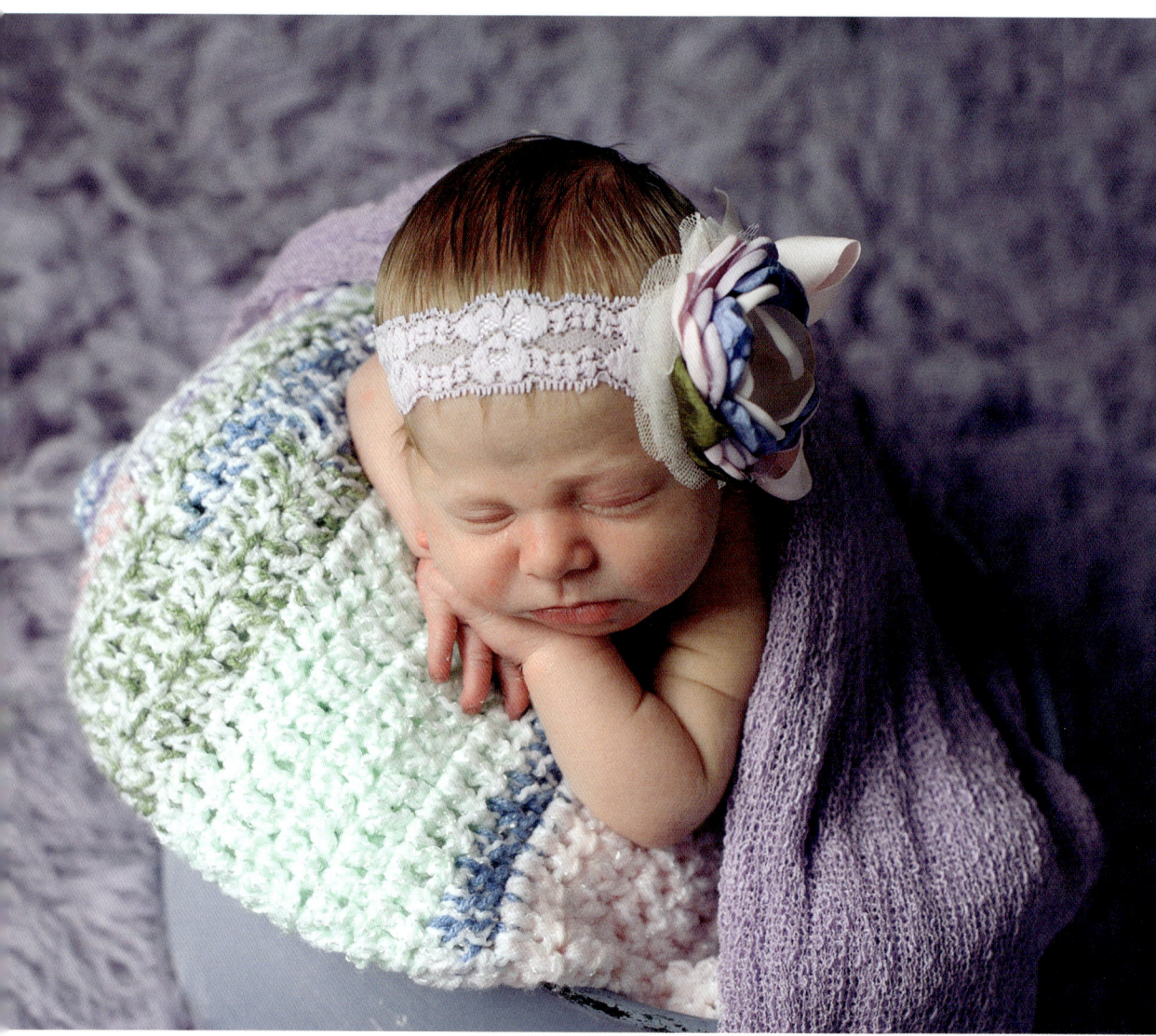

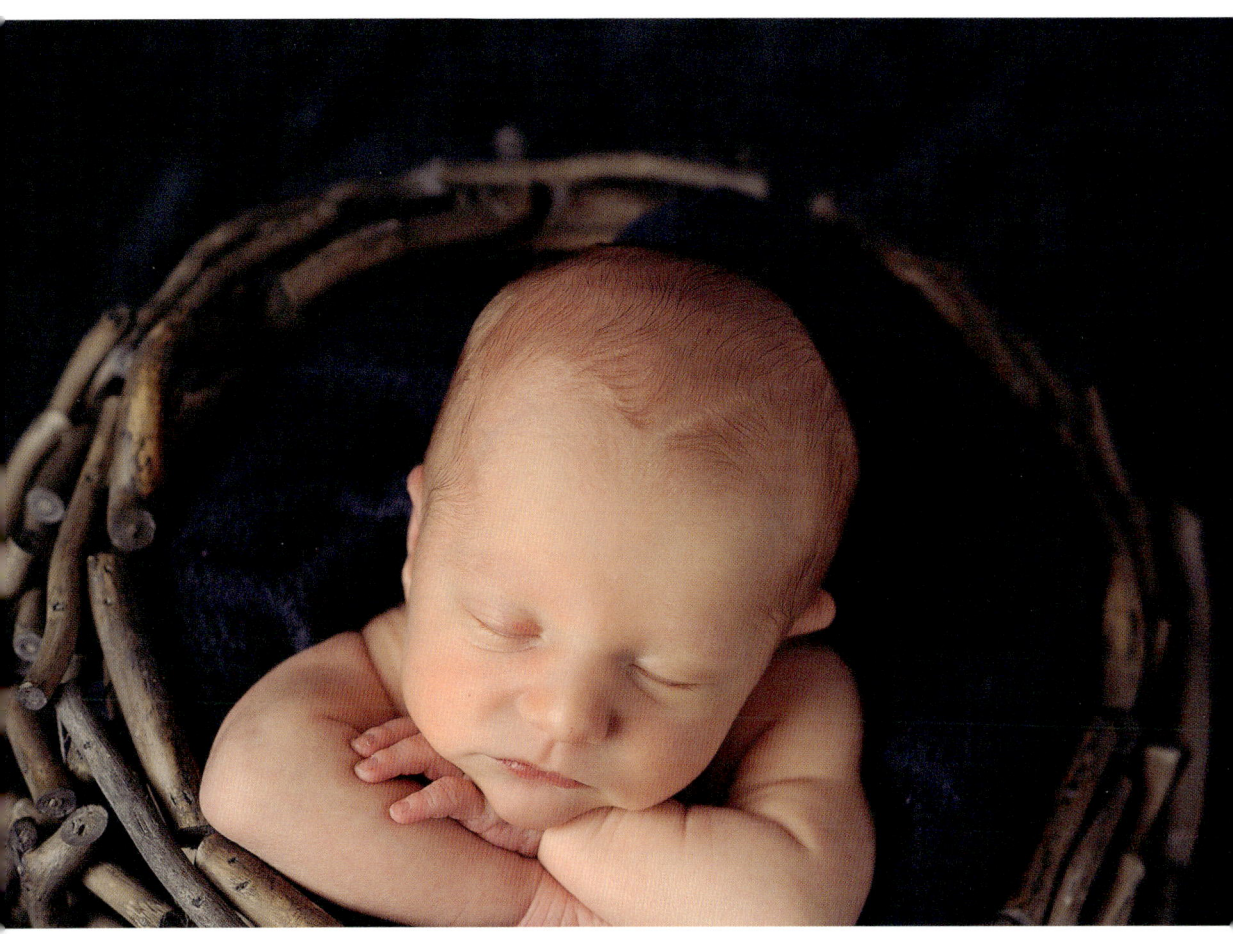

CARTER

"My favorite part of having a newborn was being able to hold and rock him—and the smell of all the baby soaps and lotions."

—Emily, mom of Carter, born August 28th, 2015

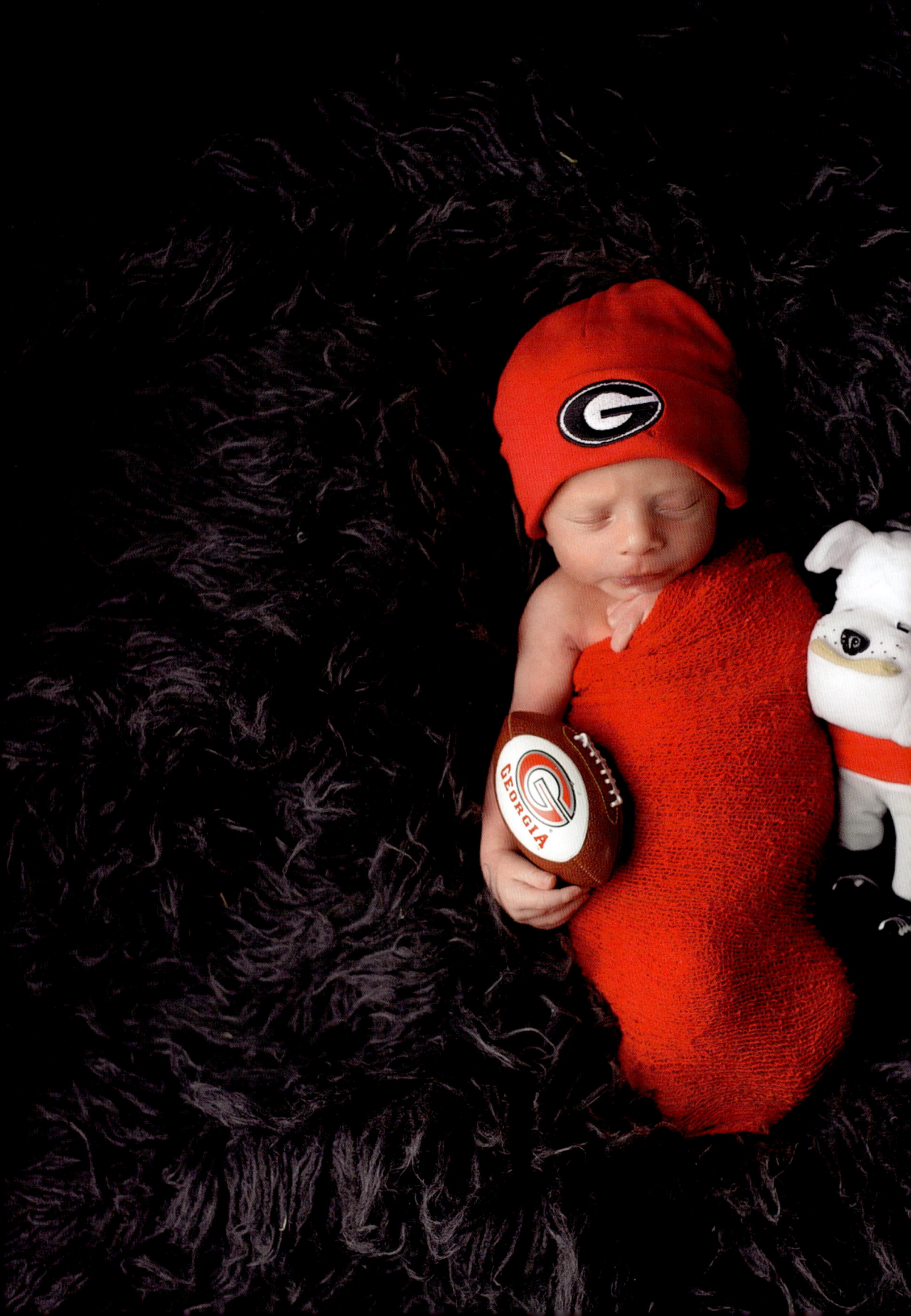

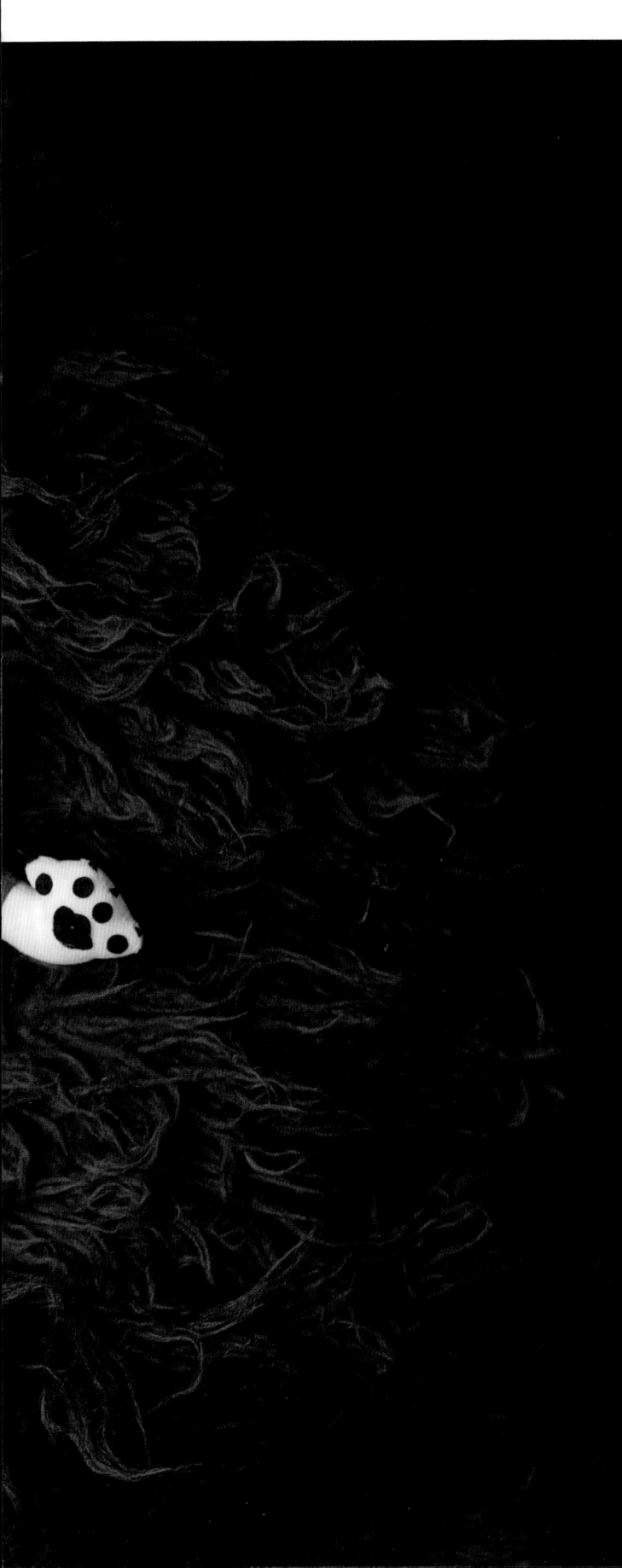

SAM

"I don't even have words to describe the first time I heard Sam's heartbeat on the ultrasound! I was just in tears, and in awe of this little person growing inside me."

—Jenn, mom of Sam,
born December 31st, 2014

ANSON

"When I first felt Anson move, I was so excited!"

—Stephanie, mom of Anson, born March 17th, 2014

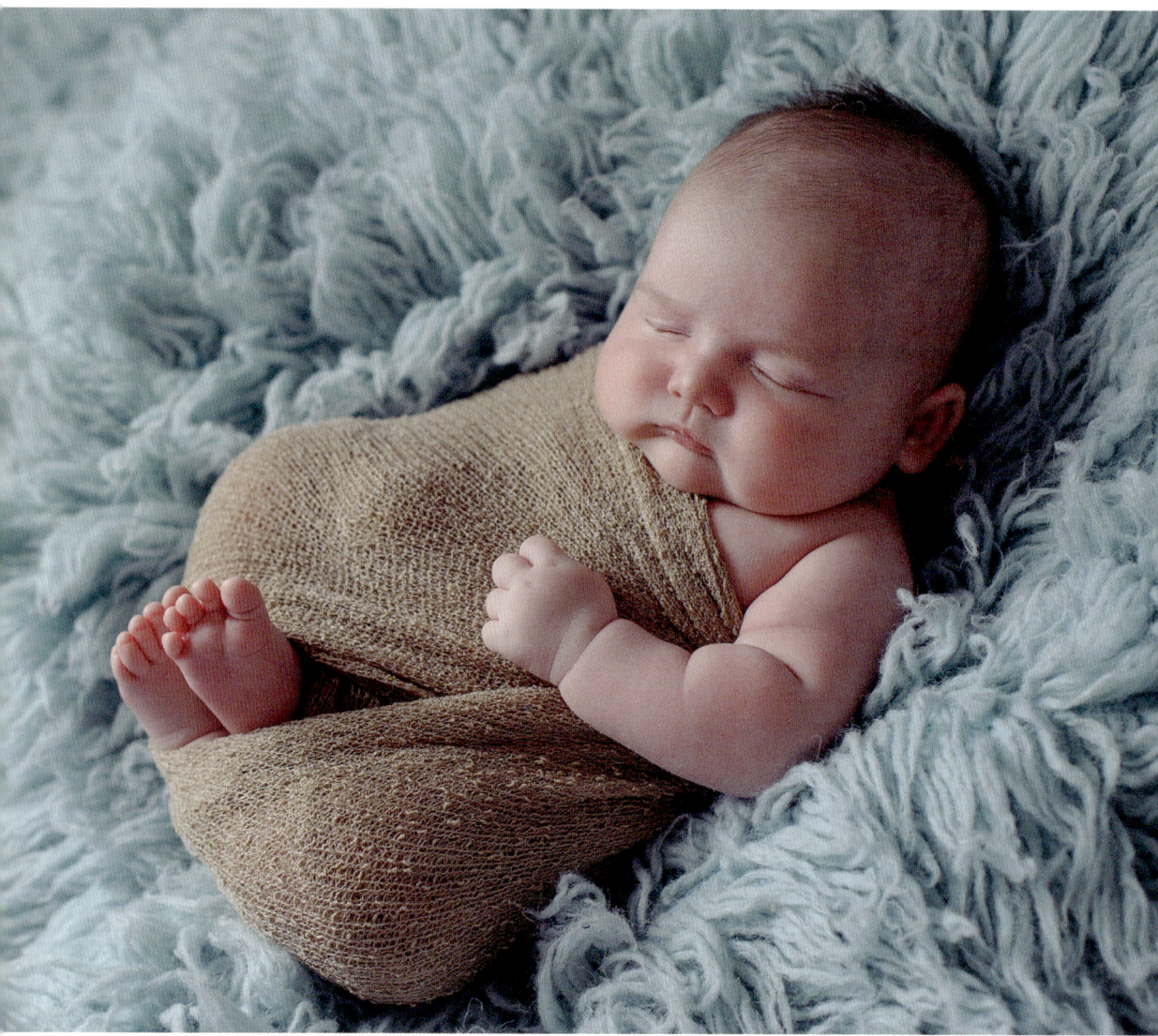

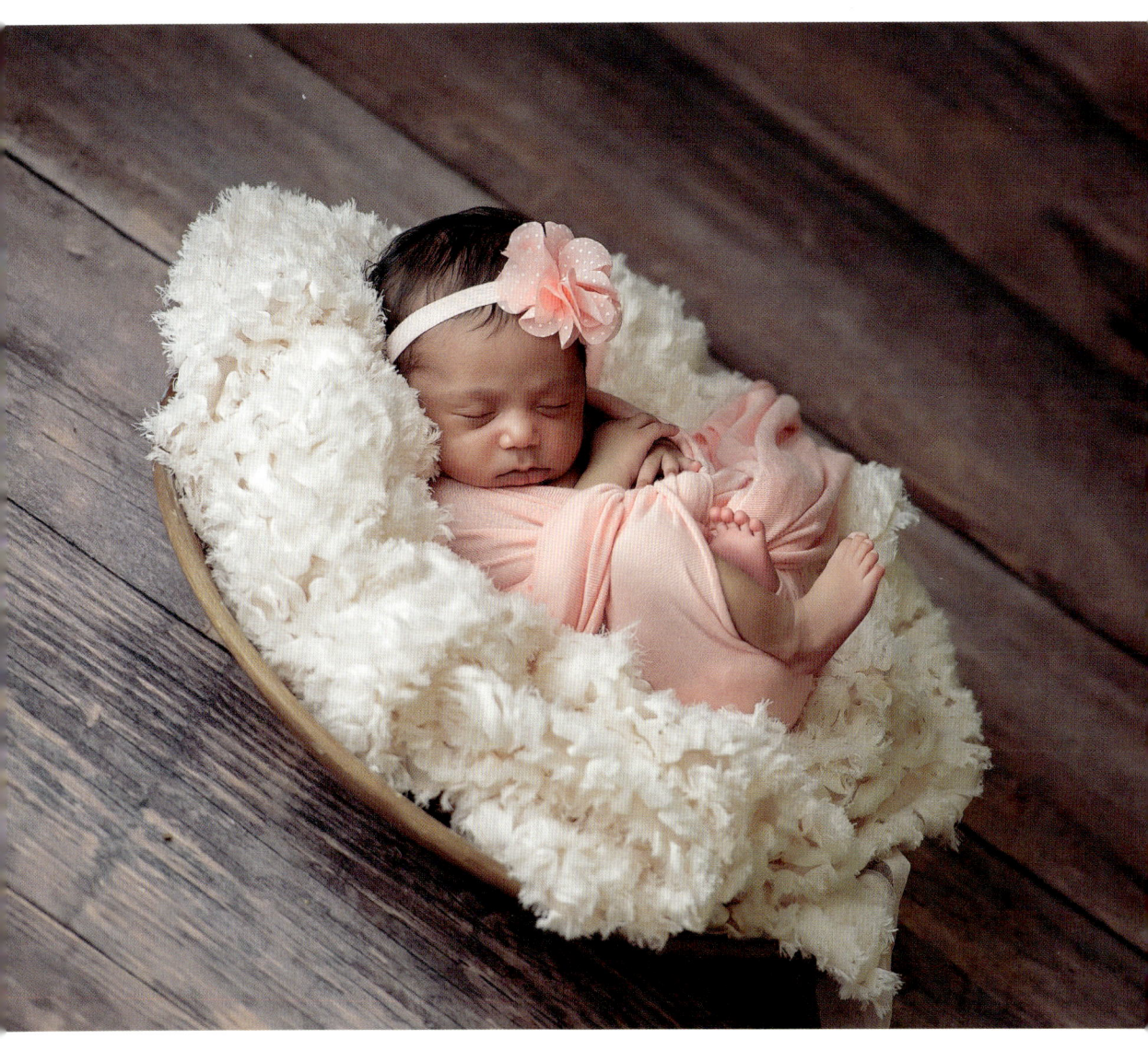

SYNOVIE

"We were over-the-moon excited when we found out we were expecting!"

—Ratnawali, mom of Synovie, born April 25th, 2018

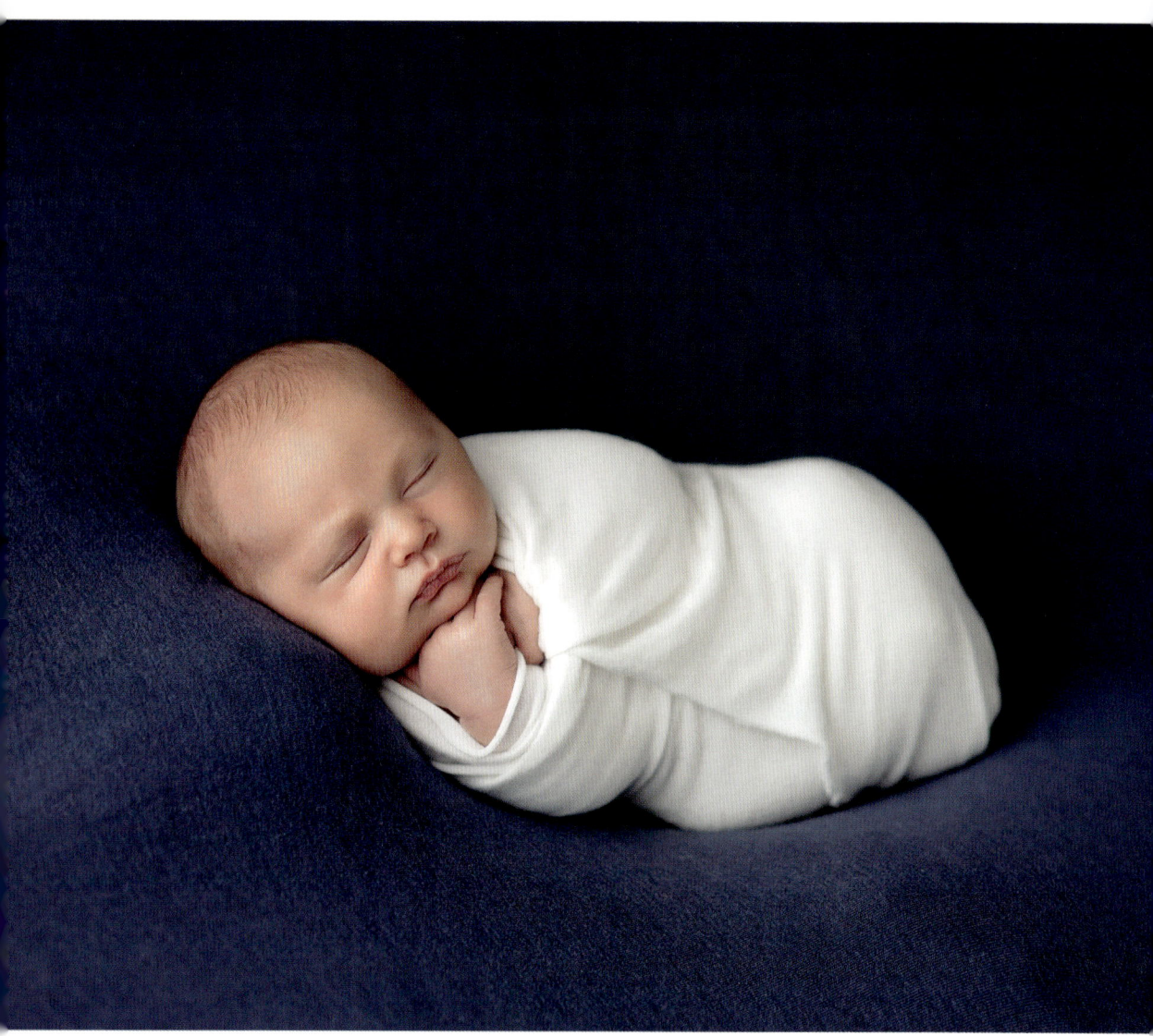

CONWAY

"One of my favorite things about being pregnant was watching my five-year-old kiss my belly and talk to the baby."

—Meredith, mom of Conway, born January 24th, 2018

ANSLEY

"The first time I saw her, I was completely consumed with love for her!"

—Megan, mom of Ansley, born July 11th, 2015

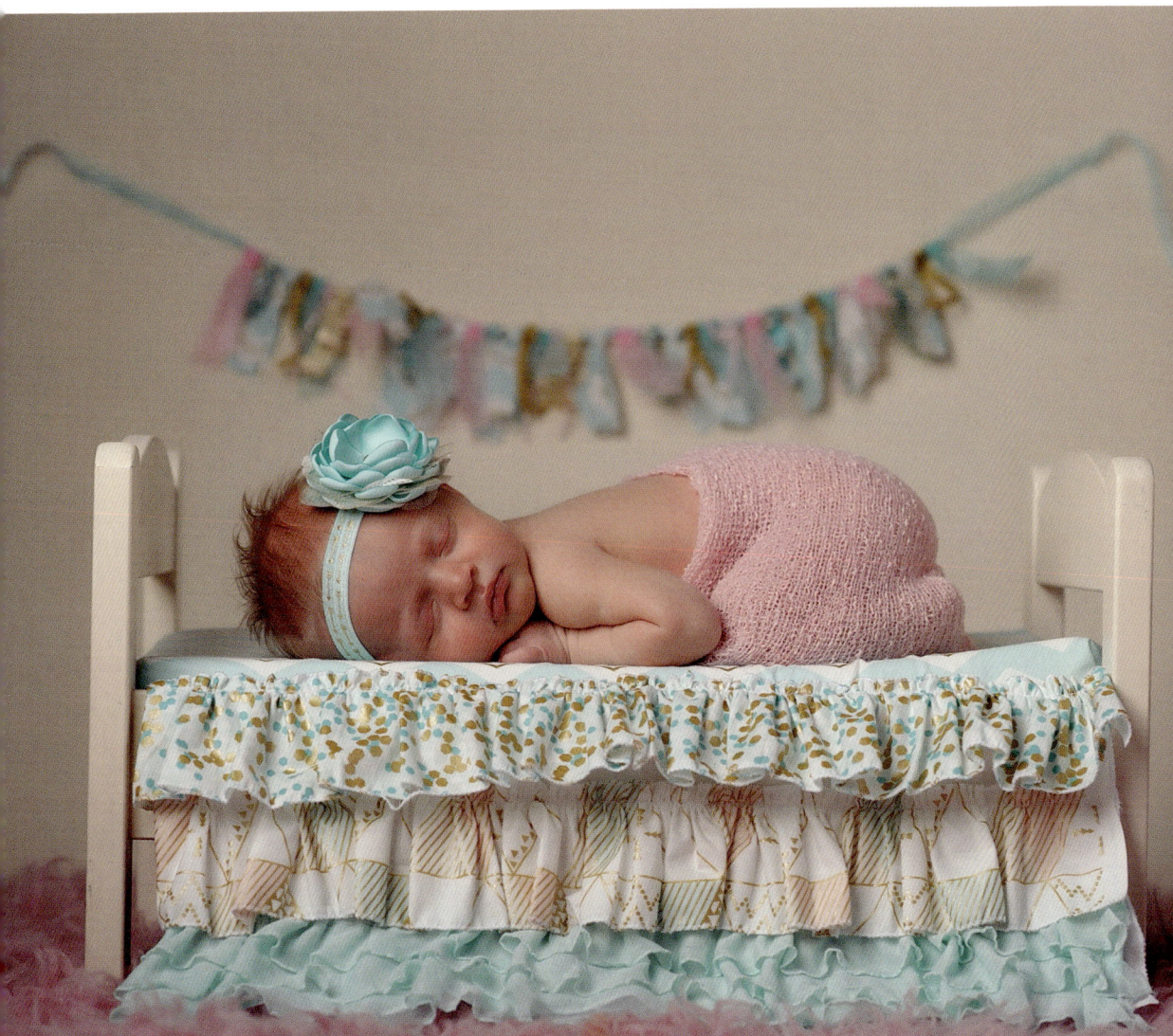

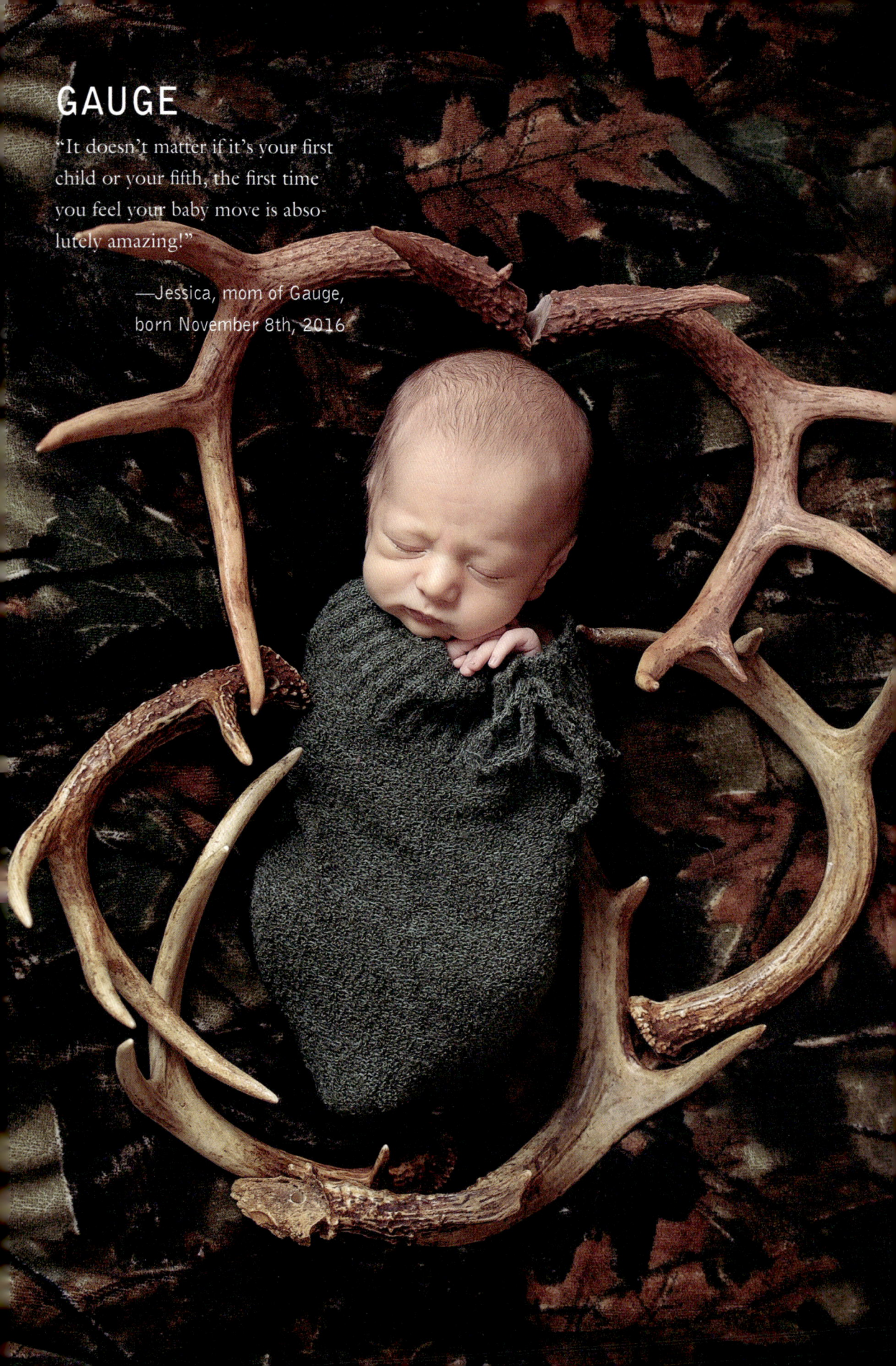

GAUGE

"It doesn't matter if it's your first child or your fifth, the first time you feel your baby move is absolutely amazing!"

—Jessica, mom of Gauge, born November 8th, 2016

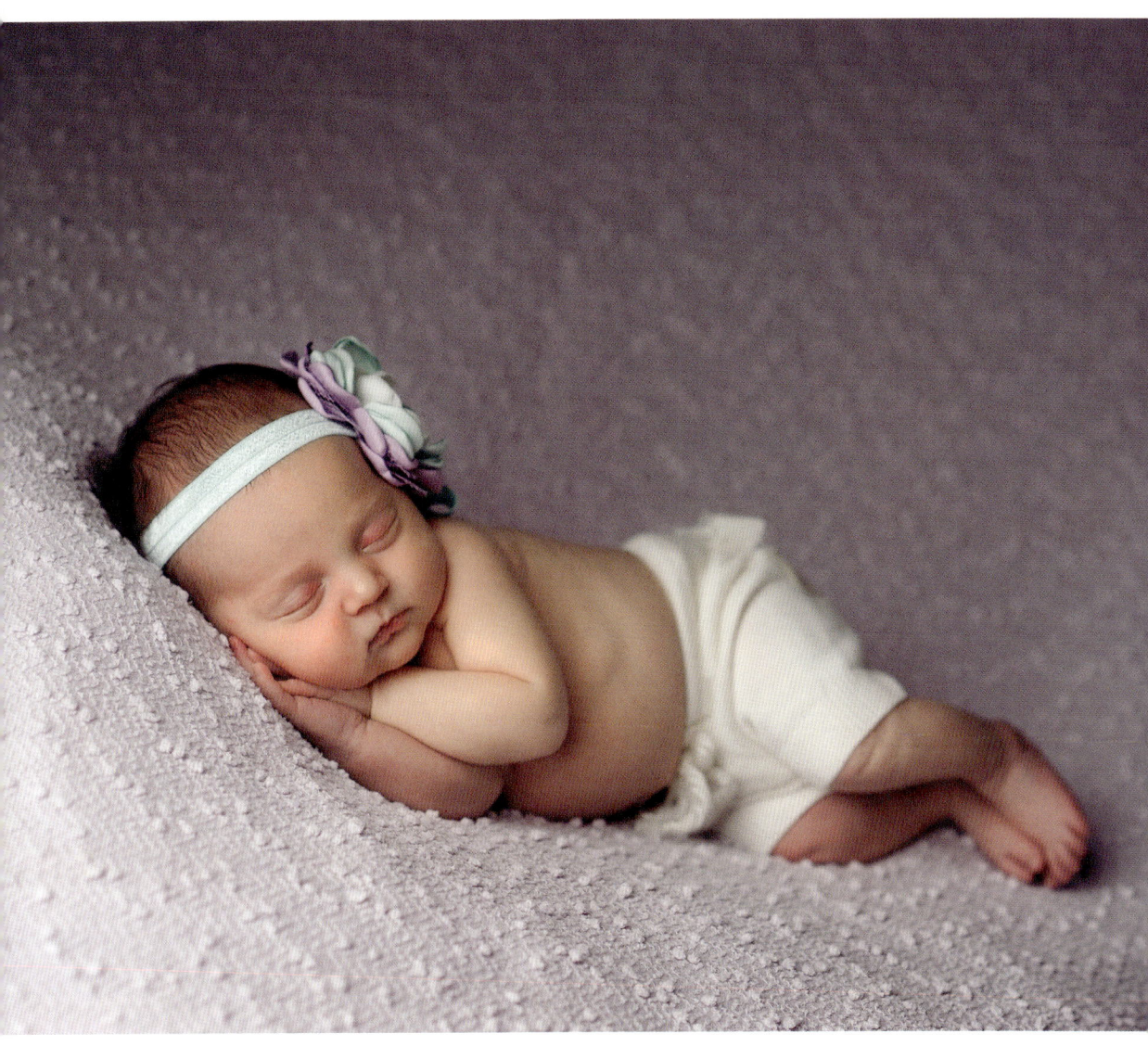

MORGAN

"The first time I saw my husband with Morgan, he was smiling and crying. He had pure joy on his face."

—Jennifer, mom of Morgan, born August 21st, 2015

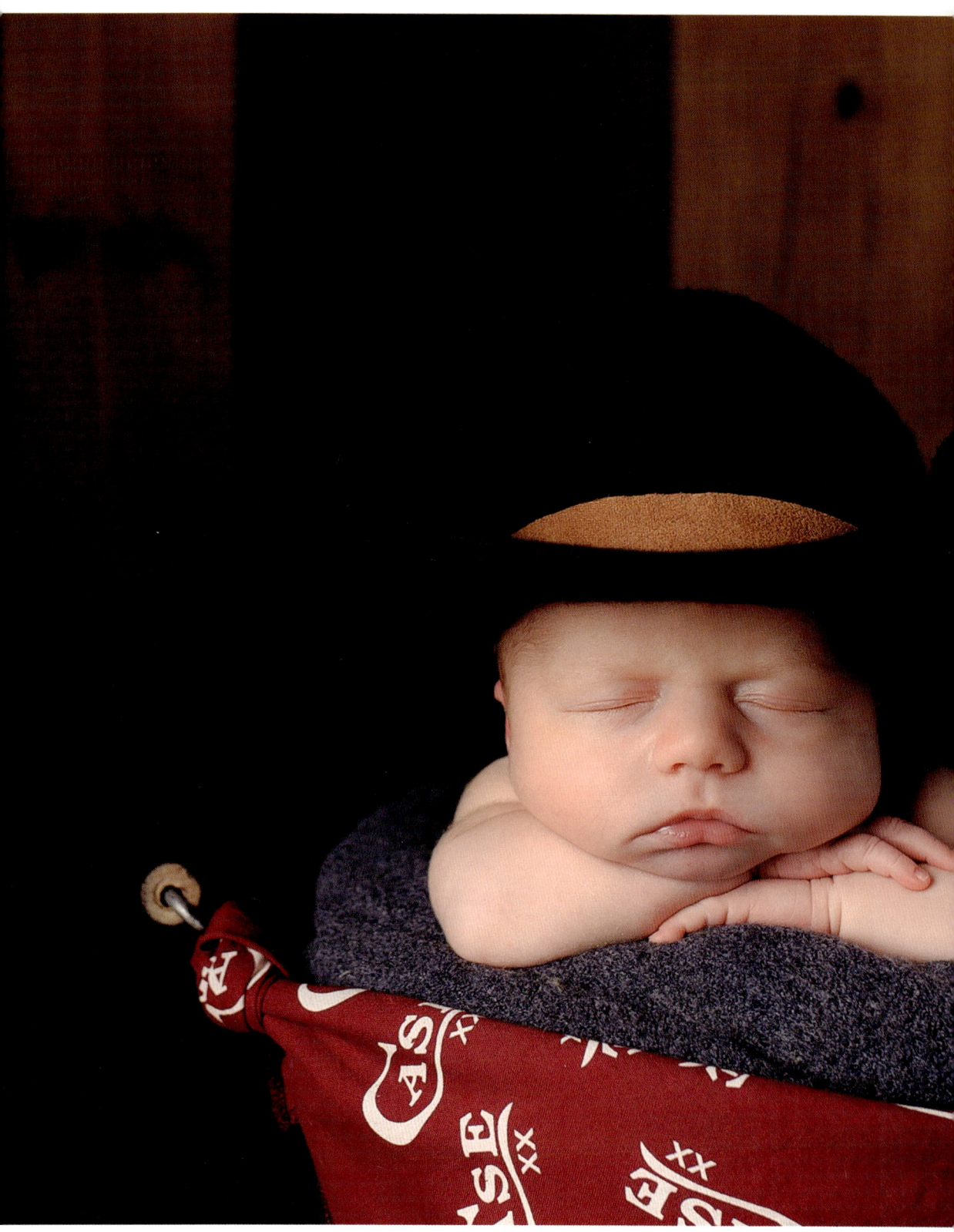

CASE

"The first time I saw Case, I was surprised at how big he was and that he had red hair!"

—Amy, mom of Case, born January 31st, 2015

WYATT

"The first time I saw Wyatt, I thought, 'Oh goodness. He is mine! This is the best day *ever!*' He was the most beautiful baby boy. He looked up at me while he was skin-to-skin with me, like he had known me forever!"

—Michelle, mom of Wyatt, born February 3rd, 2016

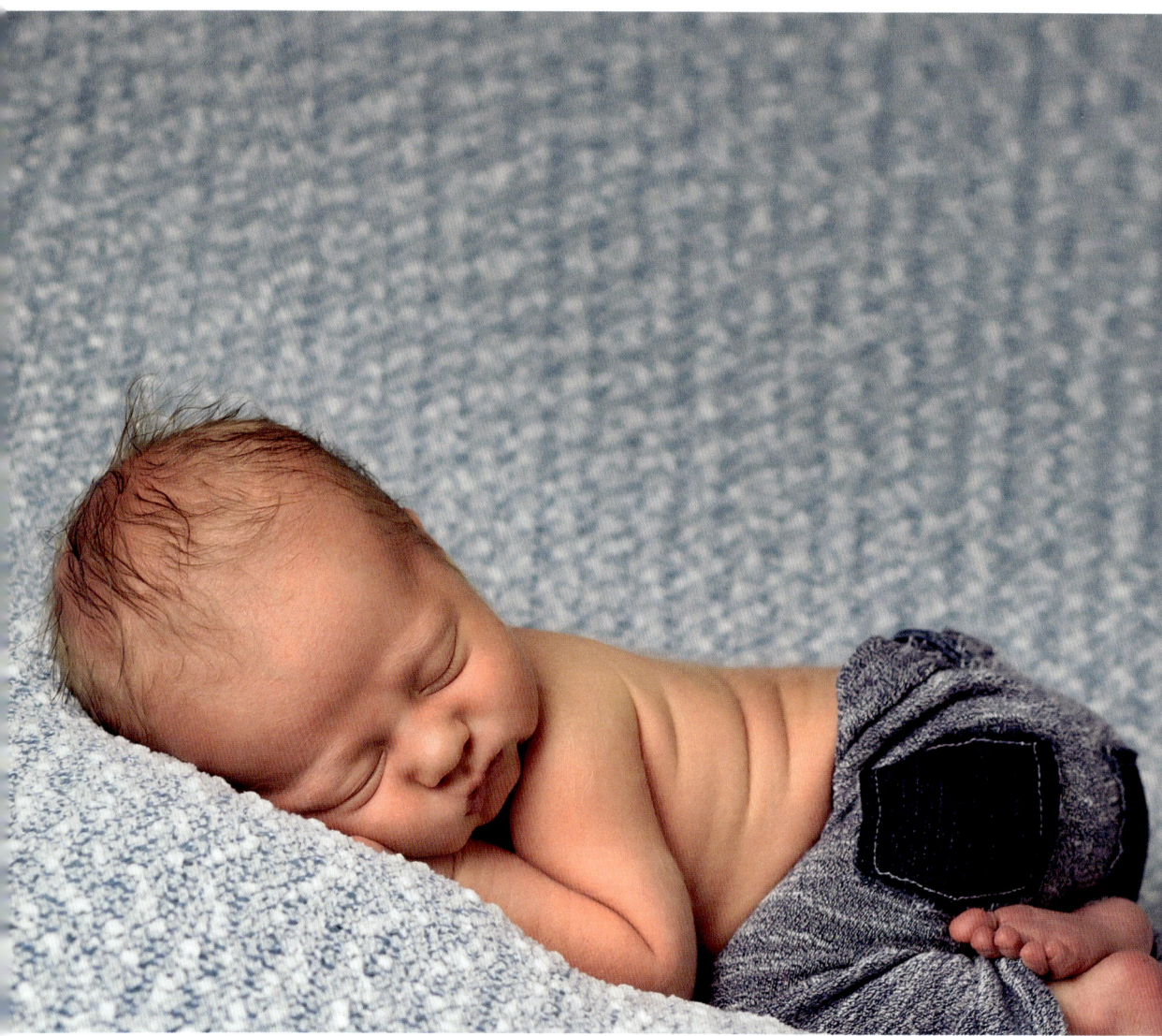

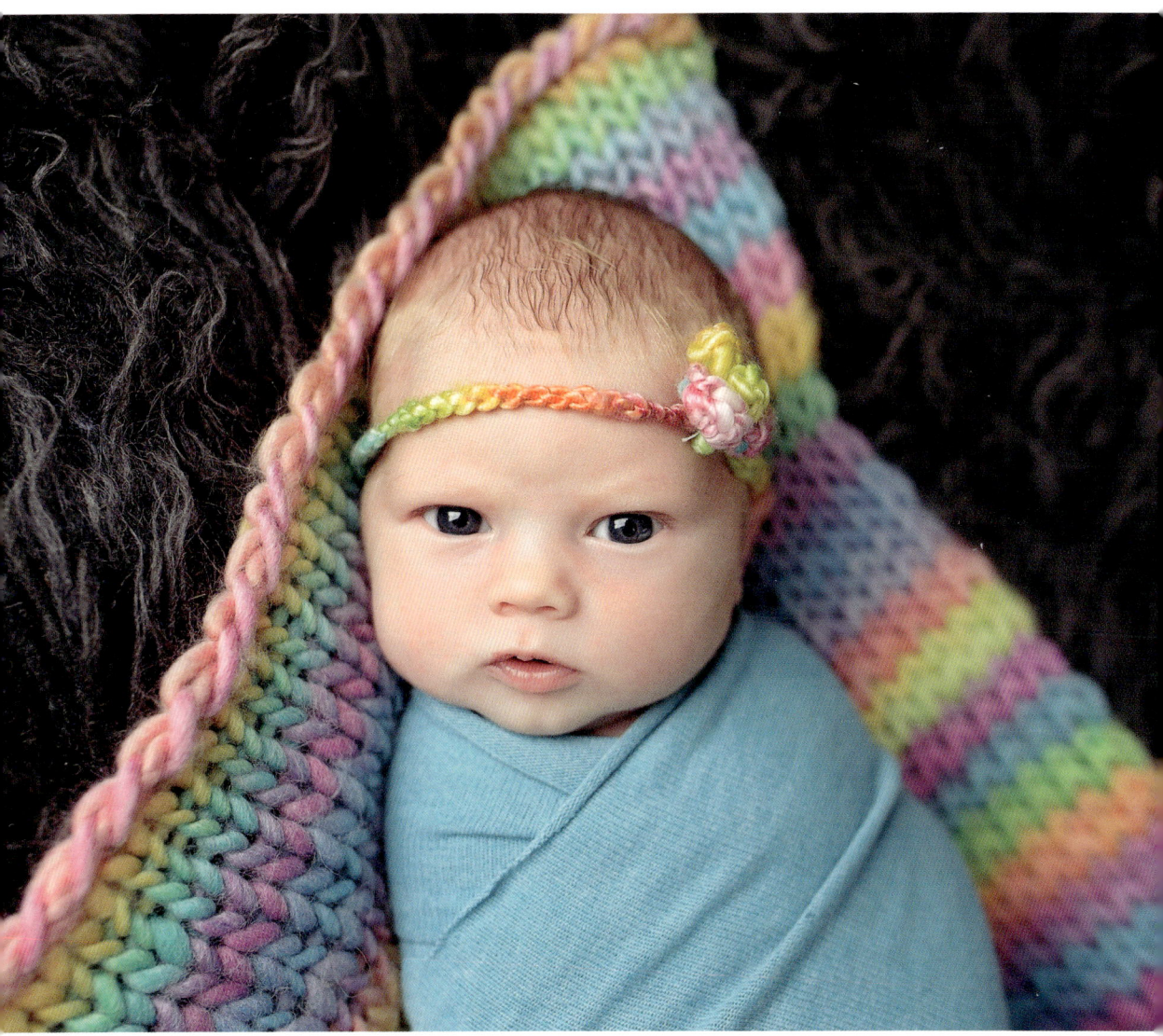

KENLYNN

"You always hear people say that there is nothing like looking into your child's eyes for the first time. It's true. I never knew how much love I could feel for another human until that moment. My heart felt like it exploded!"

—Megan, mom of Kenlynn, born September 9th, 2017

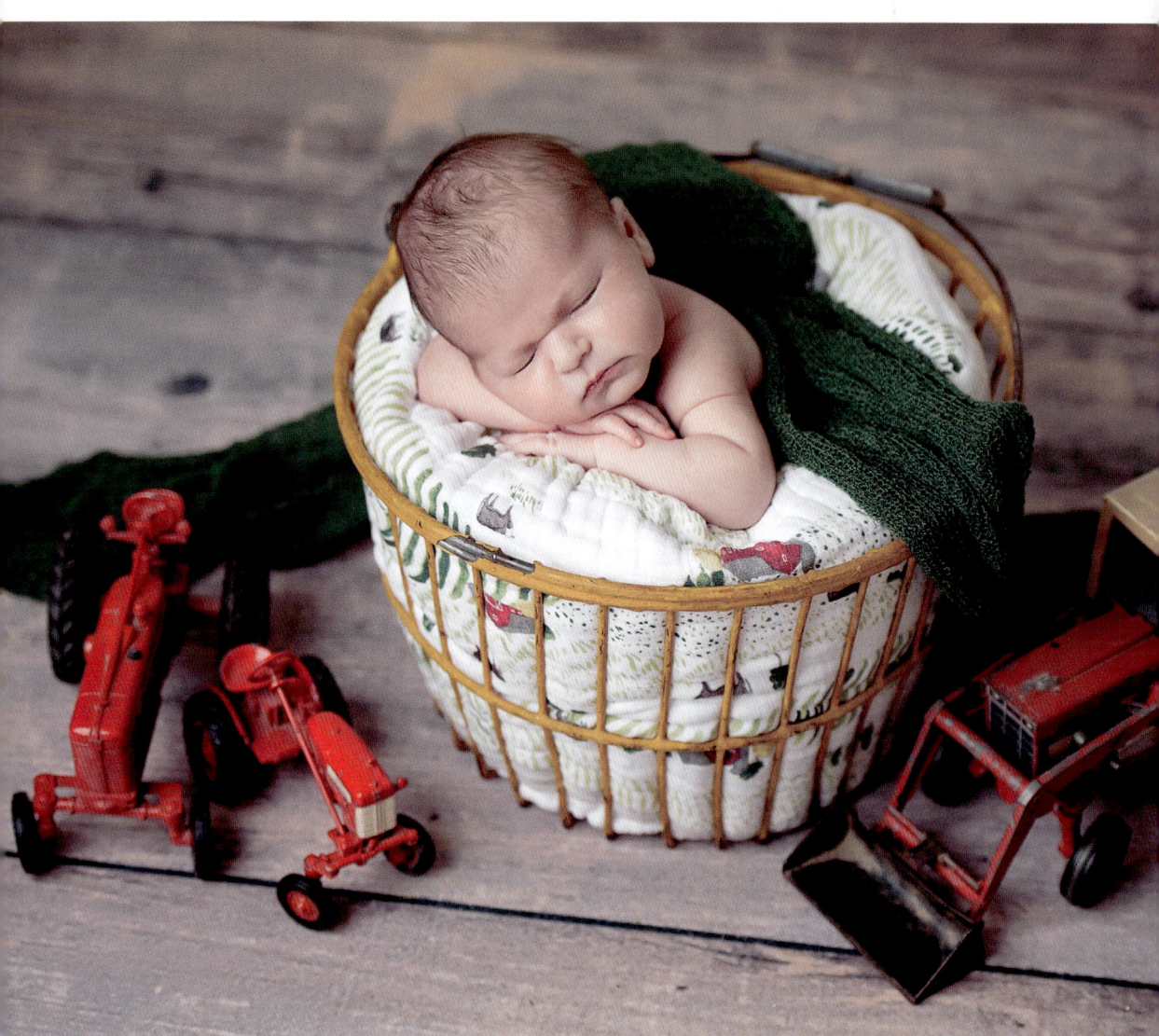

LAYTON

"I was so worried when Layton was first born. He was rushed to NICU, but it made me feel better knowing he was okay and was going to be well taken care of by the nurses."

—Erin, mom of Layton, born September 17th, 2017

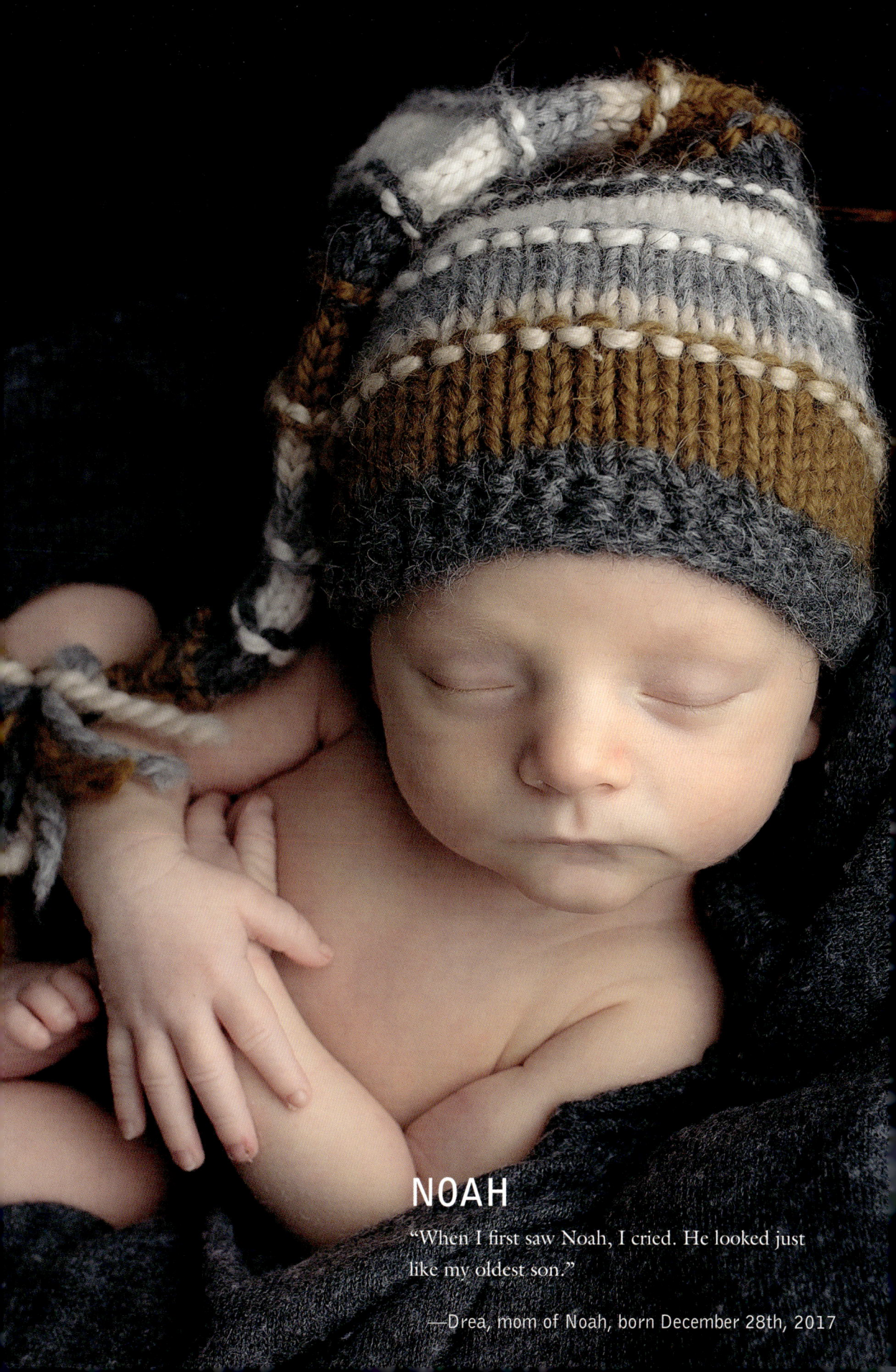

NOAH

"When I first saw Noah, I cried. He looked just like my oldest son."

—Drea, mom of Noah, born December 28th, 2017

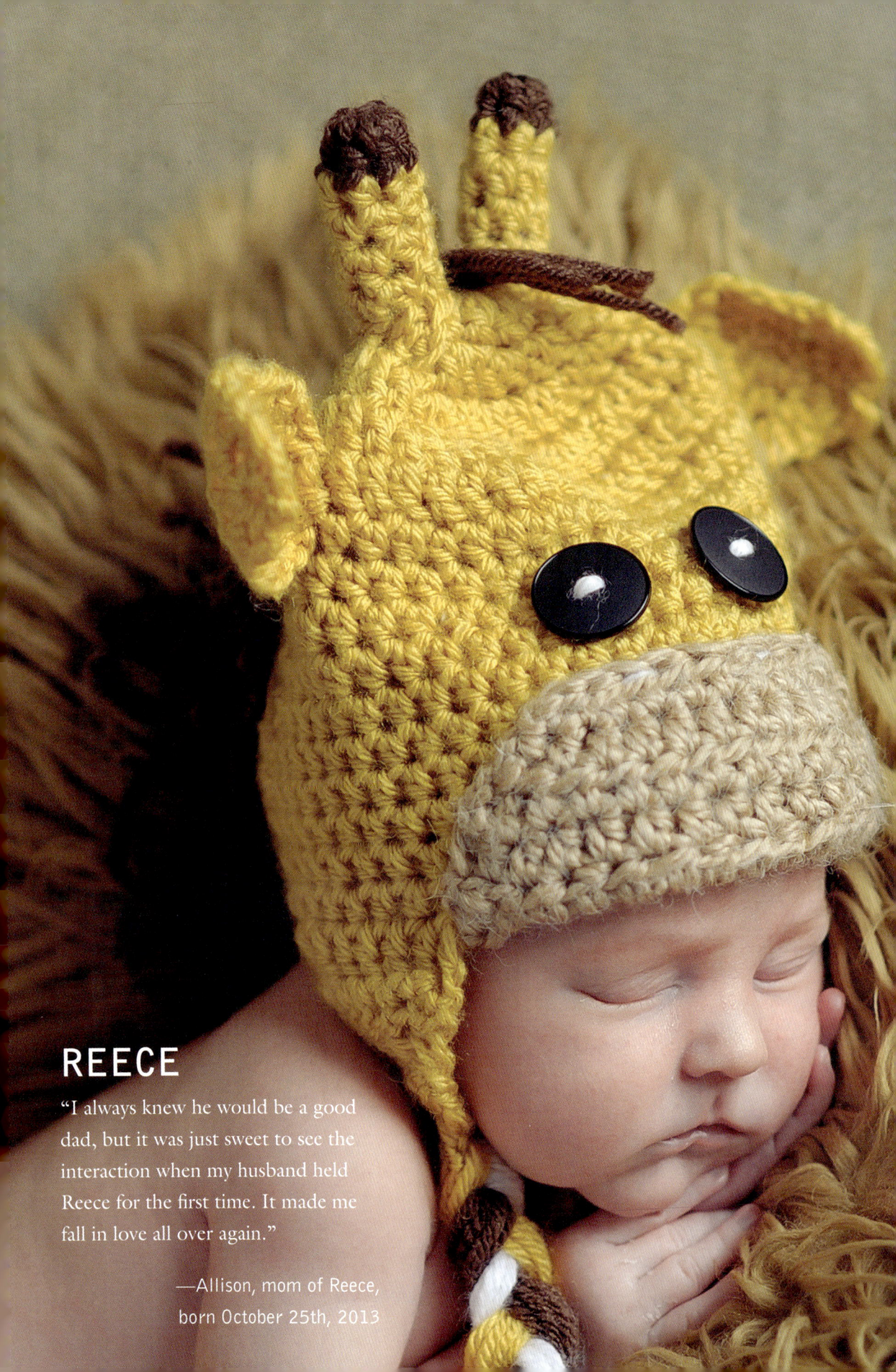

REECE

"I always knew he would be a good dad, but it was just sweet to see the interaction when my husband held Reece for the first time. It made me fall in love all over again."

—Allison, mom of Reece, born October 25th, 2013

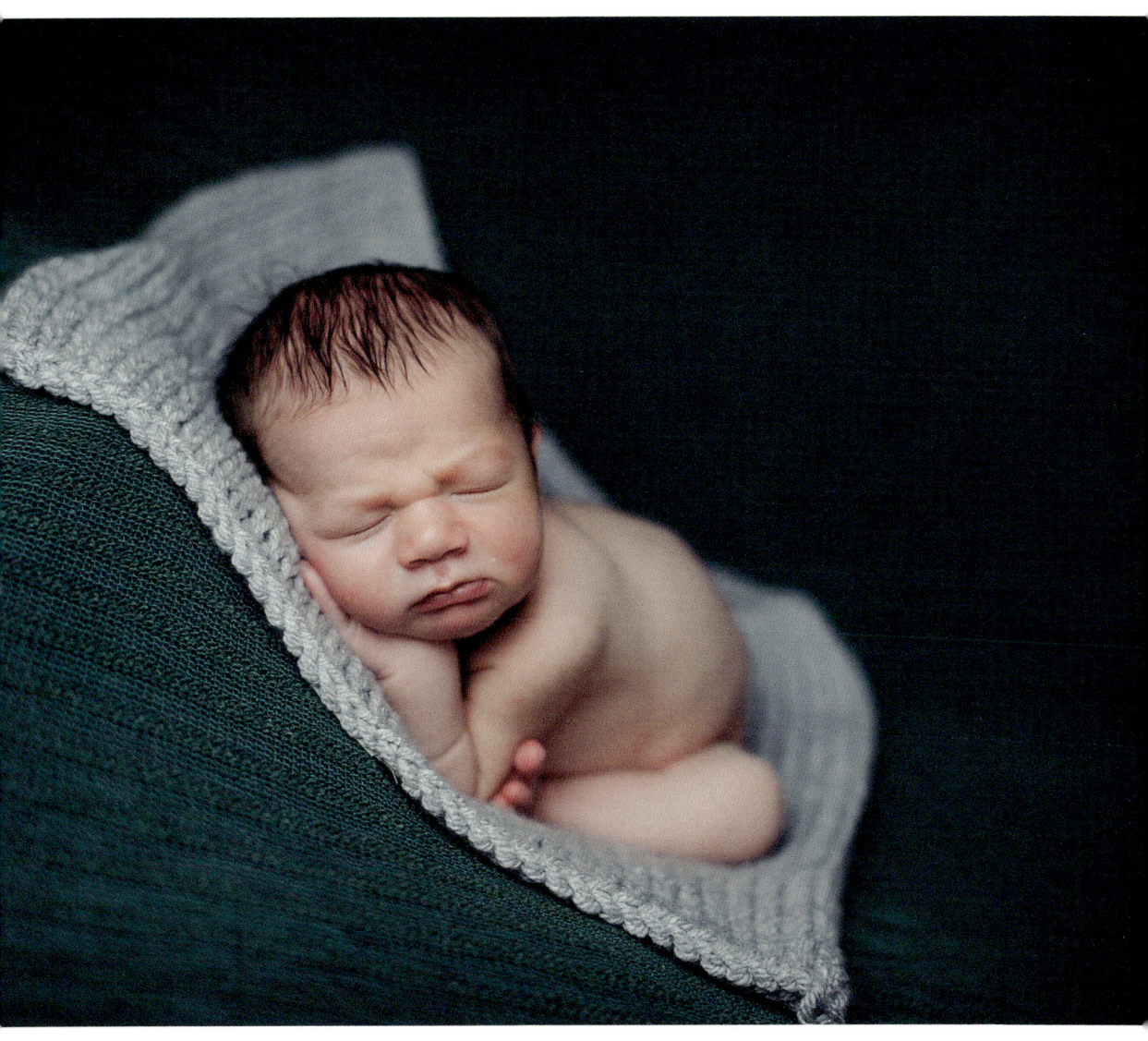

BRAXTON

"Prior to Braxton, we had a beautiful angel baby, so Braxton was a blessing and an answered prayer for us. My pregnancy was perfect; there were no issues. The moment he was born, he was put on my chest for skin-to-skin time. I just wrapped my arms around him, in awe that he was here. He cracked open his dark-blue eyes, and this mommy was wrapped."

—Melissa, mom of Braxton, born February 1st, 2014

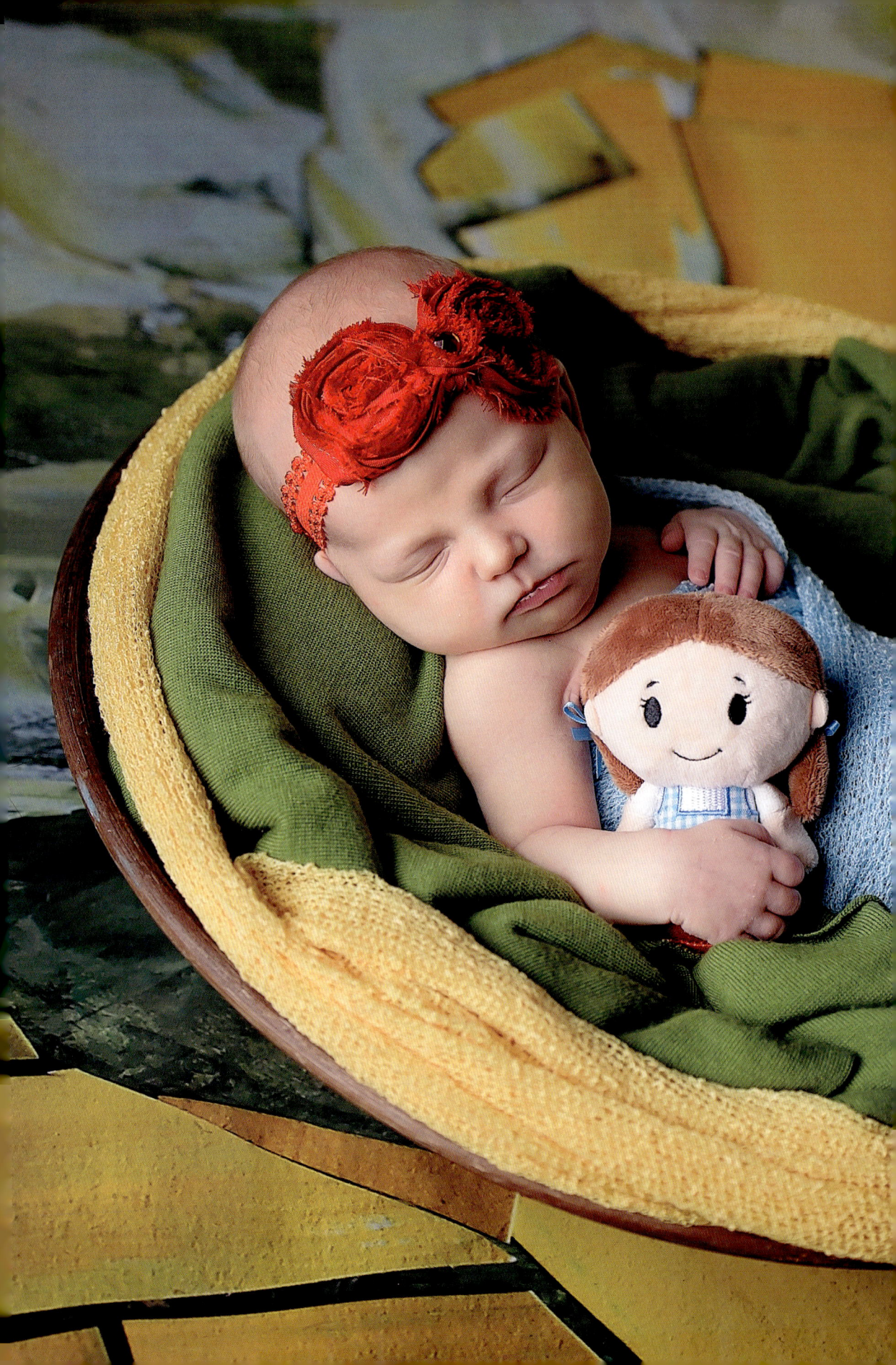

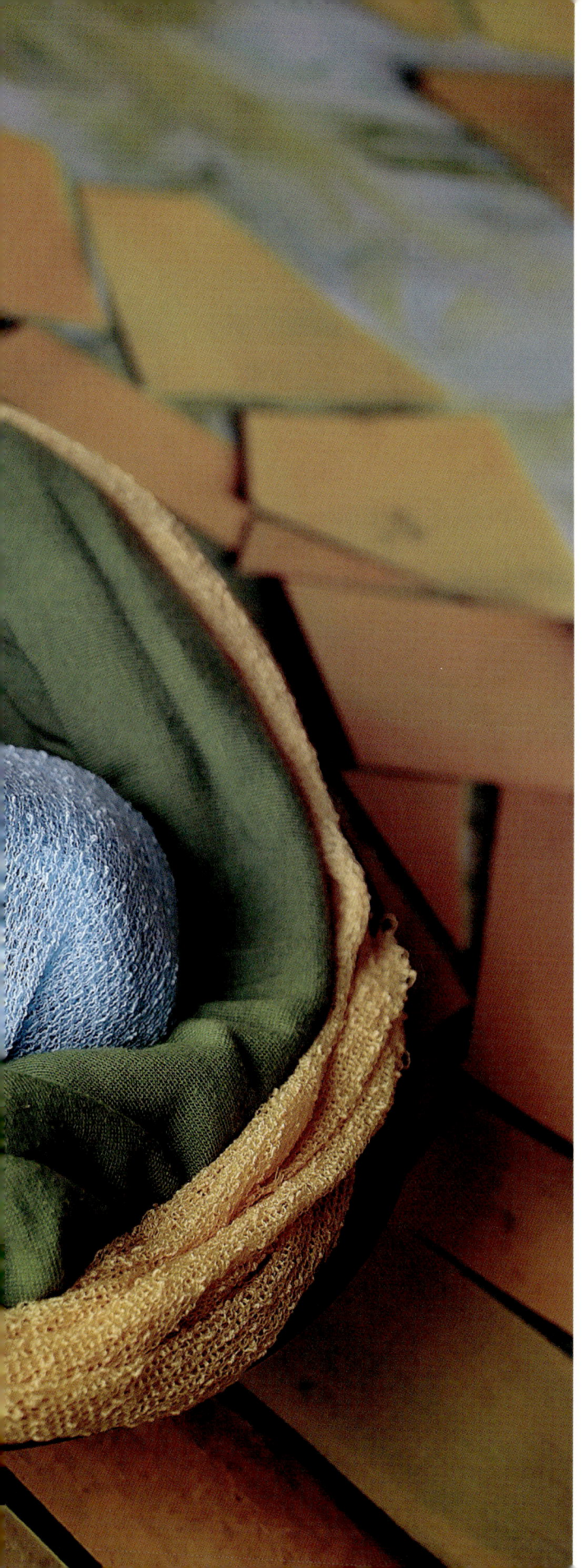

DOROTHY PEARL

"When I found out I was pregnant, I was very scared and excited—and a little protective. I felt like I had so much responsibility to protect her. Once I saw her on the ultrasound, though, it was the most reassuring feeling, knowing that her heart was beating and that she was alive and growing inside of me."

—Laurie, mom of Dorothy Pearl, born April 8th, 2017

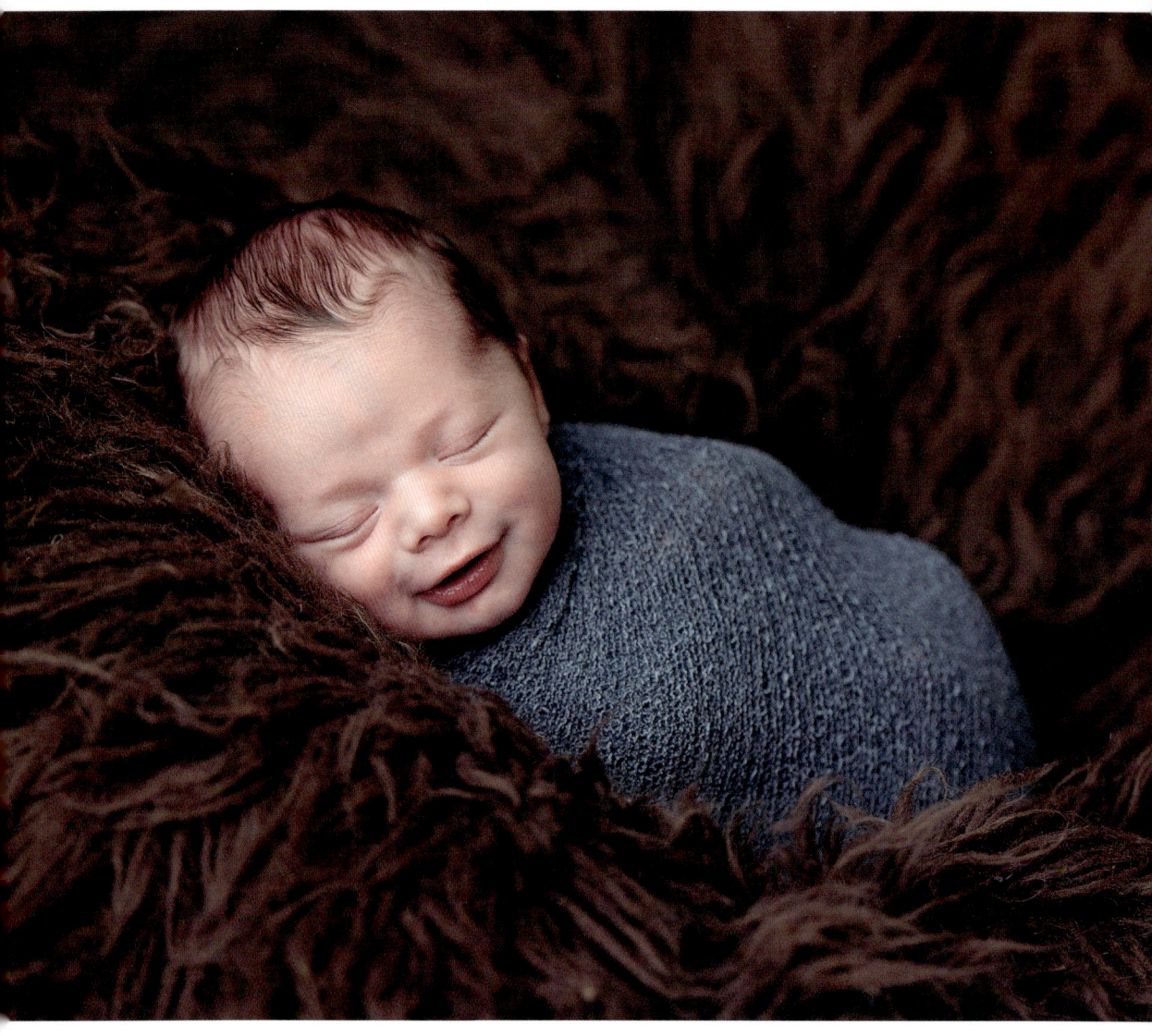

WILLIAM HENRY

"We had suffered a loss through an ectopic pregnancy followed by some fertility issues. Hearing the words 'you're pregnant' was both scary and exciting. Those nerves settled after the first trimester and it was smooth sailing from there. I was not sick or overly tired, I was really able to enjoy it. He enjoyed it too; he was a week late and induced!"

—Lindsay, mom of William Henry,
born November 30th, 2017

RUBY RAE

"The first time I saw her, it was an incredible feeling, since I had a successful VBAC. The feeling was euphoric!"

—Kayla, mom of Ruby Rae, born July 16th, 2015

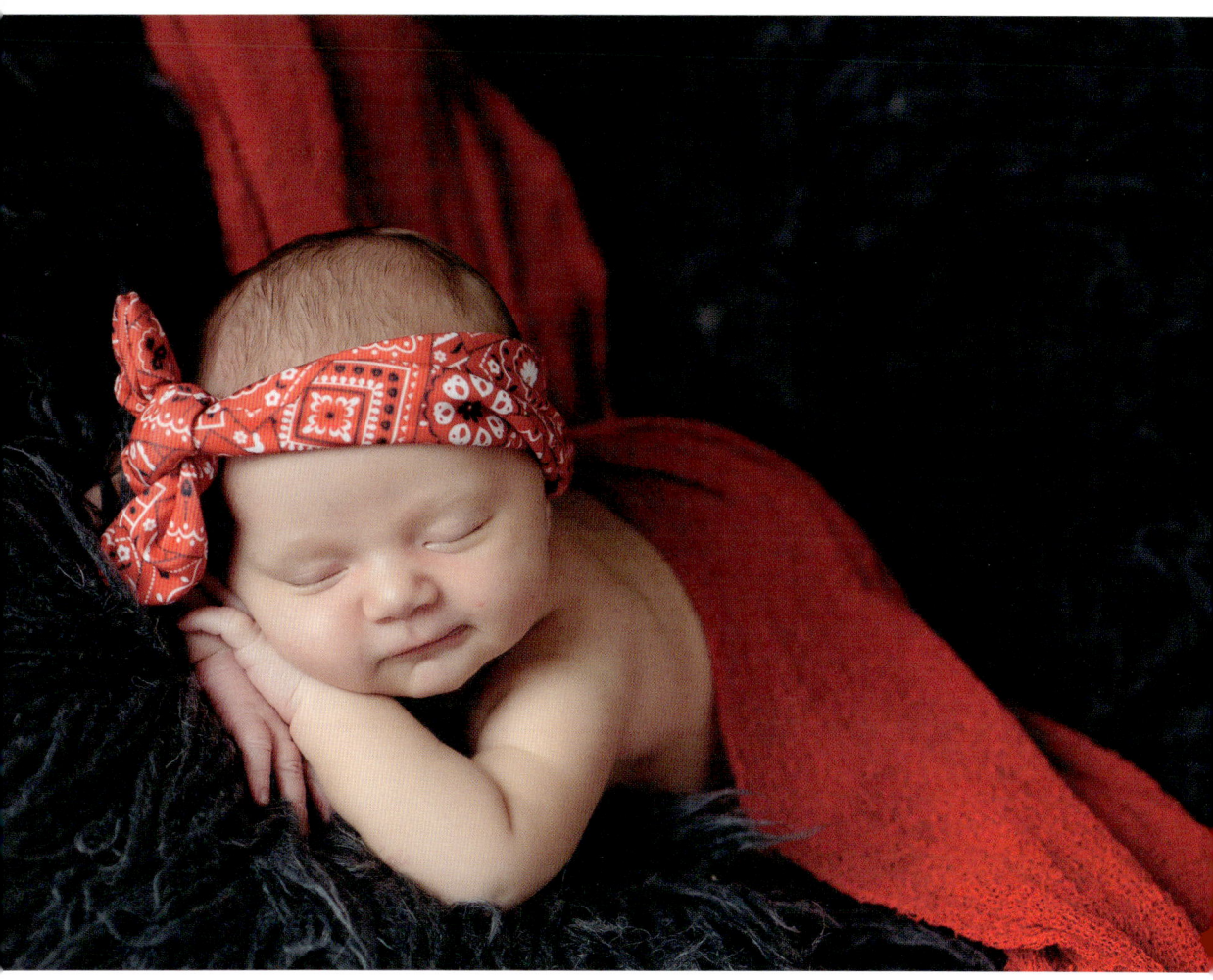

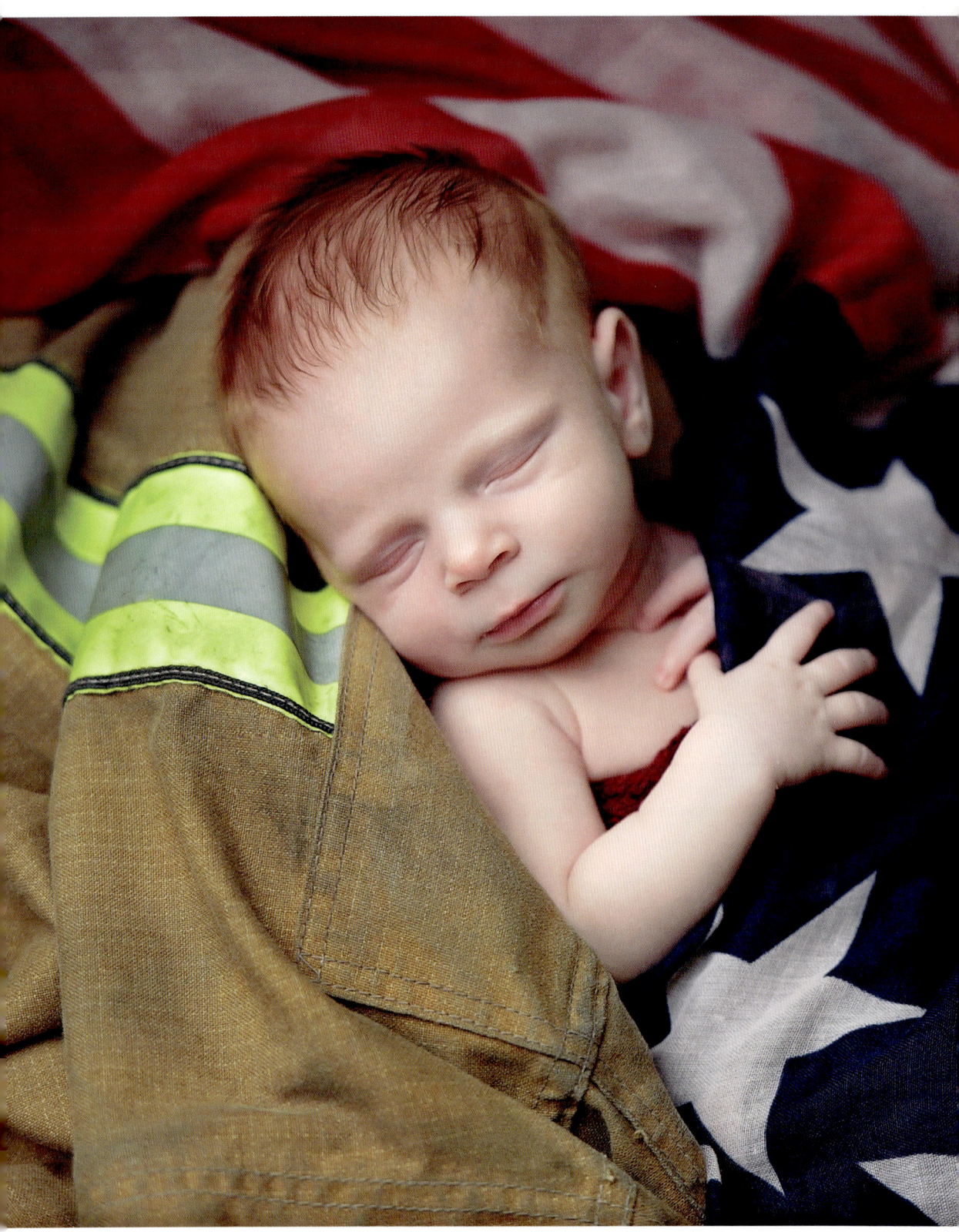

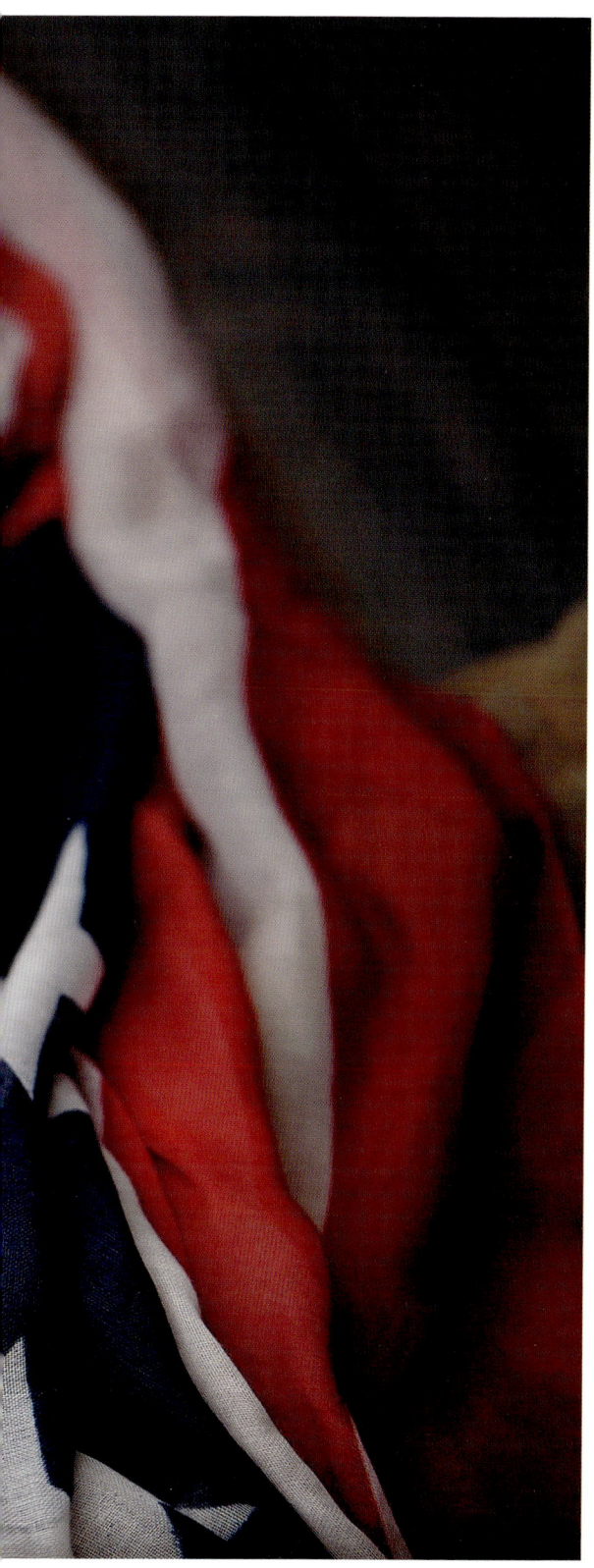

BLAINE

"I had a water birth, so the first time I saw my baby, I reached down into the water and lifted him up to the surface and onto my chest. The only thing I could think about was how perfect he was.

The most memorable moment after Blaine was born was when we got him all dried off and could see that he had red hair, just like my mom, who had passed away. It was like a part of her was with us again."

—Karlie, mom of Blaine,
born October 23rd, 2017

SETH

"During my pregnancy, I loved telling my other boys all about their new brother and watching their excitement as they waited for the arrival of 'their baby.' I loved watching how much they loved him already, before he was even born."

—Heather, mom of Seth, born June 6th, 2017

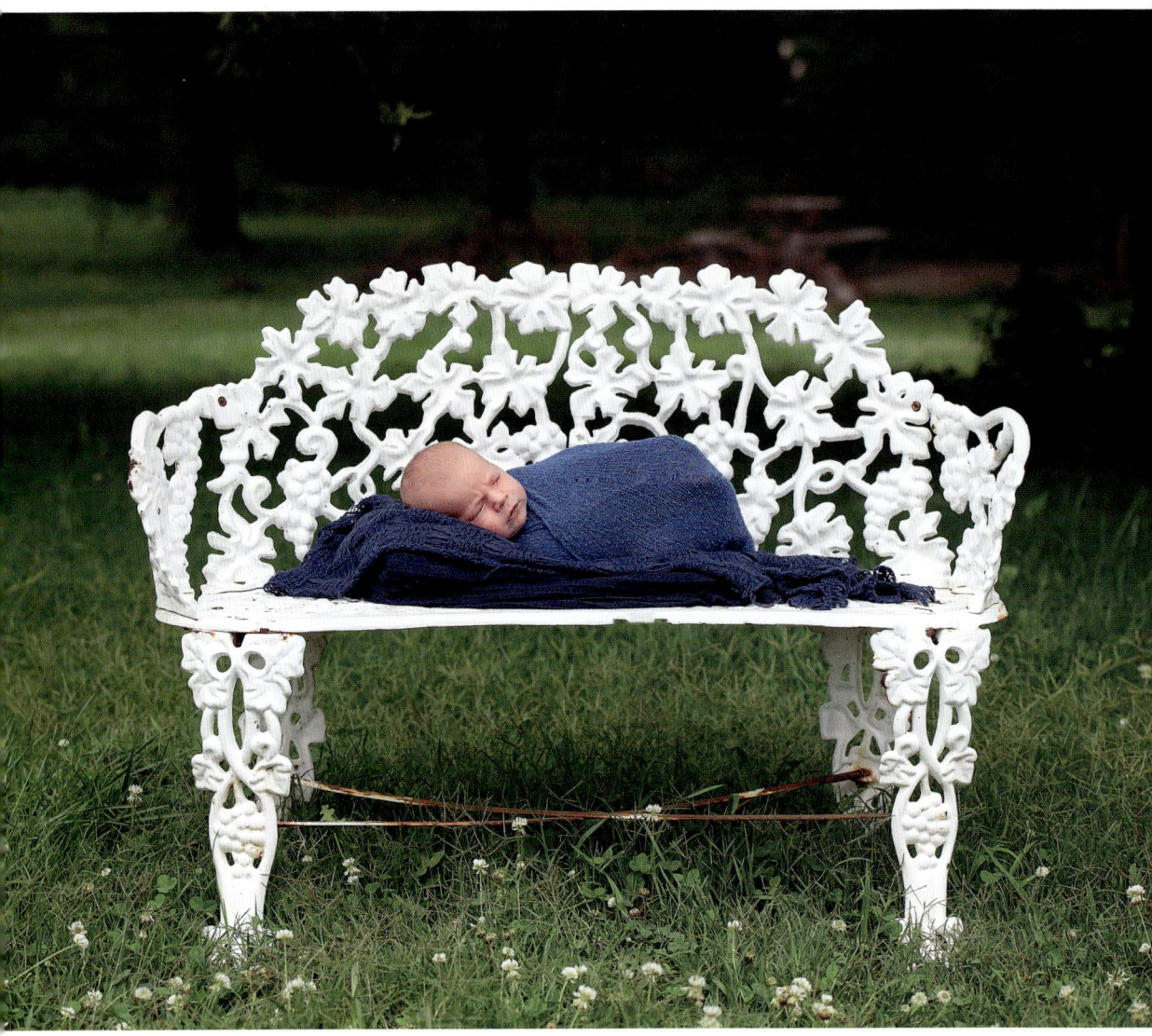

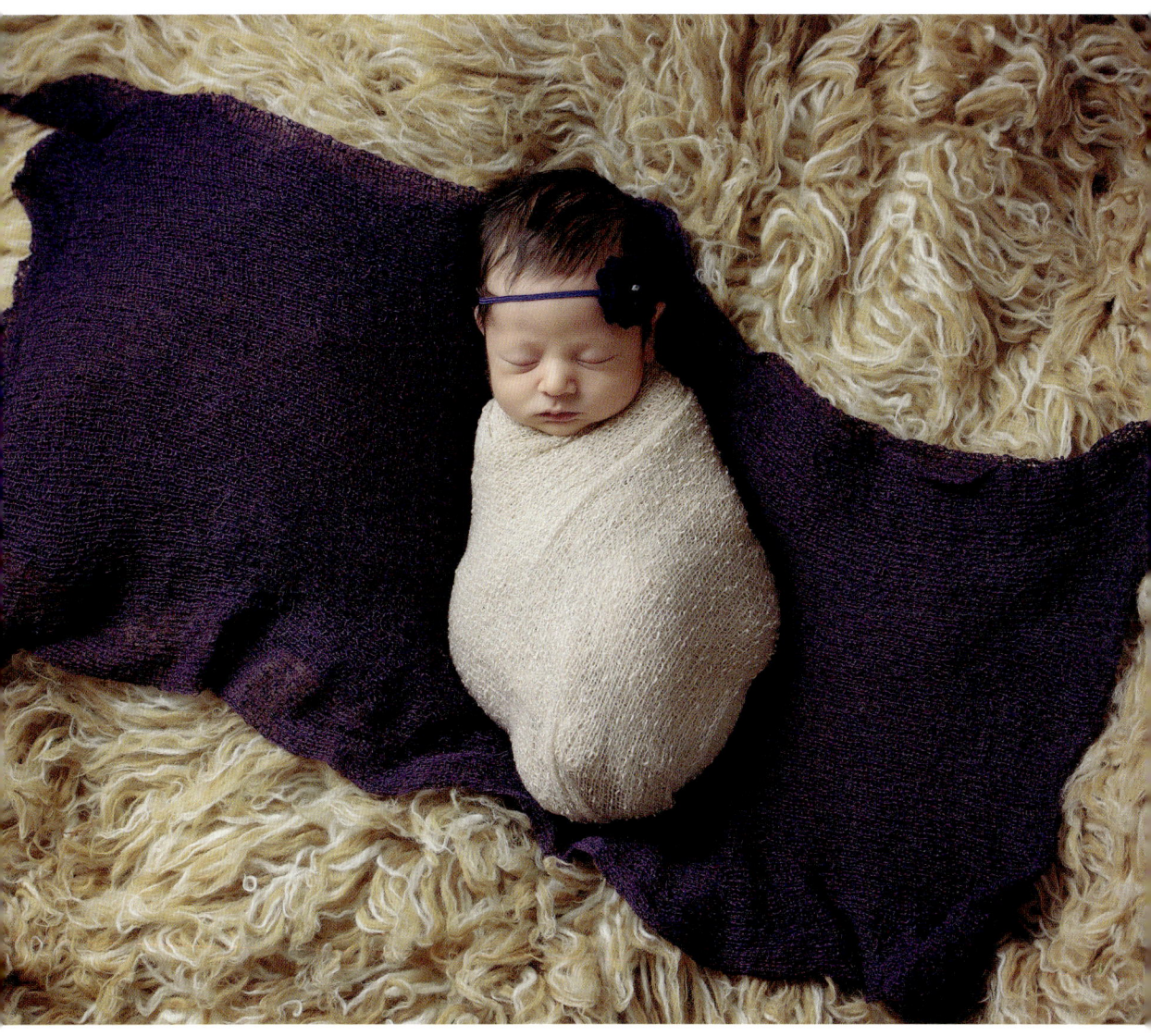

LILLIANA

"When we found out we were pregnant, I was excited and nervous, as we had waited four years after our first daughter to have another baby."

—Leah, mom of Lilliana, born October 16th, 2016

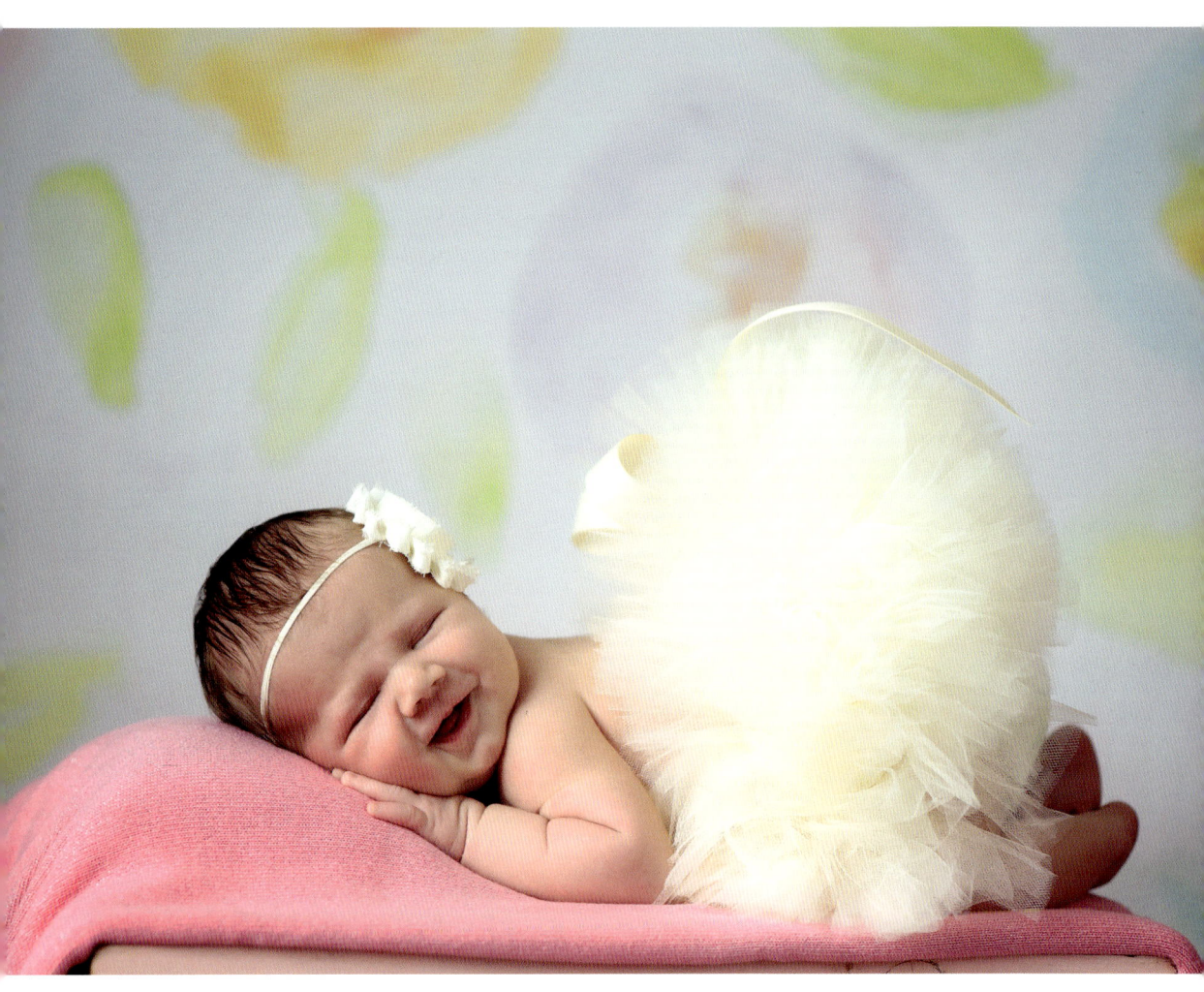

HADLEIGH

"The first time I saw my husband holding Hadleigh, everything felt absolutely perfect. Our family was complete!"

—Jessica, mom of Hadleigh, born May 5th, 2016

EDRIC

"When we came home from the hospital, we all just sat on the couch quietly with each other for a few minutes. Everyone seemed to be adjusting to life as a party of four. It was the most beautiful moment, and the first time I really felt like that was our family."

—Karen, mom of Edric, born May 5th, 2015

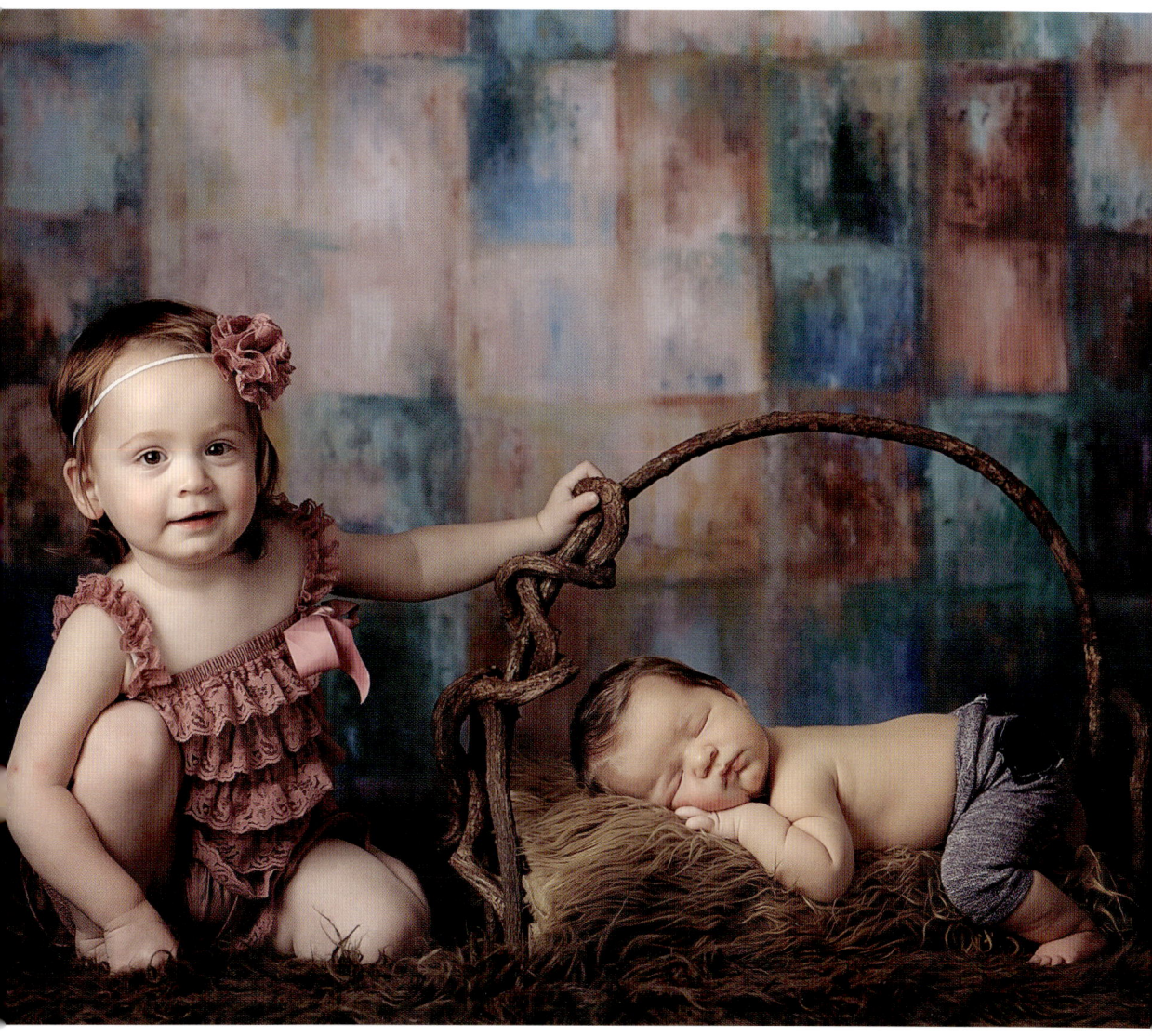

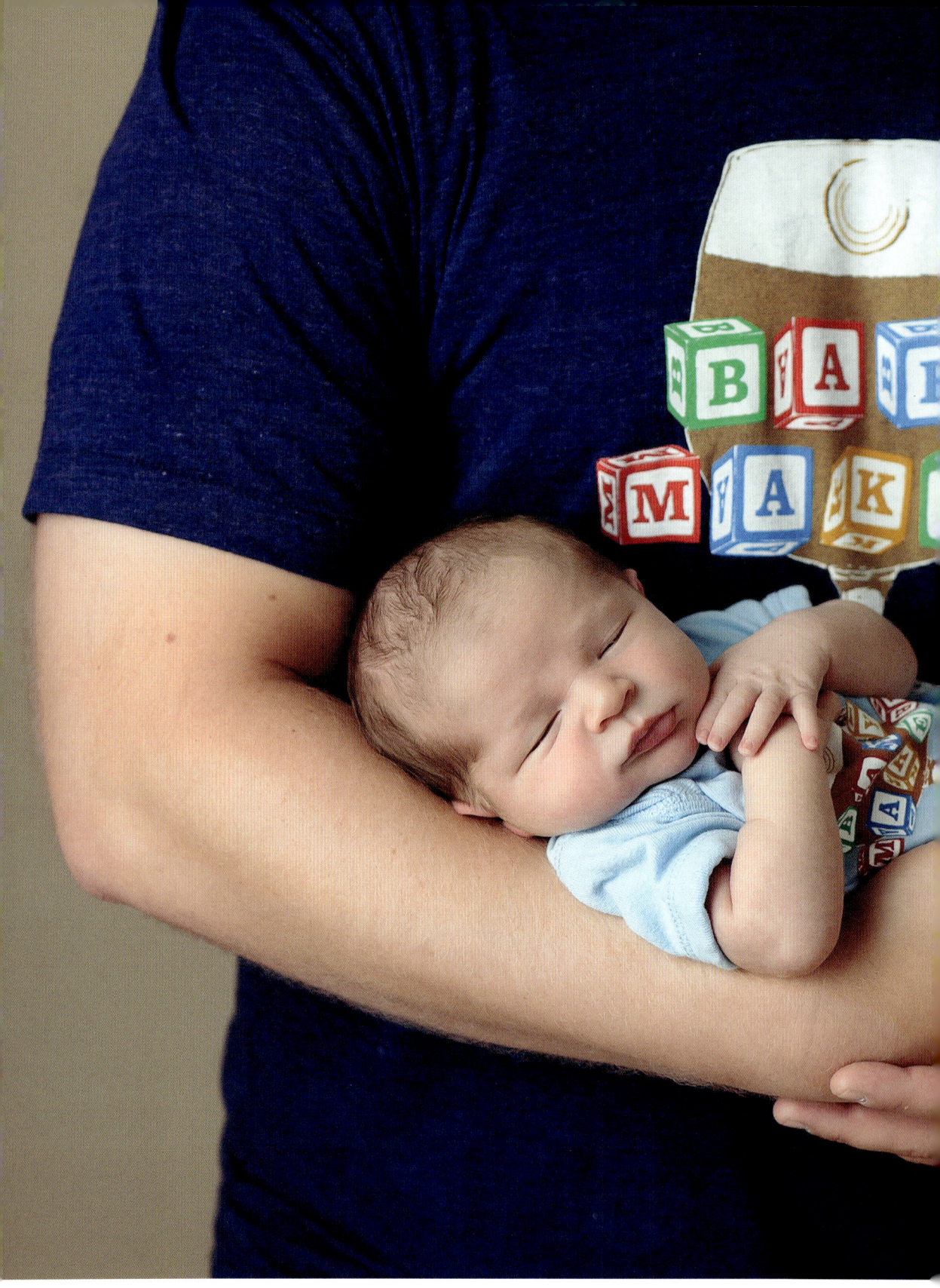

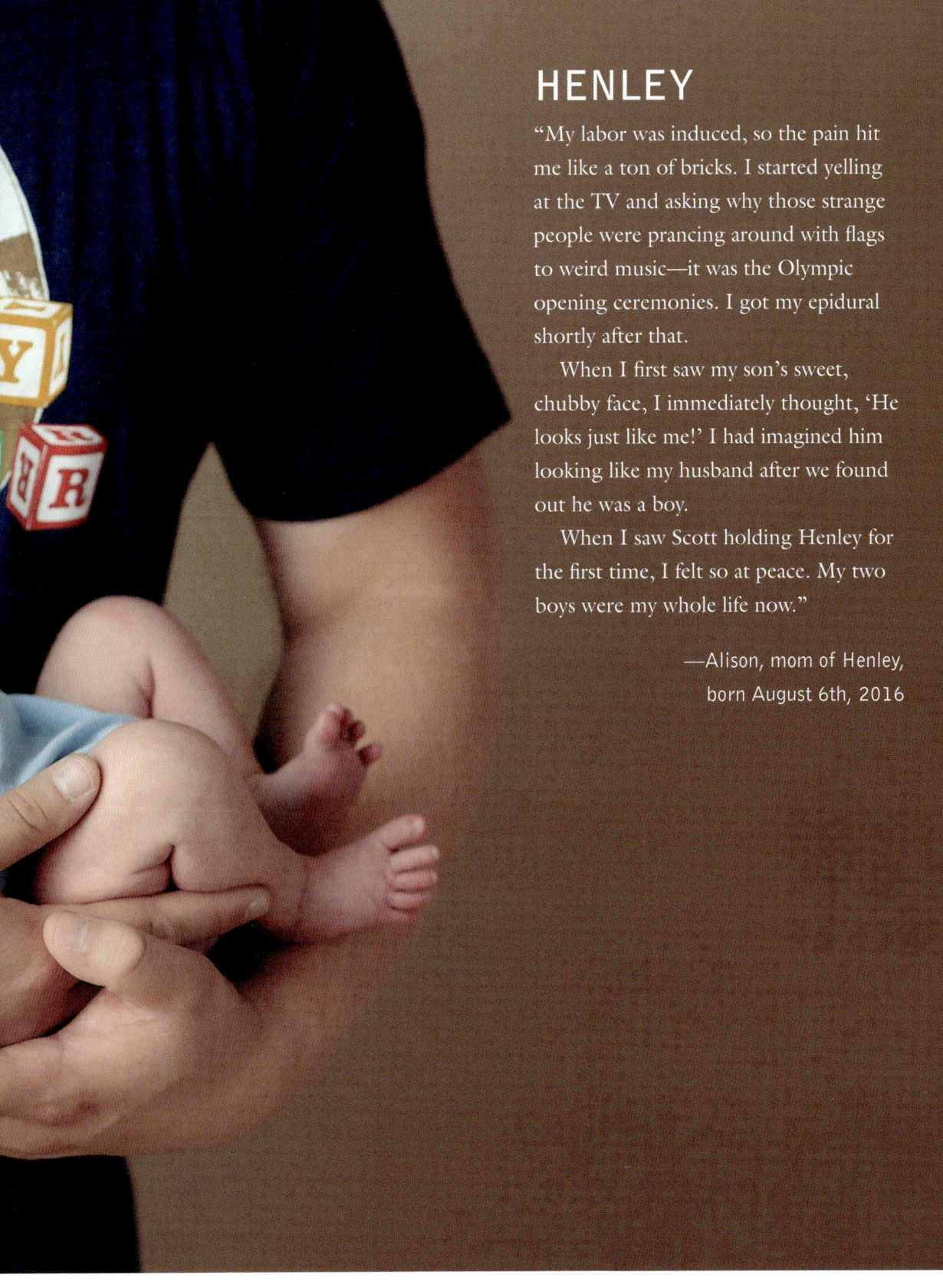

HENLEY

"My labor was induced, so the pain hit me like a ton of bricks. I started yelling at the TV and asking why those strange people were prancing around with flags to weird music—it was the Olympic opening ceremonies. I got my epidural shortly after that.

When I first saw my son's sweet, chubby face, I immediately thought, 'He looks just like me!' I had imagined him looking like my husband after we found out he was a boy.

When I saw Scott holding Henley for the first time, I felt so at peace. My two boys were my whole life now."

—Alison, mom of Henley, born August 6th, 2016

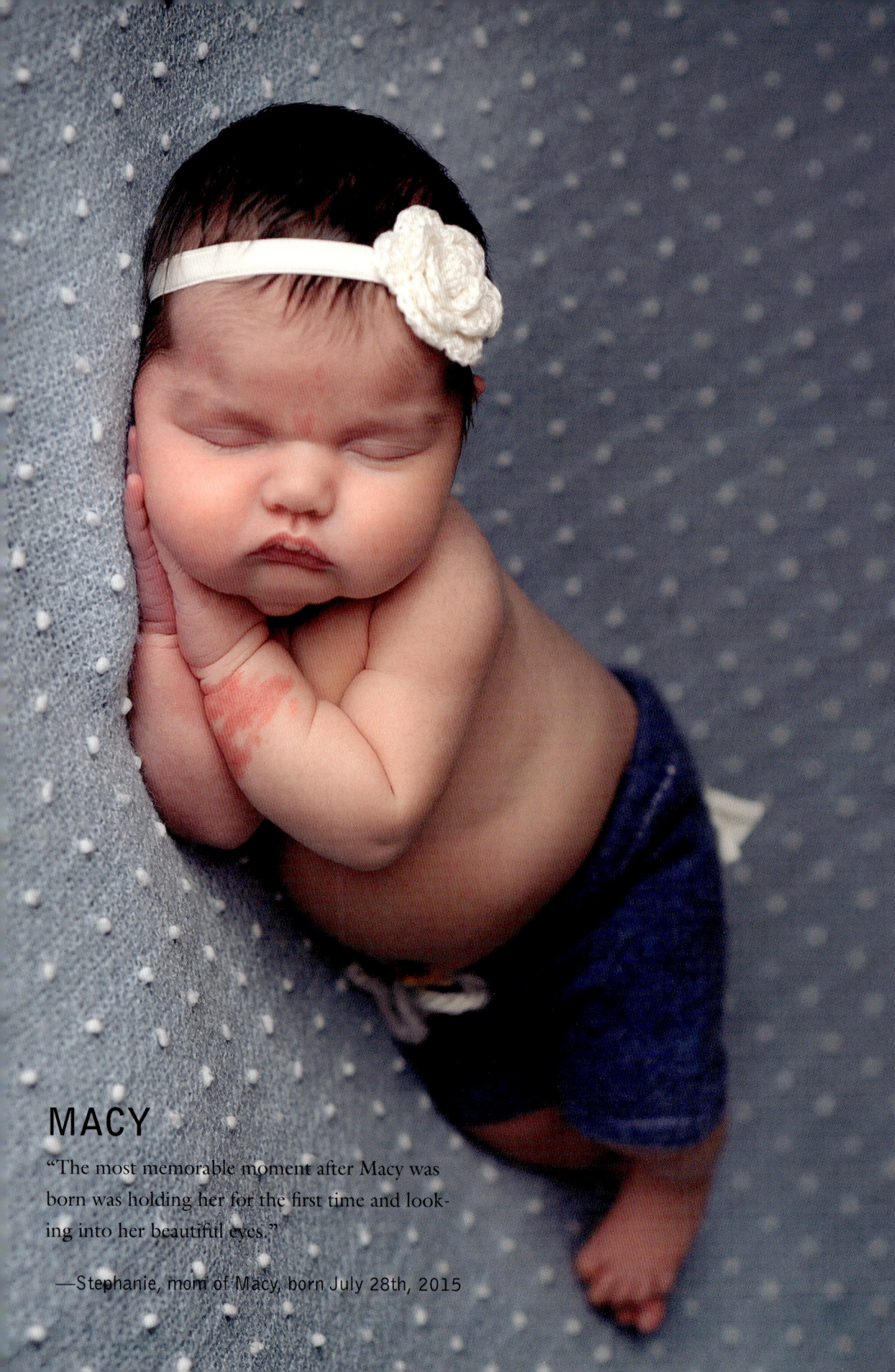

MACY

"The most memorable moment after Macy was born was holding her for the first time and looking into her beautiful eyes."

—Stephanie, mom of Macy, born July 28th, 2015

CAROLINE

"Finding out I was pregnant was exciting, but I was nervous. Having two kids exactly two years apart was a little scary, but seeing Caroline and her brother together for the first time made it all worthwhile. I'll never underestimate how lucky and blessed I am to have happy, healthy kids."

—Anna, mom of Caroline, born October 4th, 2016

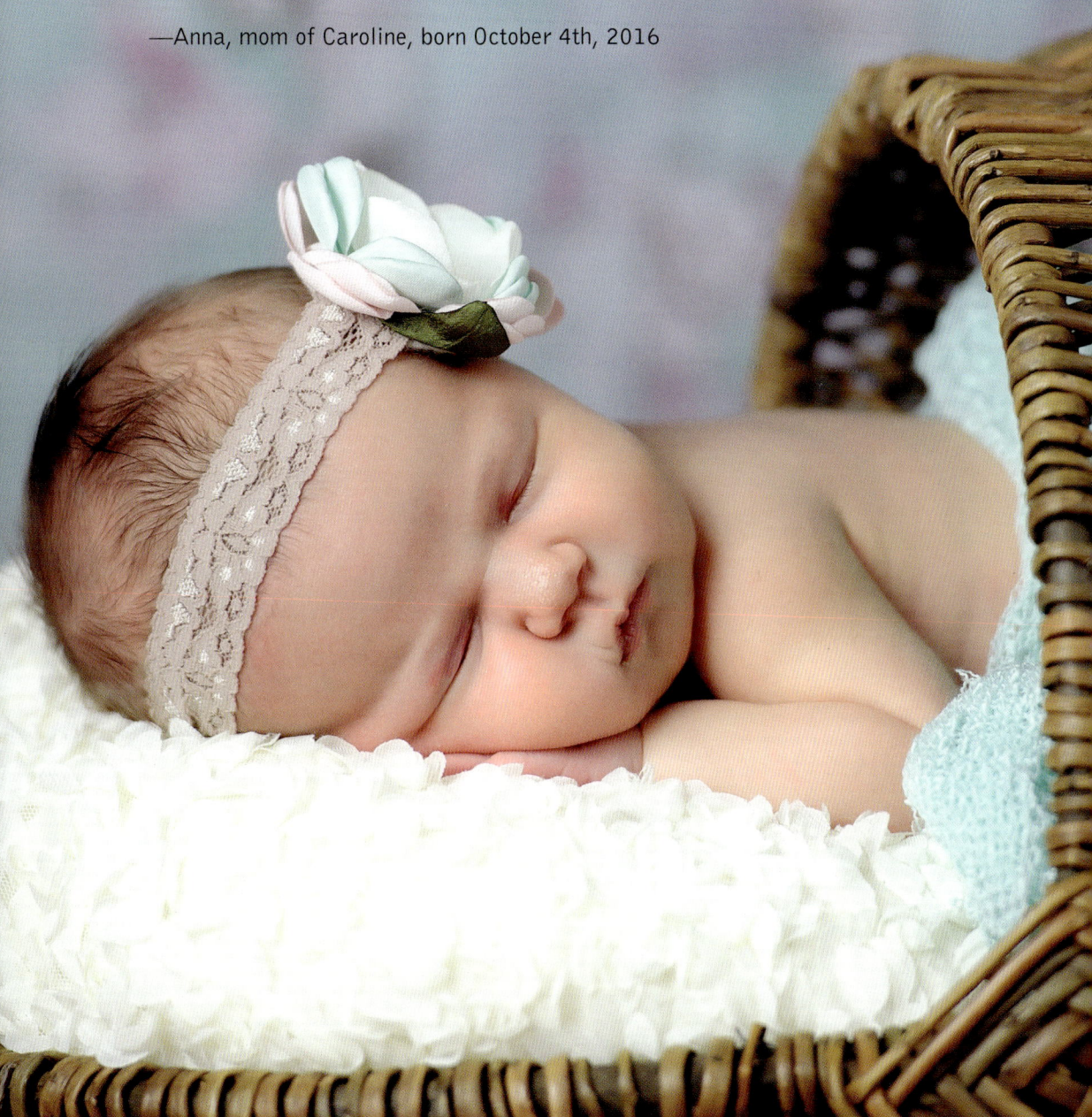

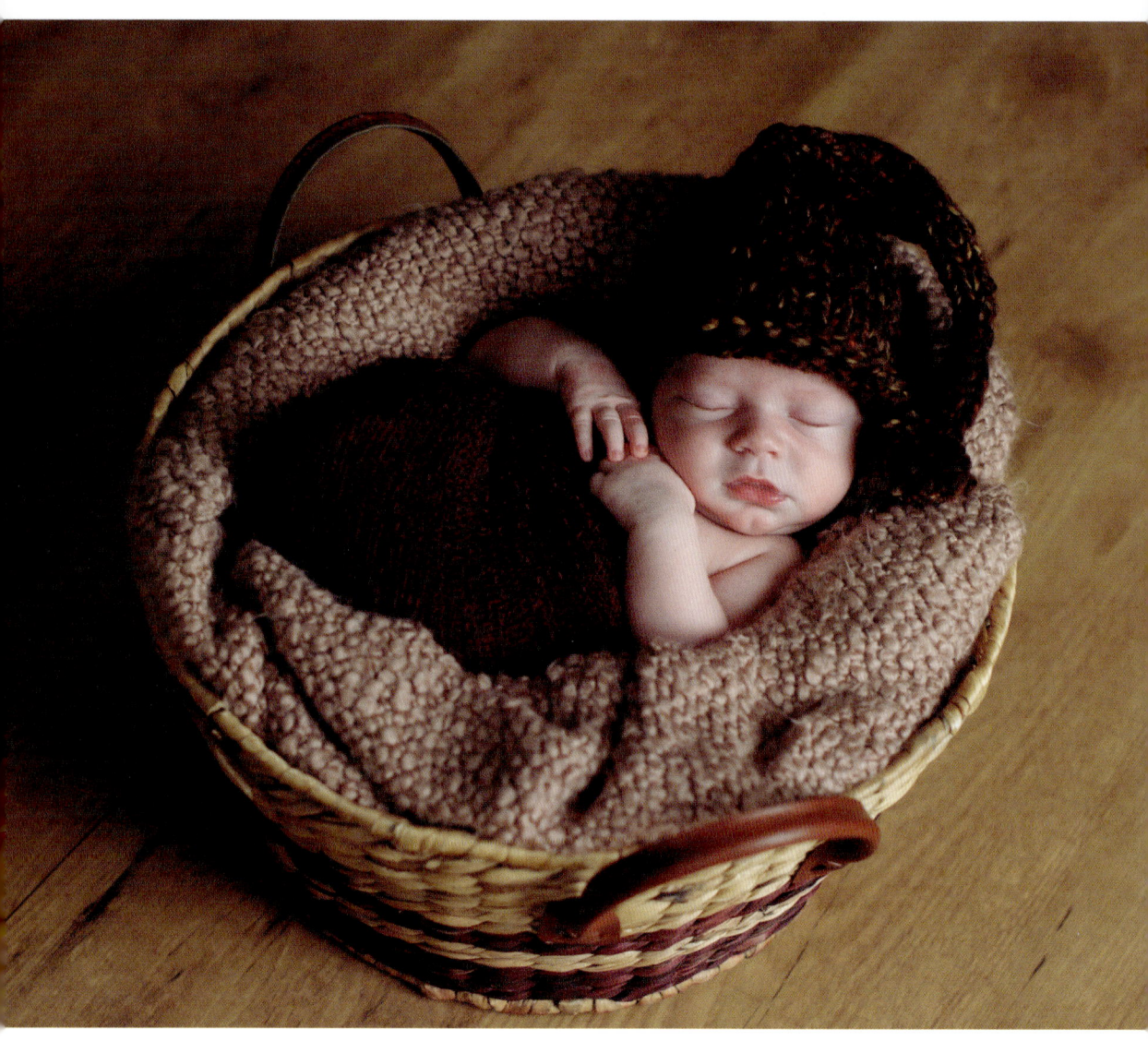

ANDREW

"My pregnancy was the longest, sweetest, most precious and miserable time!"

—Shellie, mom of Andrew, born February 7th, 2013

EMMA

"I loved introducing Emma to her big sister. It was so sweet to see them together. My oldest just wanted to be a little mama. She loved holding Emma and changing her diaper."

—Nicole, mom of Emma, born June 17th, 2014

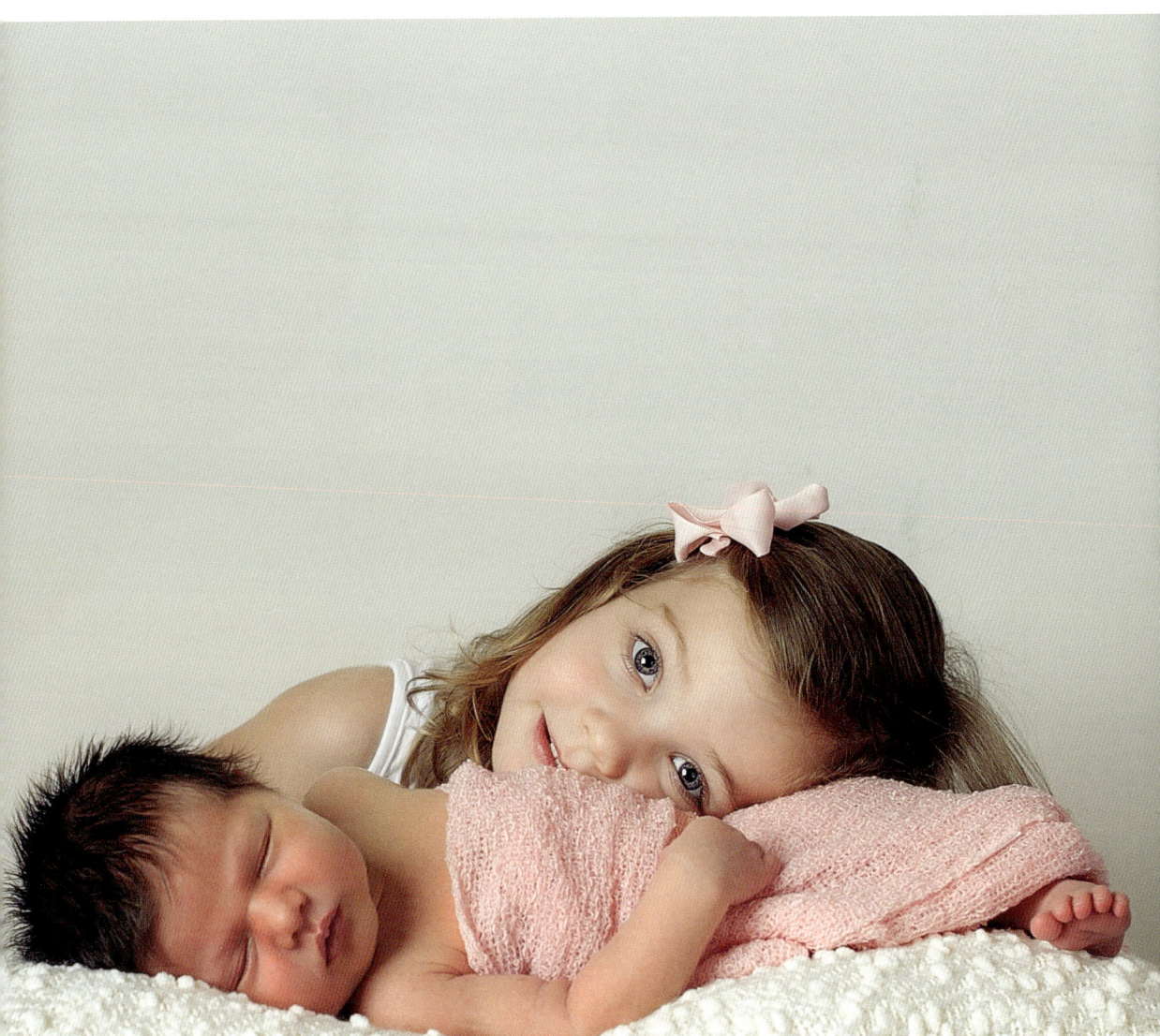

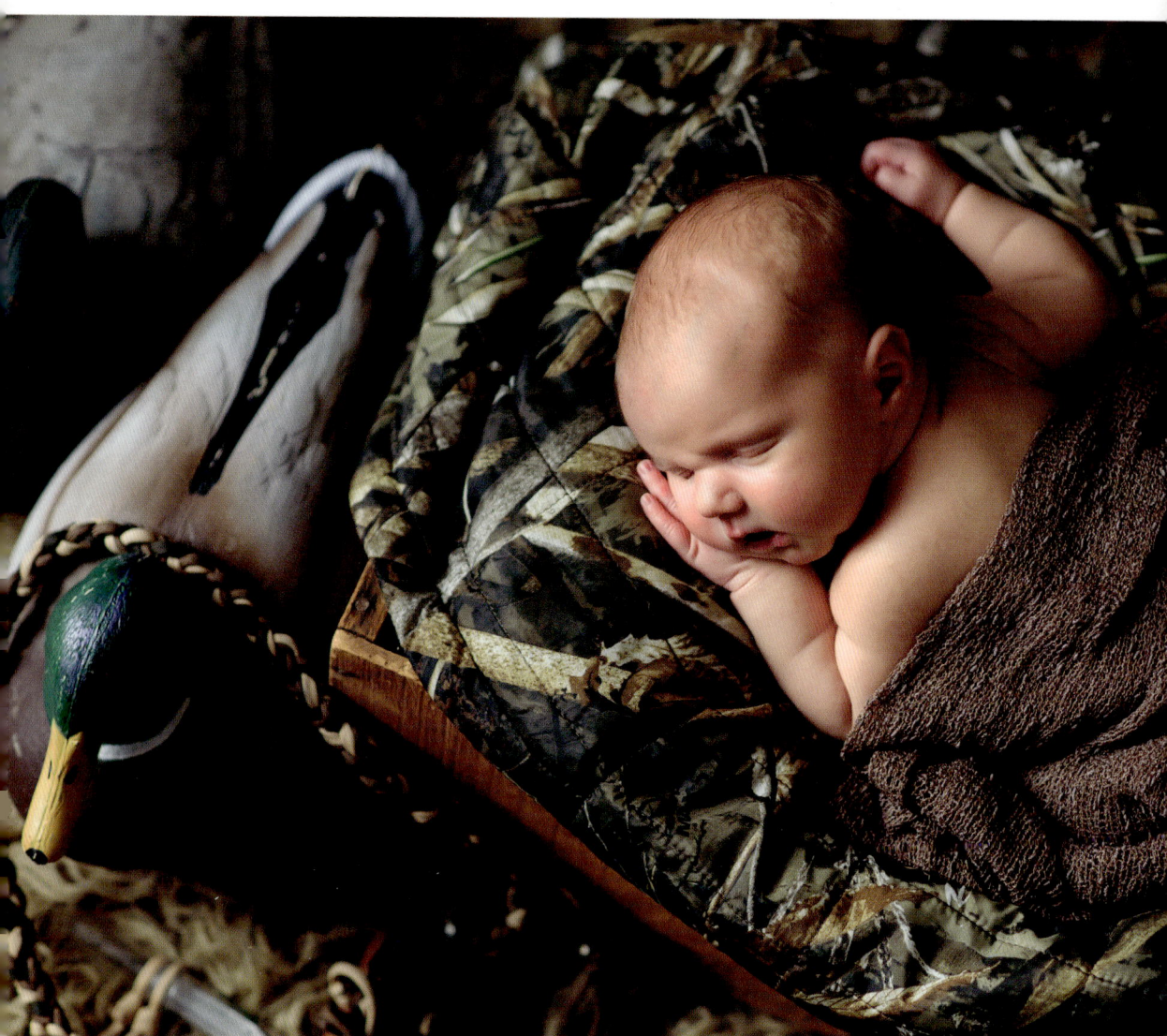

DRAKE

"My husband, Marc, was deployed to Iraq when I was pregnant with our daughter, so we were happy for him to be home so we could experience this pregnancy together."

—Tara, mom of Drake, born February 20th, 2016

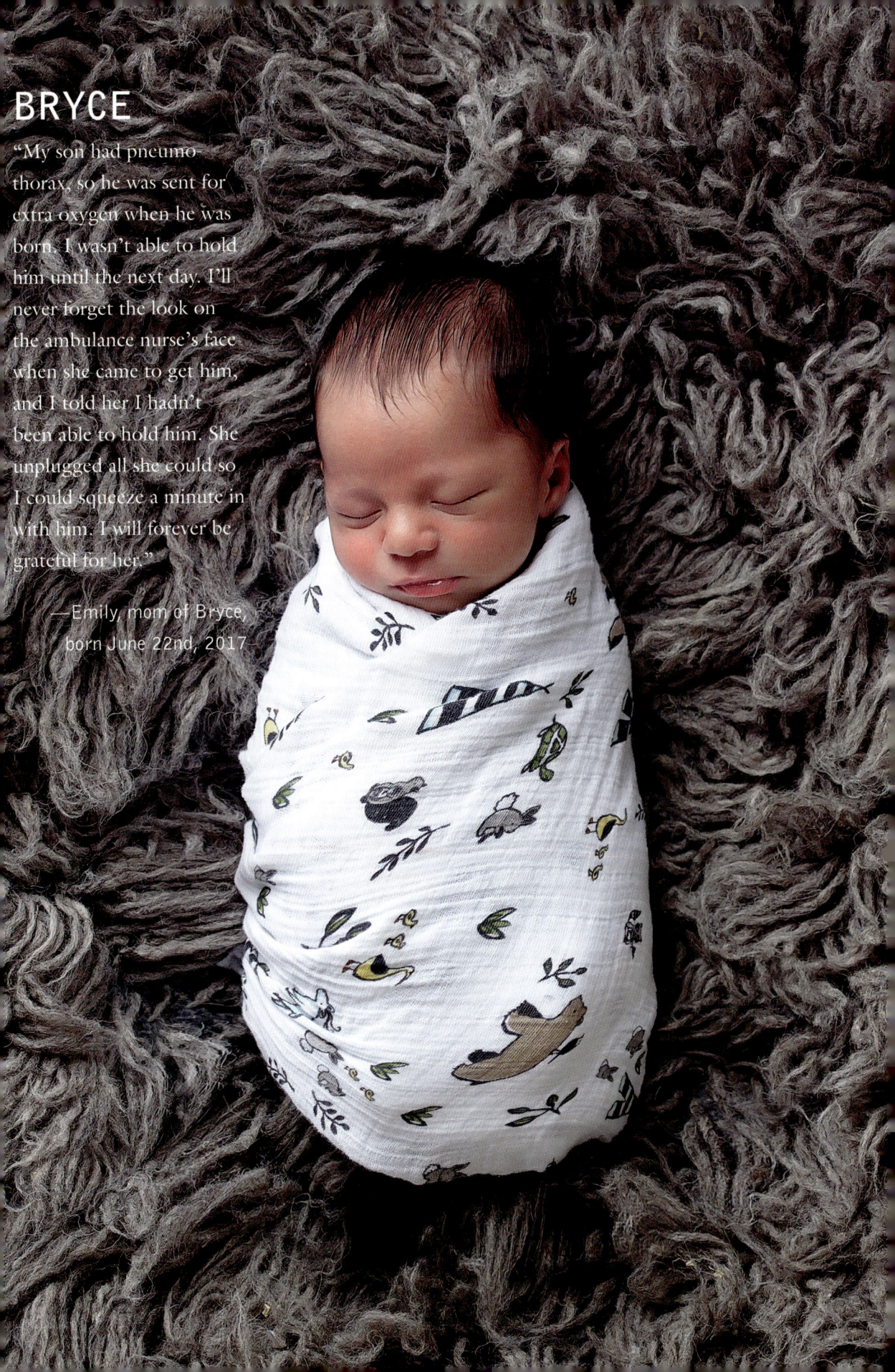

BRYCE

"My son had pneumo-
thorax, so he was sent for
extra oxygen when he was
born. I wasn't able to hold
him until the next day. I'll
never forget the look on
the ambulance nurse's face
when she came to get him,
and I told her I hadn't
been able to hold him. She
unplugged all she could so
I could squeeze a minute in
with him. I will forever be
grateful for her."

—Emily, mom of Bryce,
born June 22nd, 2017

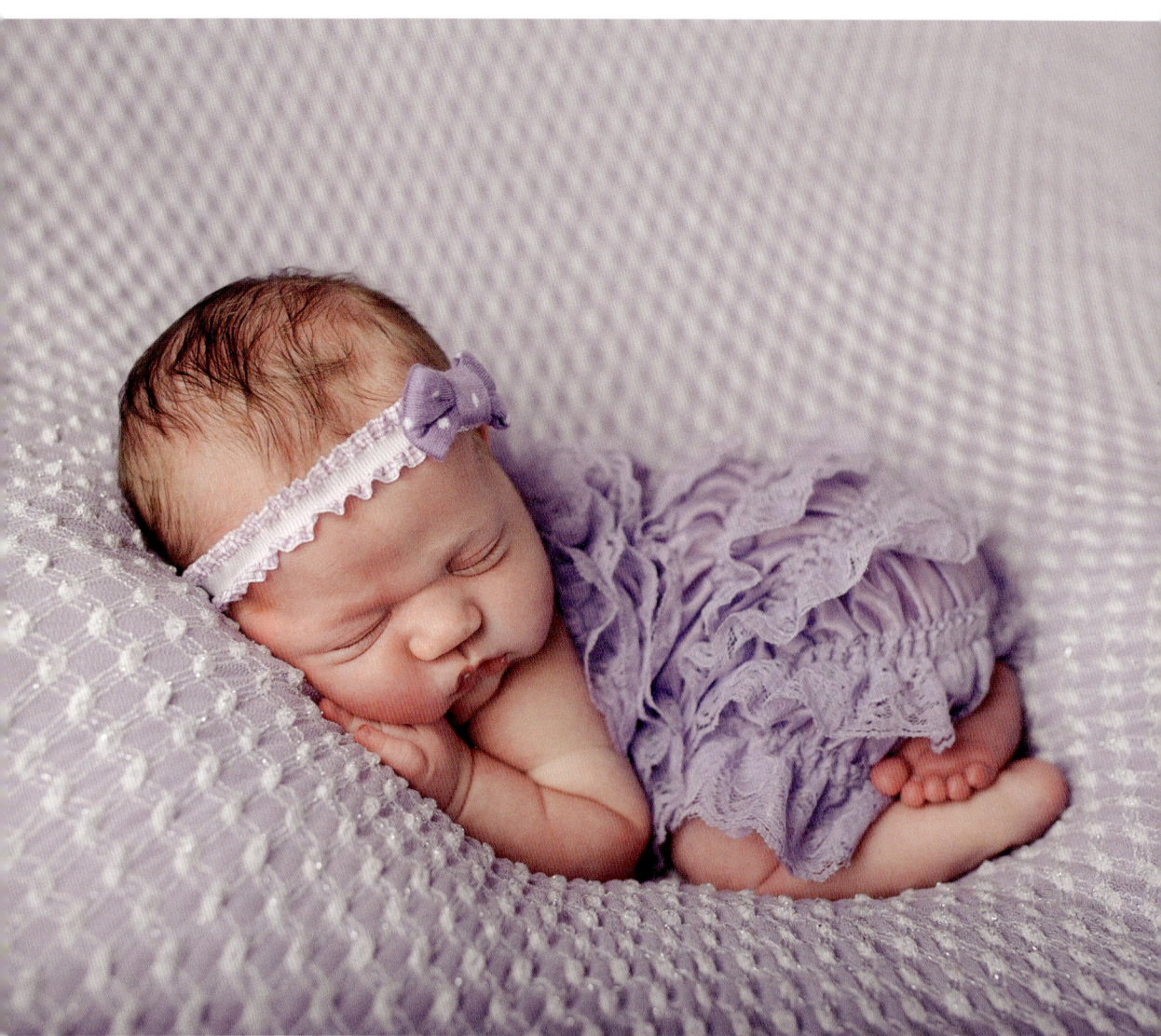

ALLISON

"The first time I held her, she snuggled right up on my chest, with her head at my neck, and just laid there and let me love on her."

—Jamie, mom of Allison, born December 24th, 2014

DAWSON

"I will never forget that my water broke while I was in the garden, picking tomatoes!"

—Nicole, mom of Dawson, born August 5th, 2017

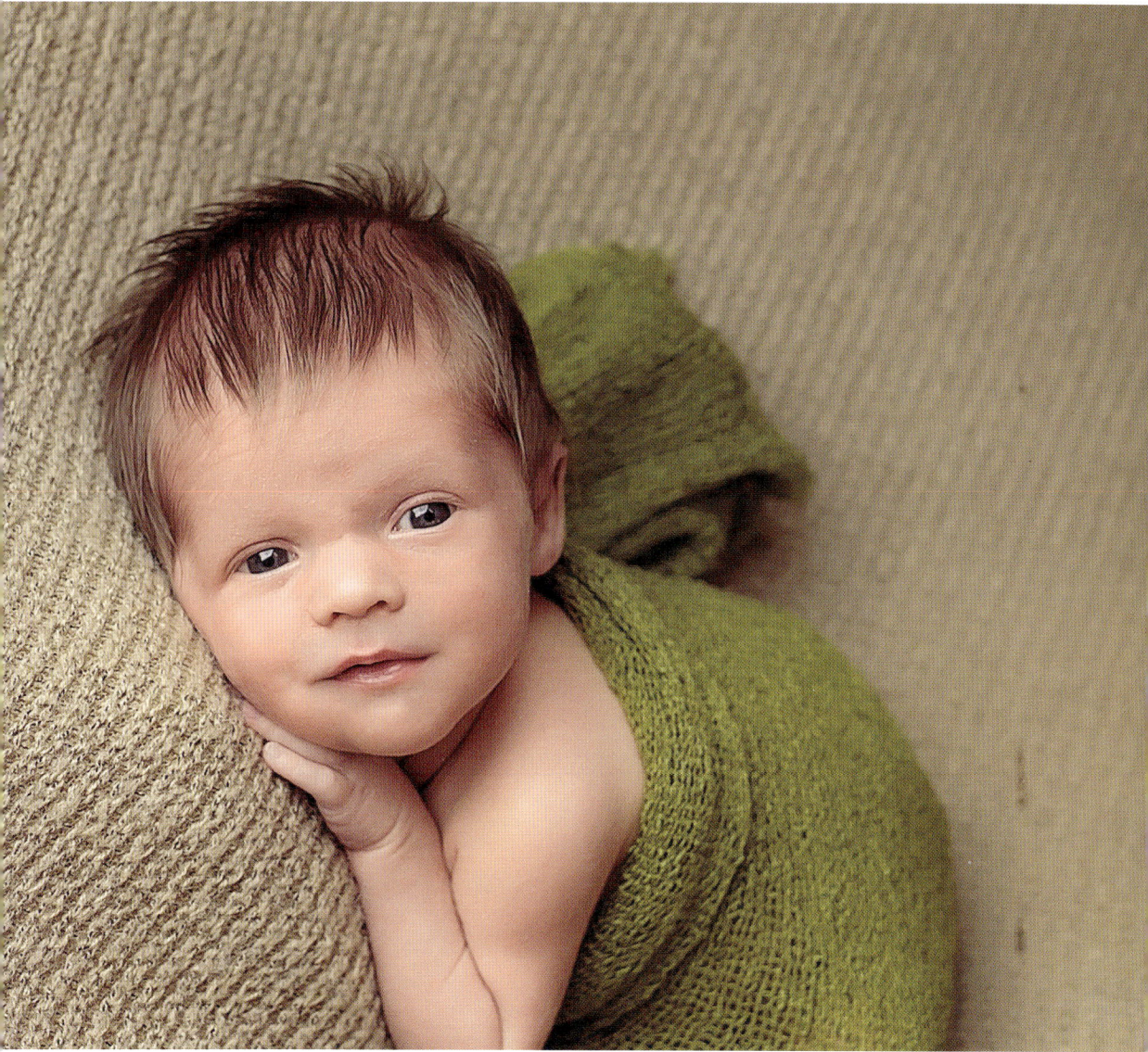

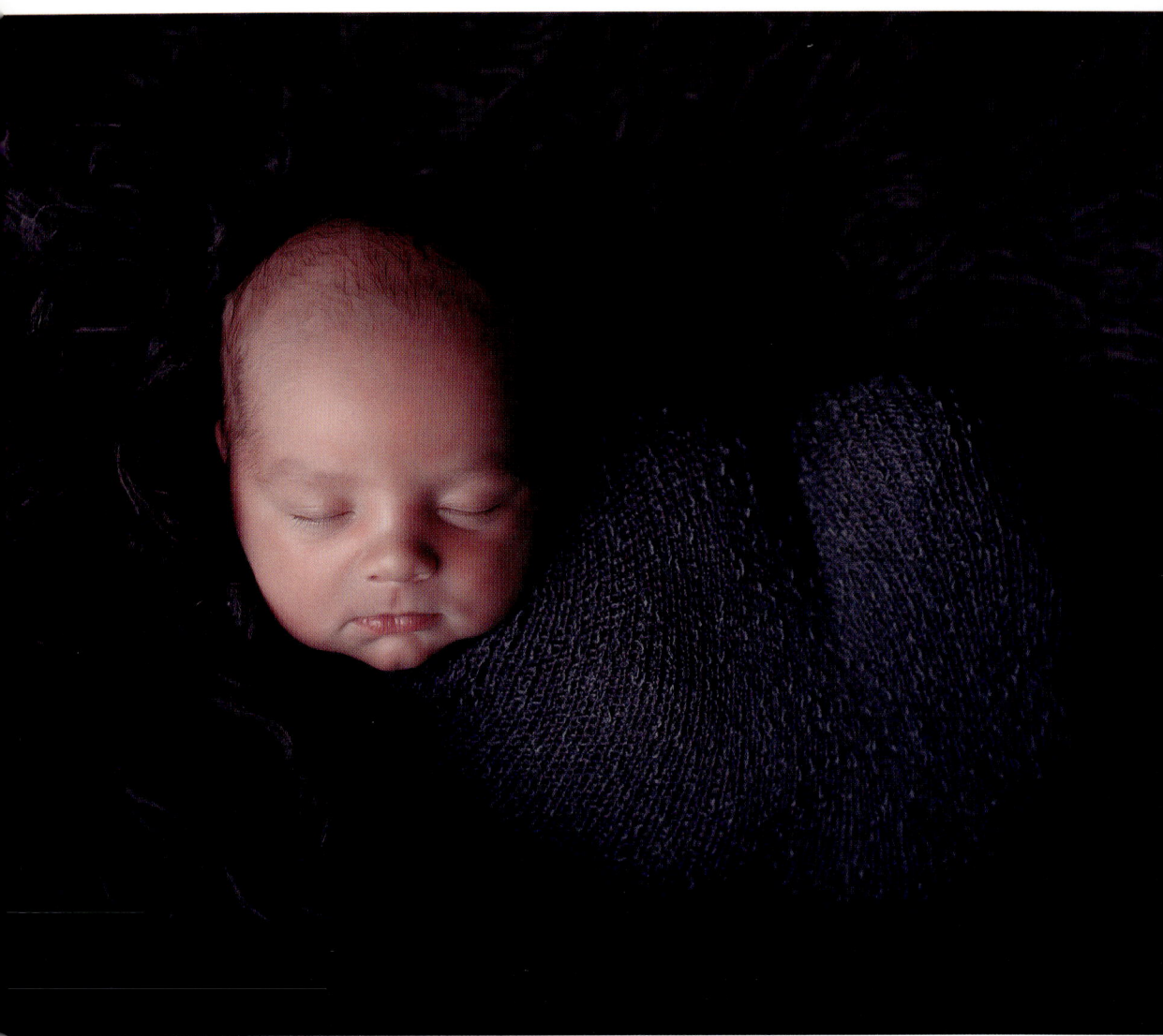

HOLDEN

"I loved being pregnant. I never felt alone. I used to just sit around by myself, rub my belly, and talk to my sweet baby. It was the most comforting feeling I'd ever had. There is also nothing like feeling your baby move for the first time. That's when it finally seems real that there is a life growing inside you."

—Holly, mom of Holden, born December 23rd, 2014

PAYTON

"When I found out I was pregnant, I was shocked! She was a big surprise. Throughout my pregnancy, I loved just laying back and watching my stomach move around when she kicked."

—April, mom of Payton, born December 21st, 2013

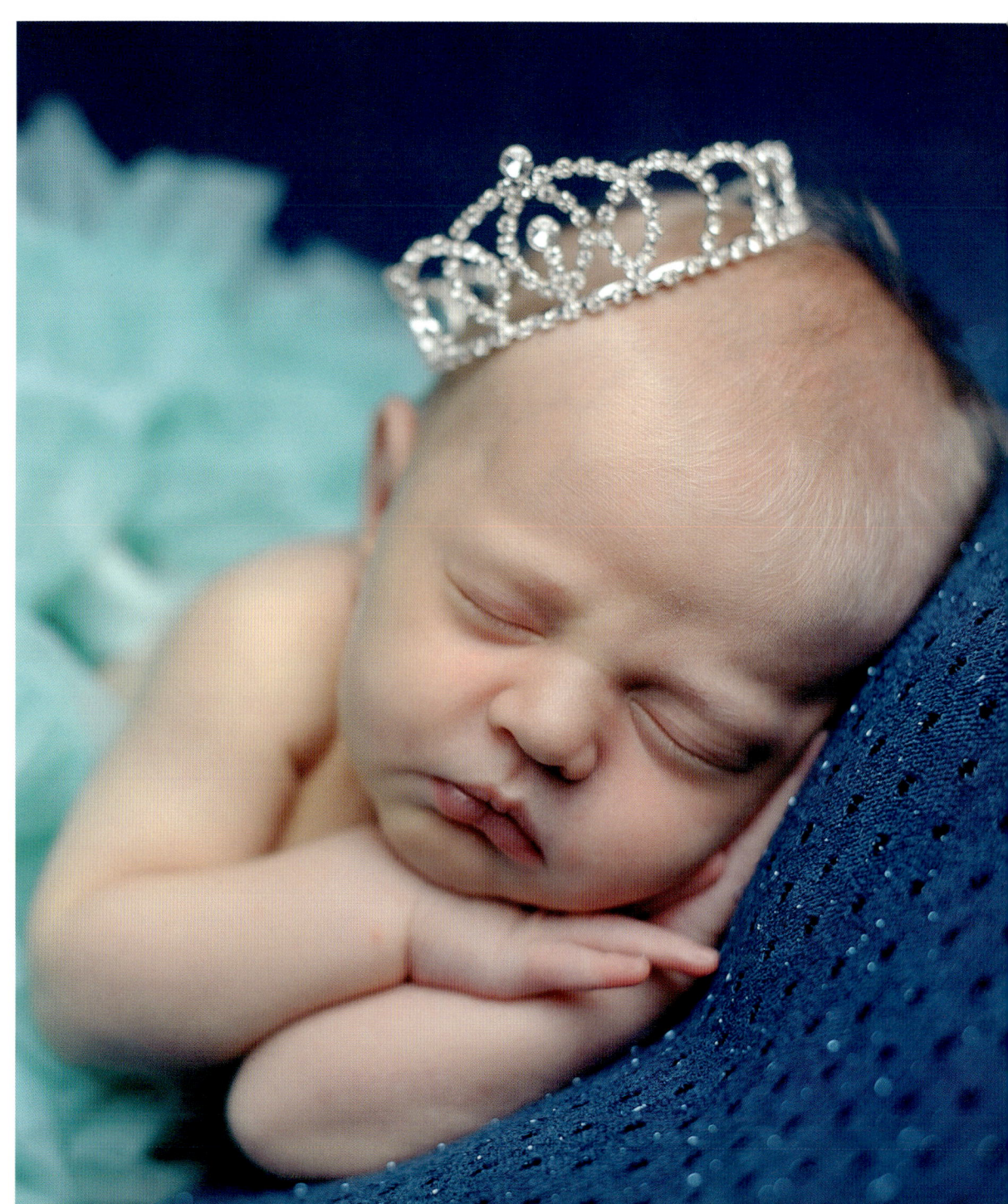

MACIE & MADDIE

"1,460 days of praying, vasectomy reversal, uterine polyp removal, four failed Clomid rounds, two failed IUIs, 69 shots, countless doctor's visits/blood draws/ultrasounds, one successful IVF transfer of two embryos, approximately $30K invested total, and one *amazing* God!"

—Amanda, mom of Macie & Maddie,
born October 2nd, 2017

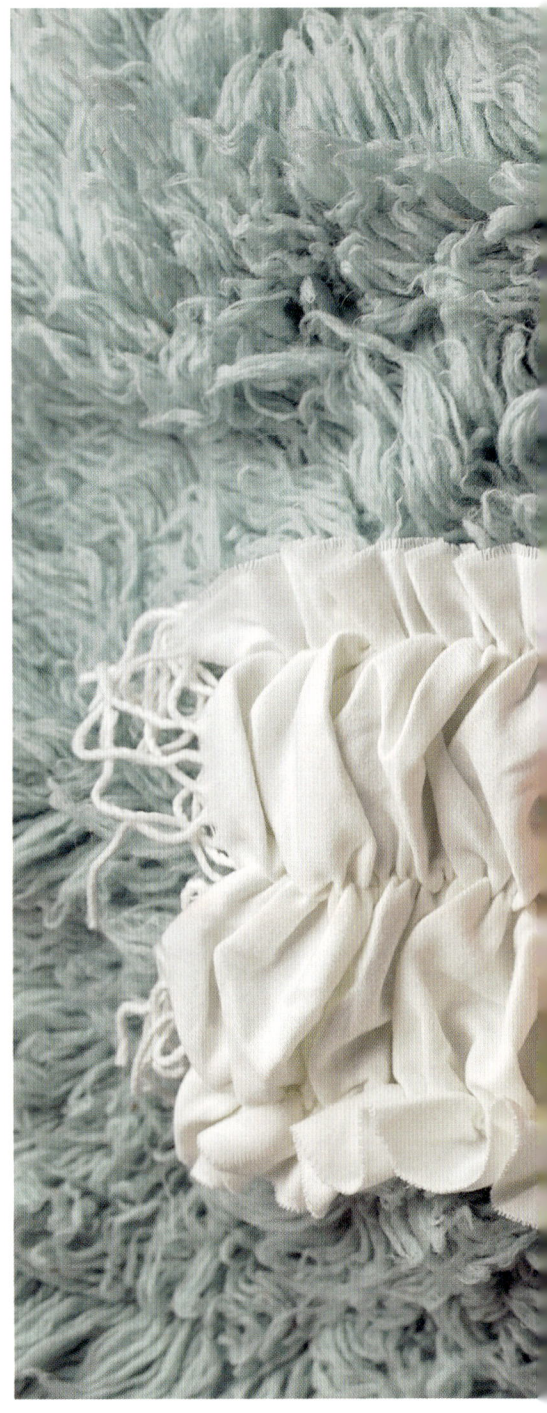

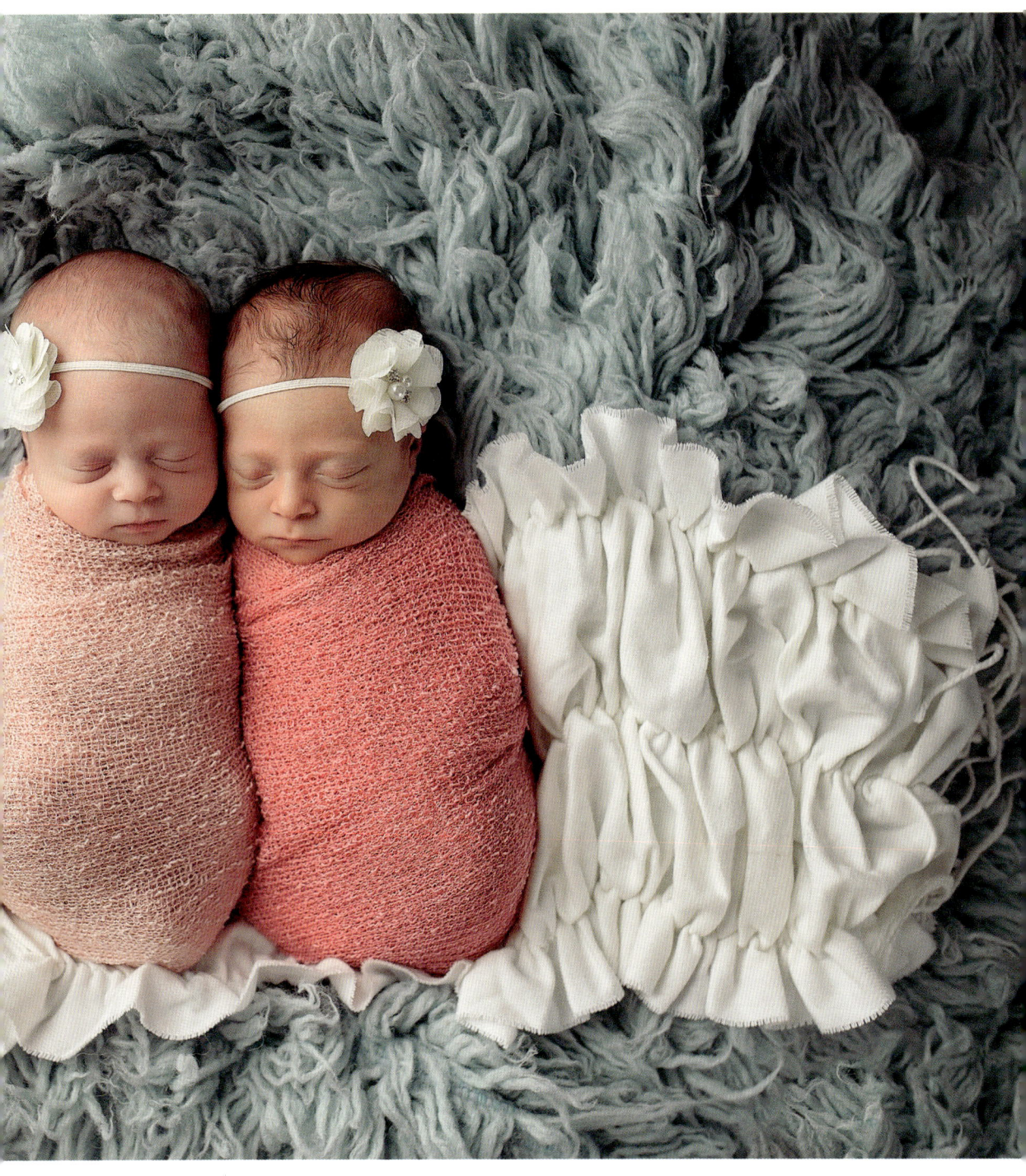

HENRY

"I was so excited to go into labor on my own, since I was induced with my first. I also felt like I was in uncharted territory, and all I could do was focus on my contractions. After a long labor, I was so happy to finally be holding Henry and excited that he looked just like me, since my older son looks just like my husband!"

—Ashli, mom of Henry, born April 2nd, 2018

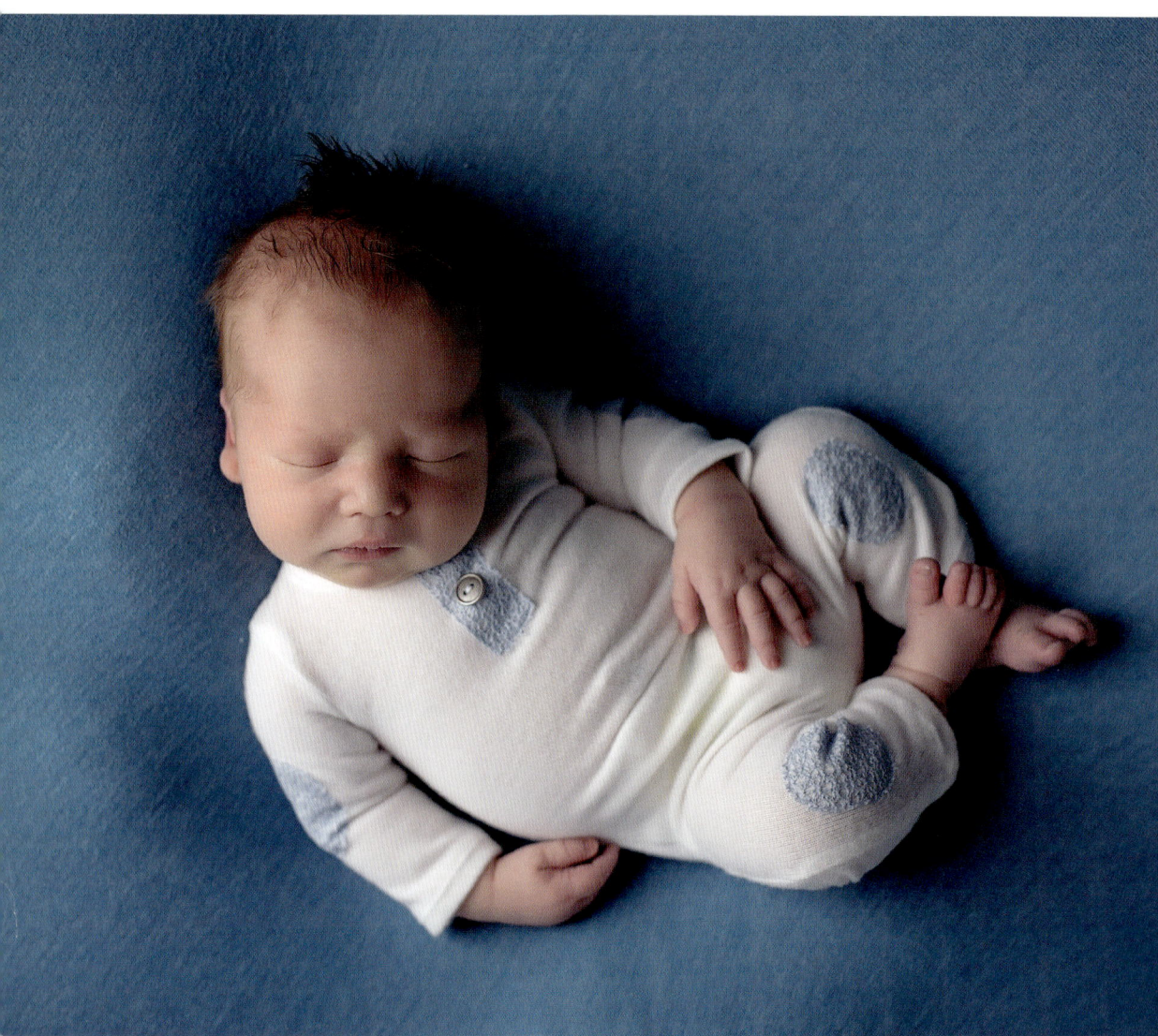

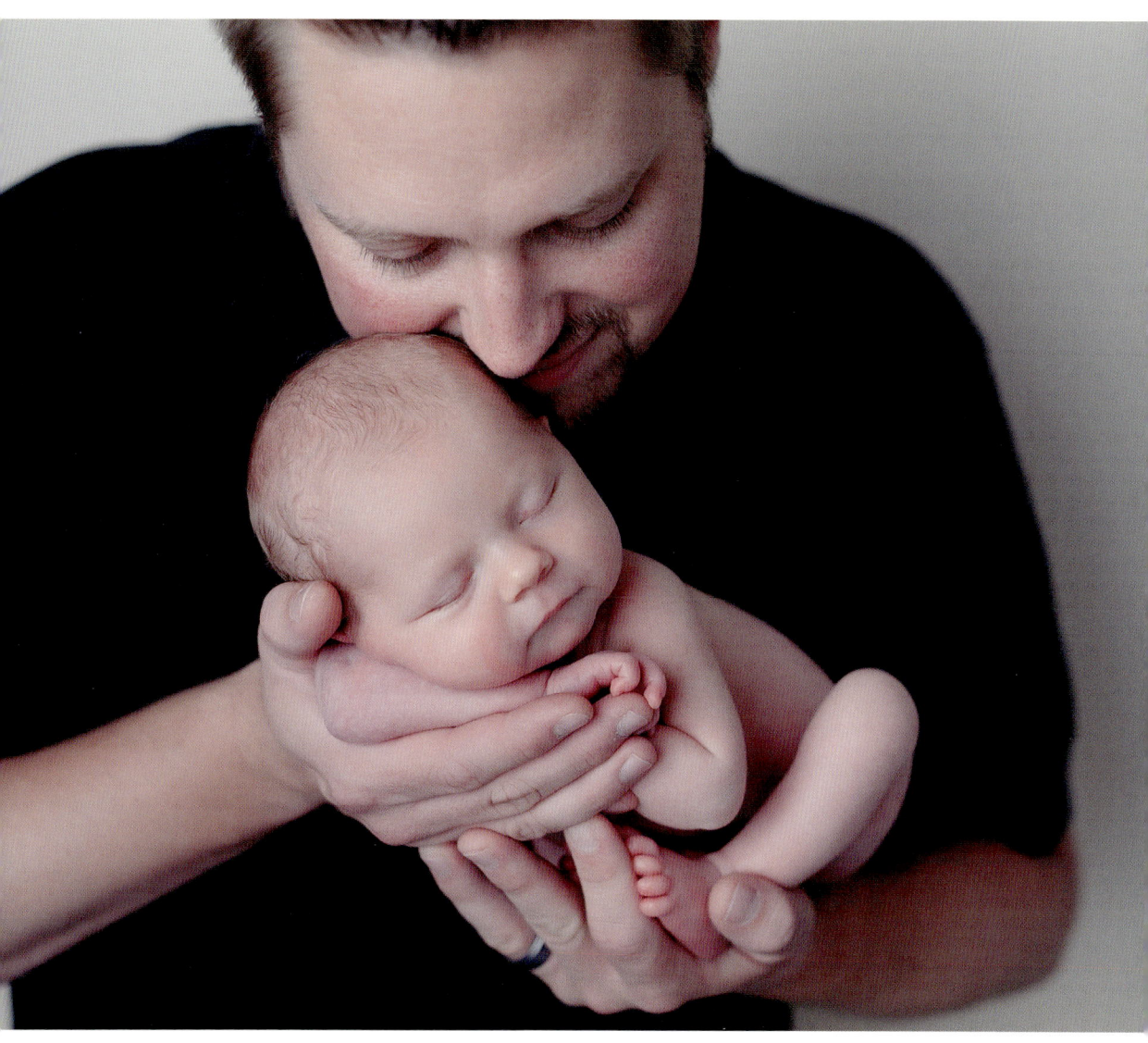

LAYNA

"Nothing prepares you for experiencing your husband as a father. It was heart-meltingly beautiful!"

—Megan, mom of Layna, born August, 14th, 2013

ELLA JEWELL

"Holding your child for the first time awakens a part of your heart that you never knew was asleep."

—Amanda, mom of Ella Jewell,
born October 3rd, 2017

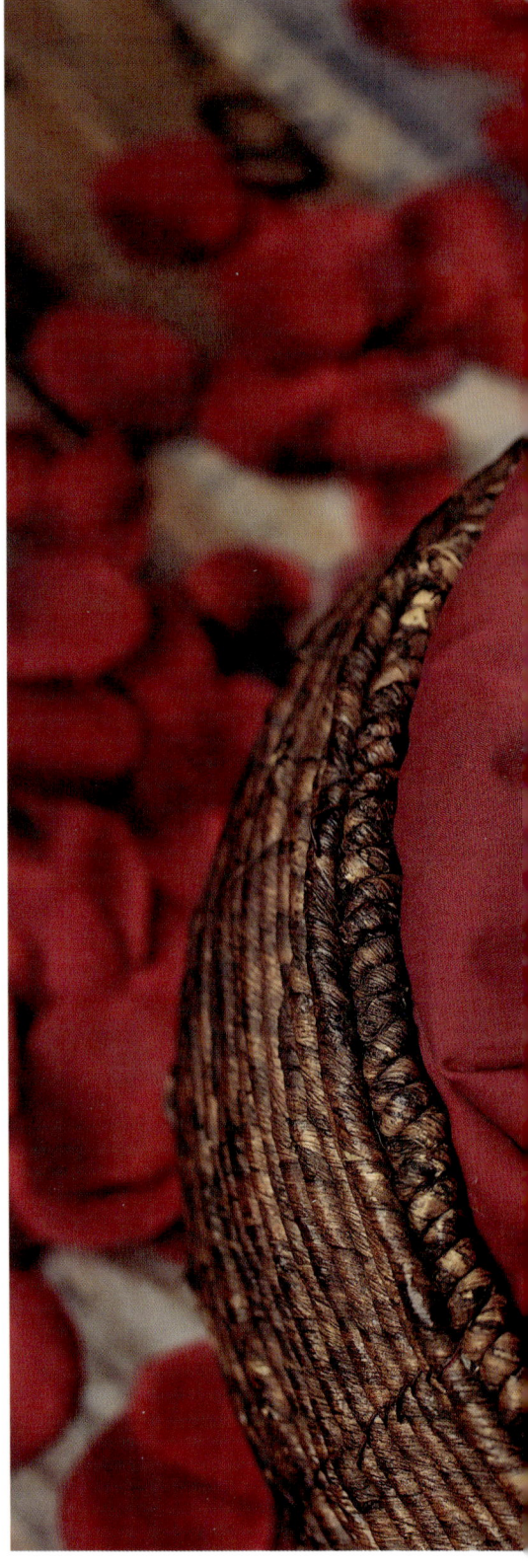

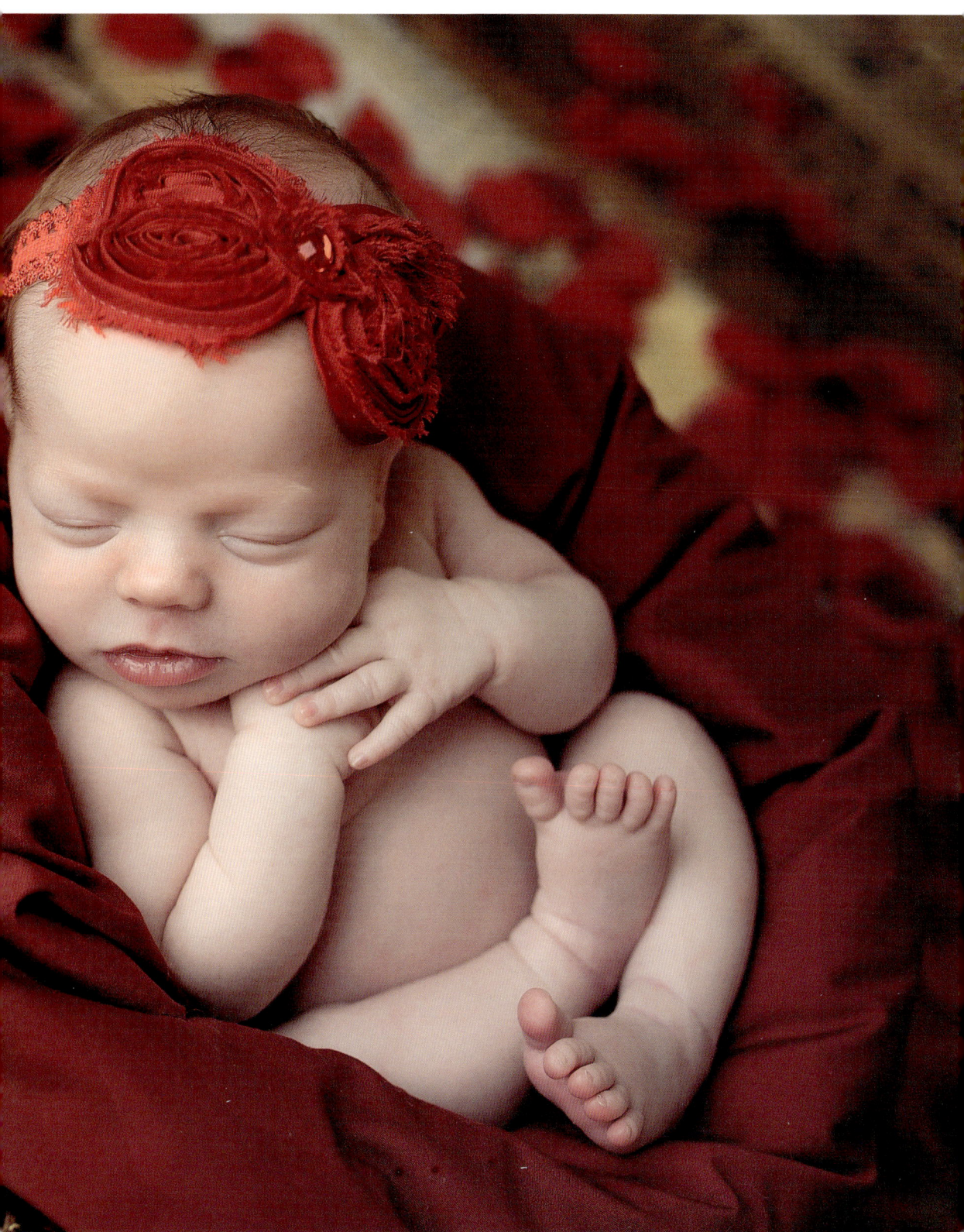

CARTER

"I was a terrified bundle of nerves the day of our first ultrasound appointment. We had been in this position two times before, with a sad outcome of little to no heartbeat that ended in miscarriage. I told the ultrasound technician that I didn't want to look; I was too nervous. I closed my eyes and almost immediately, she said, 'Jamie, open your eyes.' There on the screen was a flickering heartbeat. At about eight weeks along, it was a strong heartbeat of 183 beats per minute. I cried and cried. I was so relieved and happy. I remember it like it was yesterday."

—Jamie, mom of Carter, born July 19th, 2013

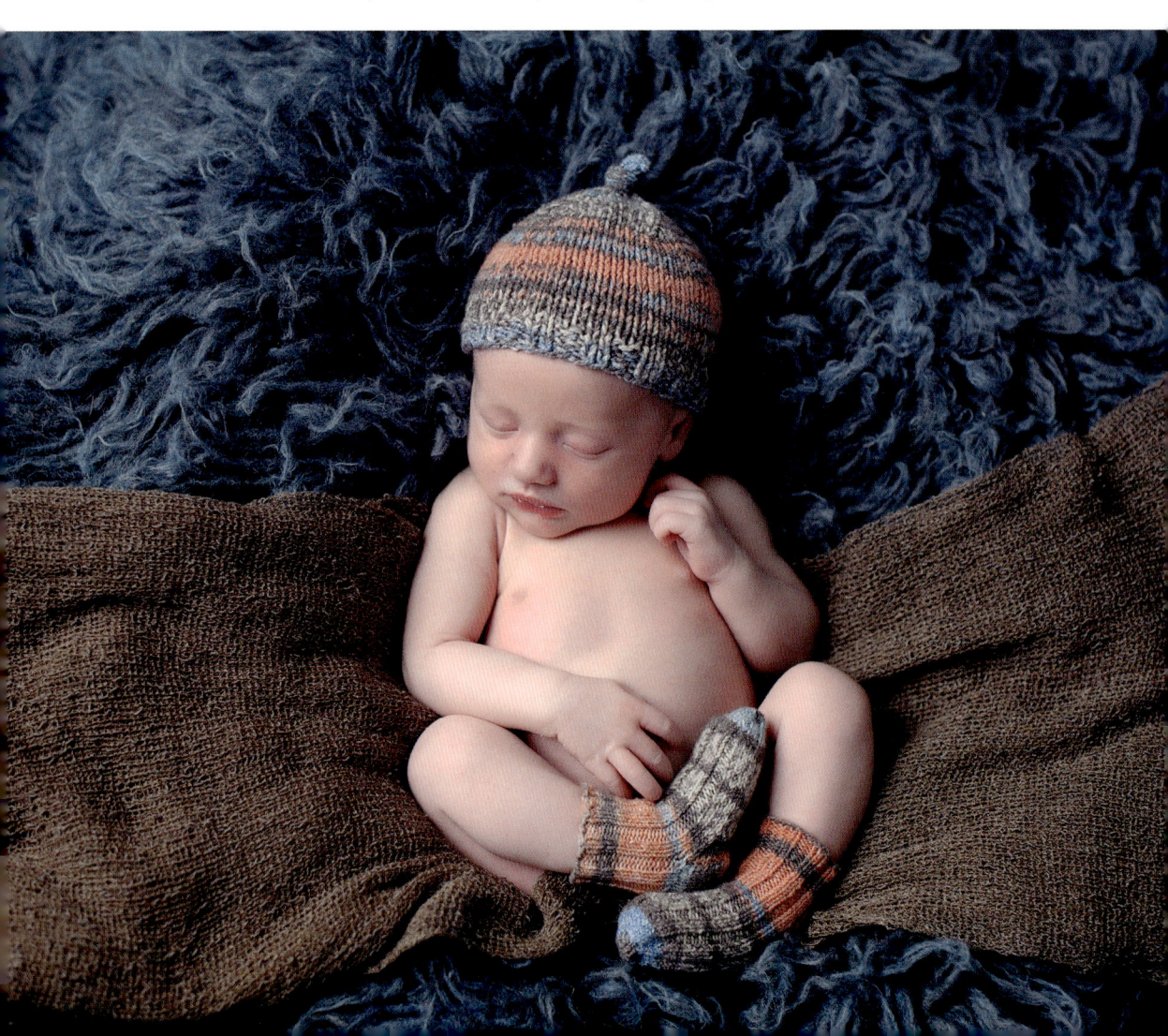

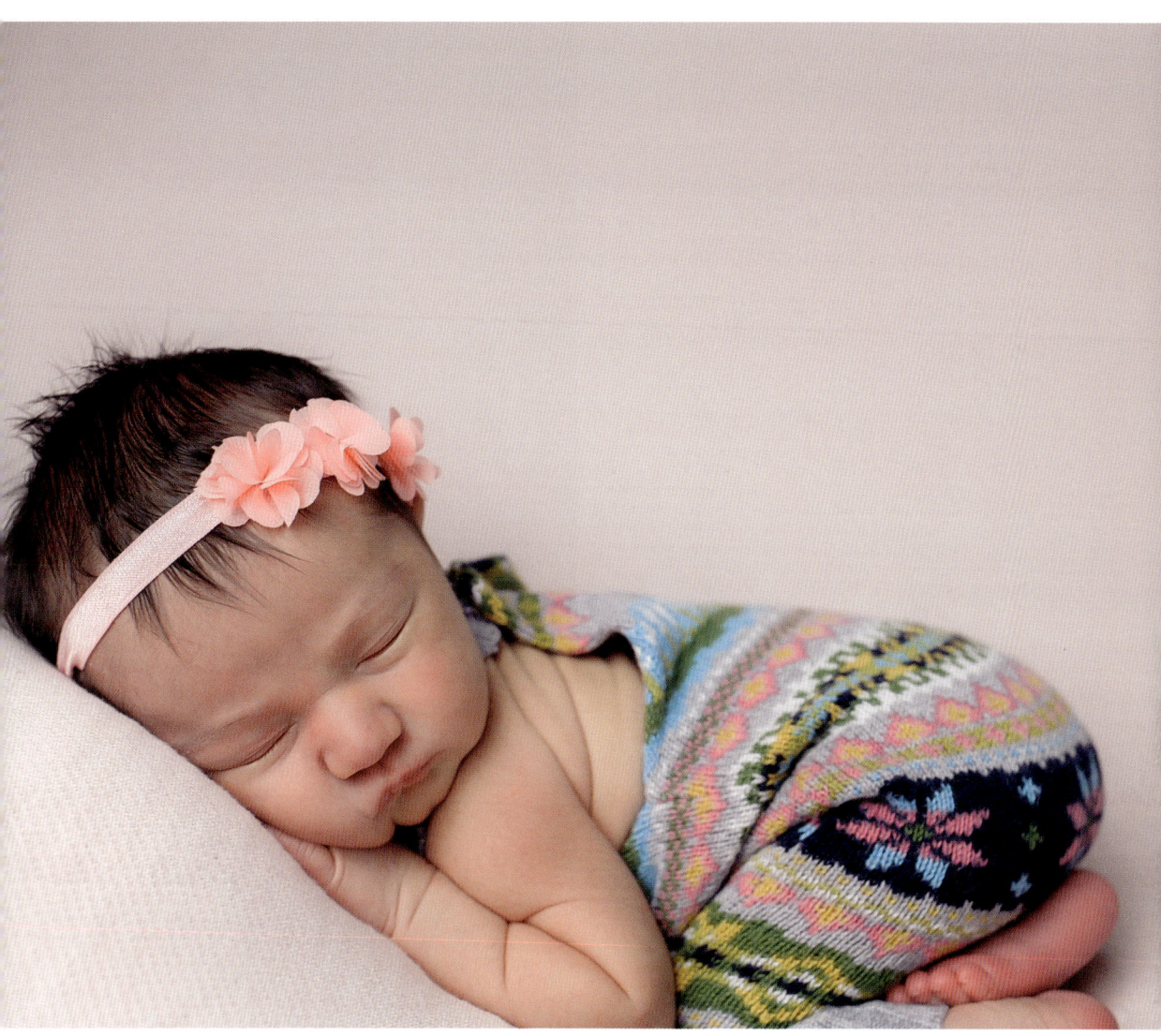

BELLAMY

"I remember the first time she smiled. I was rocking her
in my arms and singing to her . . . and in the midst of her
sleep, she smiled."

—Kendra, mom of Bellamy, born December 15th, 2014

COLE

"When I found out I was pregnant, I was so overjoyed and felt incredibly blessed that we were chosen to be parents to a sweet baby!"

—Sara, mom of Cole,
born March 9th, 3013

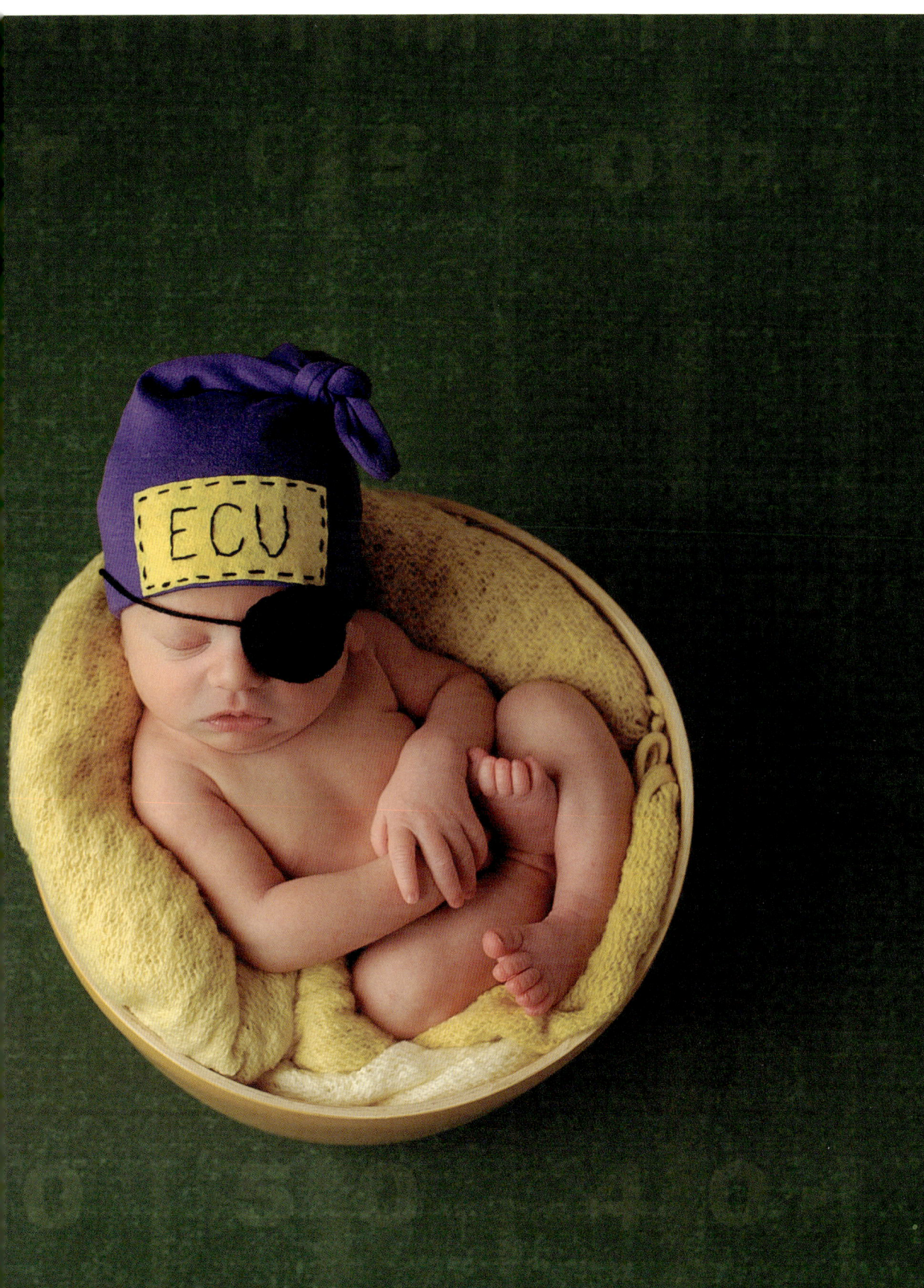

JACKSON

"When I first saw Jackson, I felt overwhelmed with joy.
My cup was running over with pure happiness that I'd
never felt before."

—Ashley, mom of Jackson, born October 28th, 2012

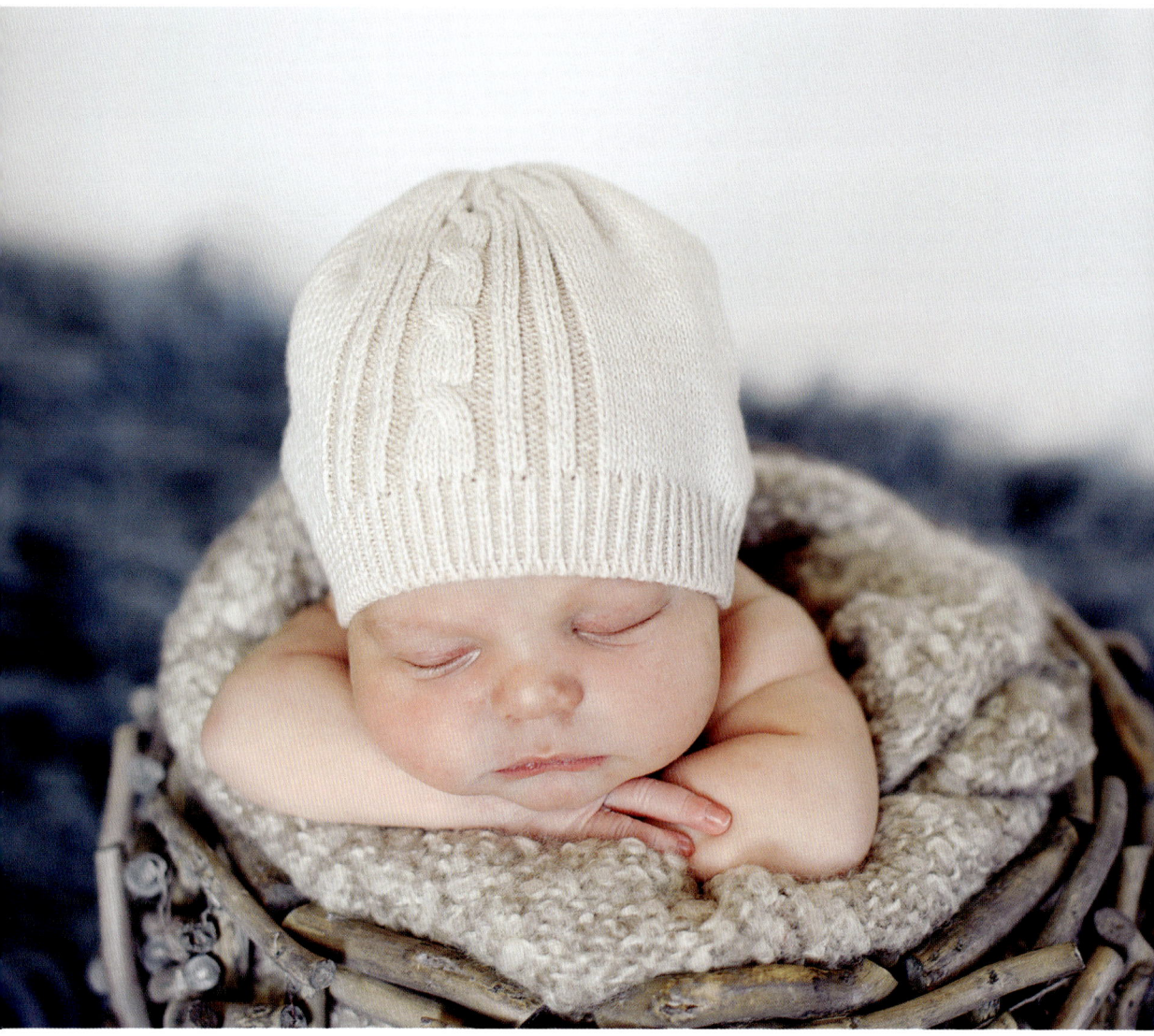

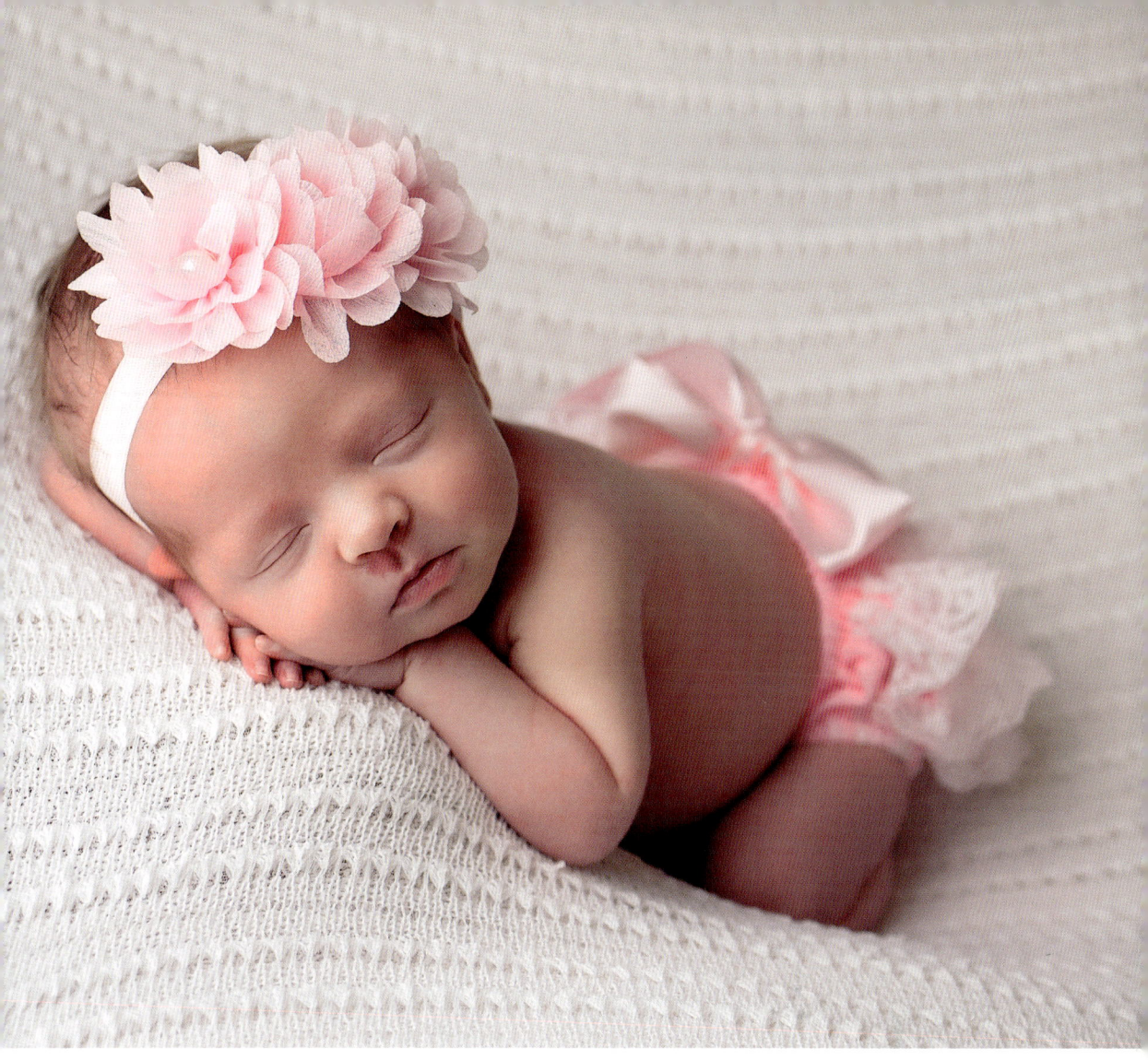

NORA

"The first time I saw Nora on an ultrasound, I cried. I had always dreamed of the day that I would find out I was pregnant, but actually seeing my little nugget and listening to that sweet heartbeat was something I never imagined could have been so amazing. They always say it is love at first sight when you see your child for the first time, and they are right. I knew the moment I saw Nora that nothing could compare to the love I felt for her."

—Lindsay, mom of Nora, born November 25th, 2017

CAROLINE

"This was my third pregnancy, and I already had
two boys, so I truly believed this would also be
a boy. When we went for an anatomy scan, the
nurse placed the probe on my stomach, and I immediately yelled, *'That's a girl!'* I probably scared
everybody in the office, but I was so shocked and
excited, I didn't know what to do with myself.
I told my husband I never realized how much I
wanted a daughter until that moment."

—Laura, mom of Caroline,
born December 22nd, 2014

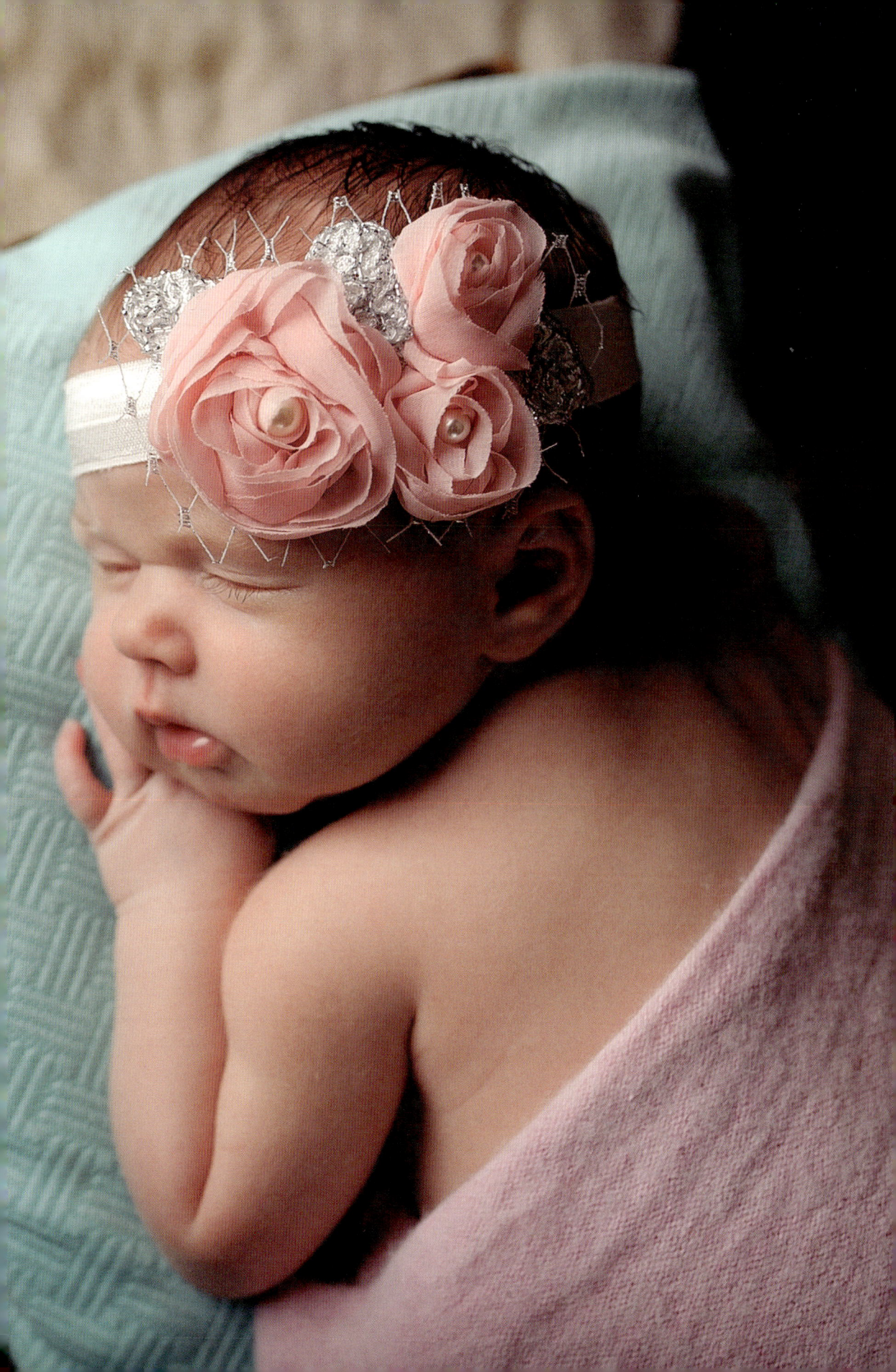

HAILEY

"My husband and Hailey would play even before she was born. She always knew when her daddy touched my belly, and would start kicking like crazy. Once he moved his hand, she would stop."

—Crystal, mom of Hailey, born November 18th, 2015

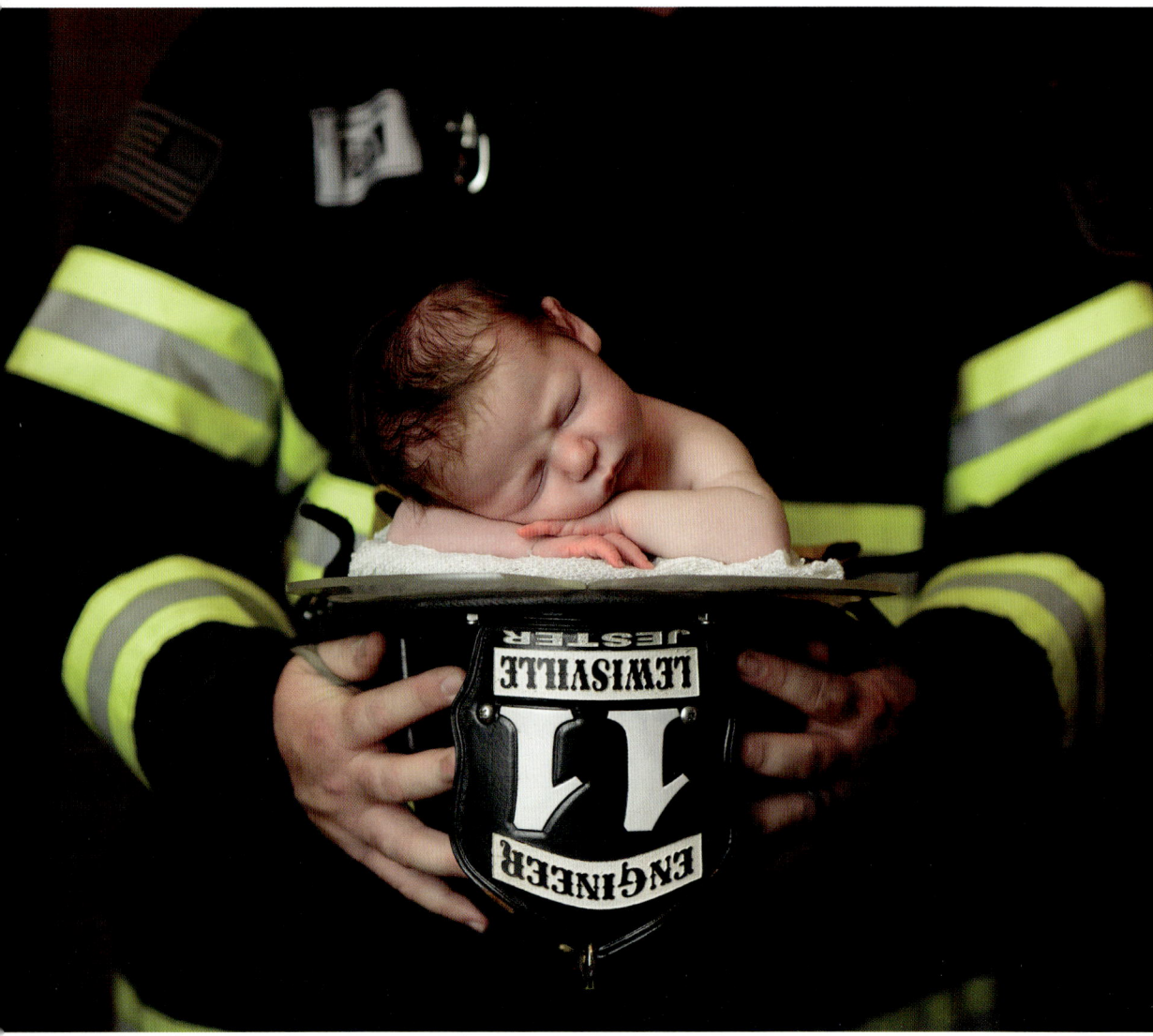

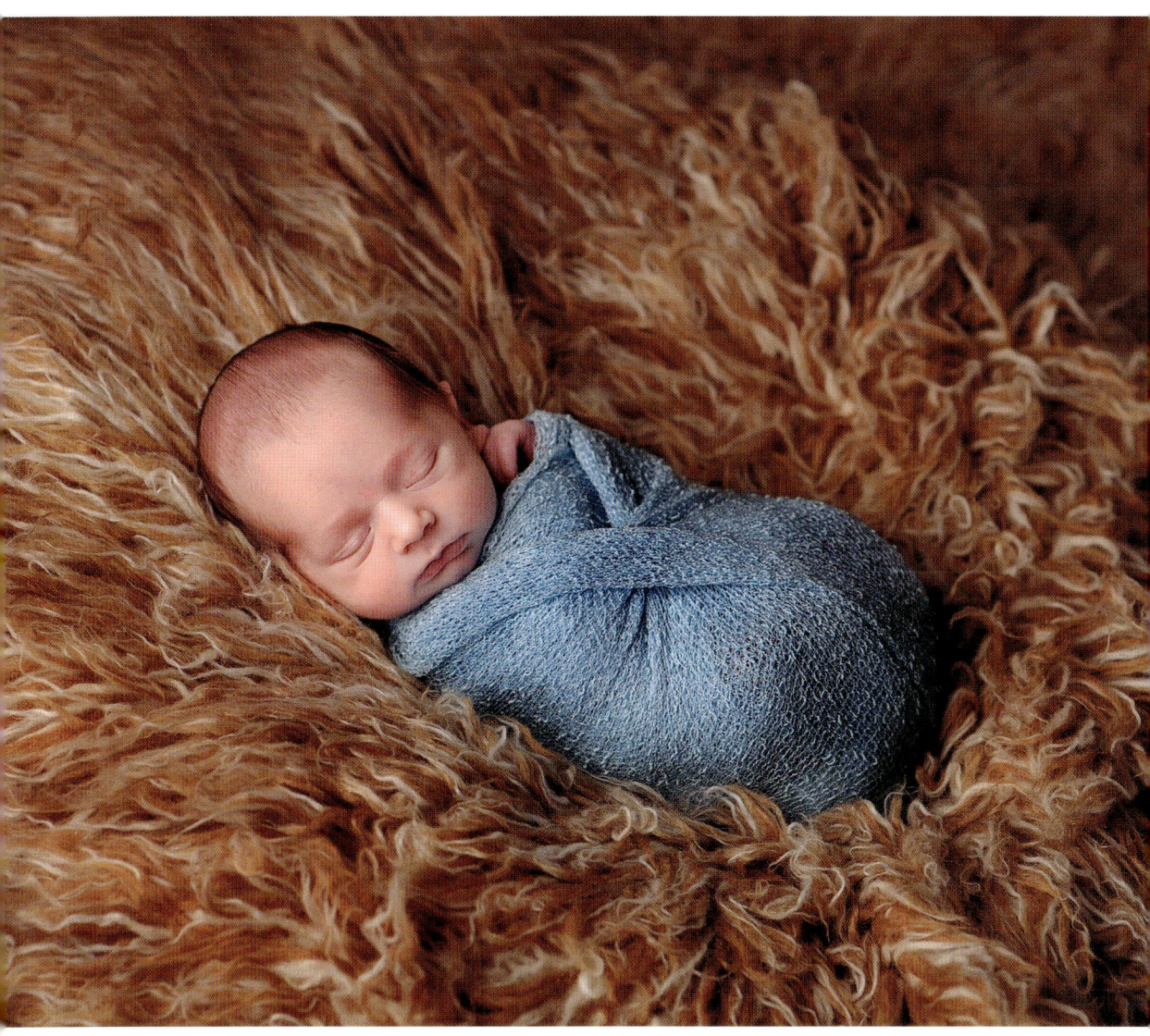

ABEL

"After my second child was born, I decided to have my tubes tied. But I guess there were other plans for me, because I became pregnant with Abel! I knew that having him was meant to be."

—Bridgett, mom of Abel, born May 22nd, 2015

BRADEN

"Instant love. As soon as I saw his precious face and they laid him on my chest, I couldn't believe he was really here, and he was what was growing in me all that time. I couldn't believe we made something so sweet."

—Kelly, mom of Braden, born February 1st, 2018

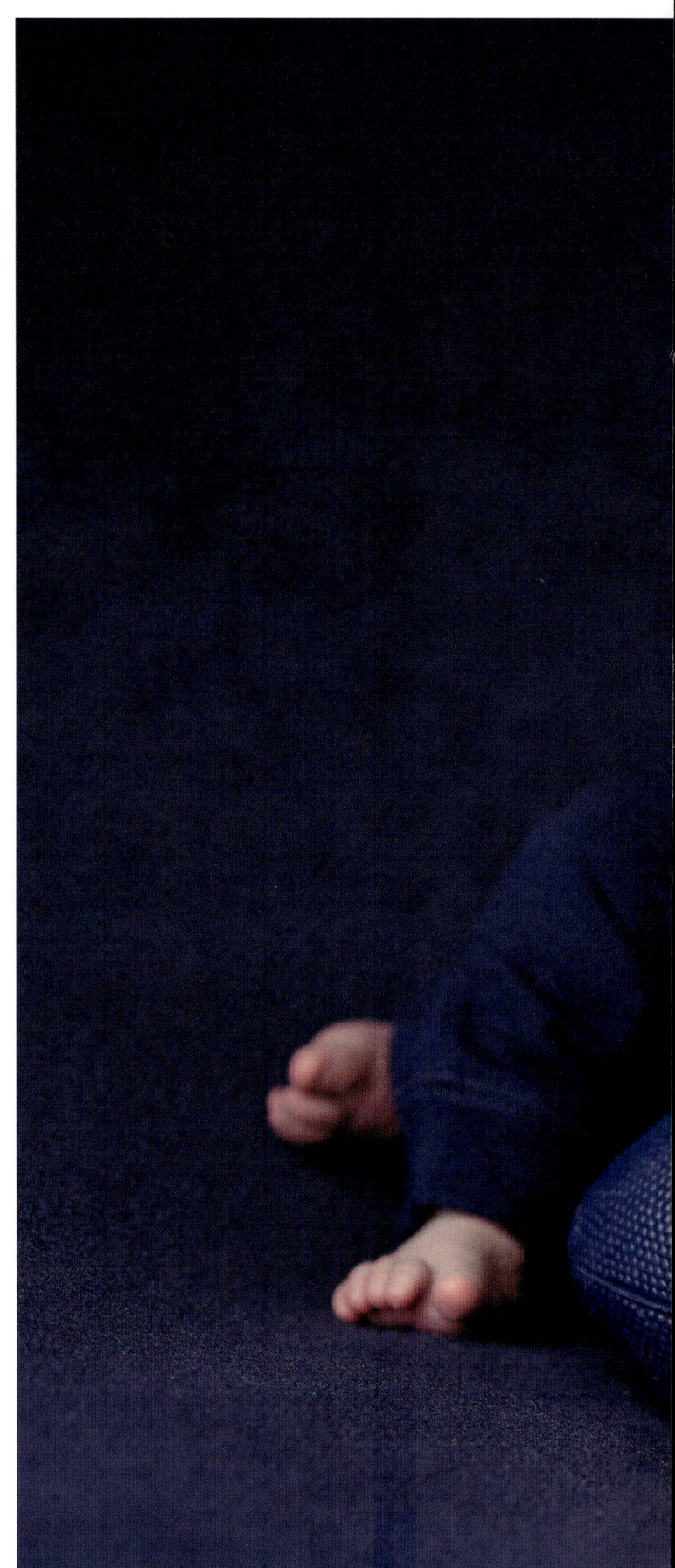

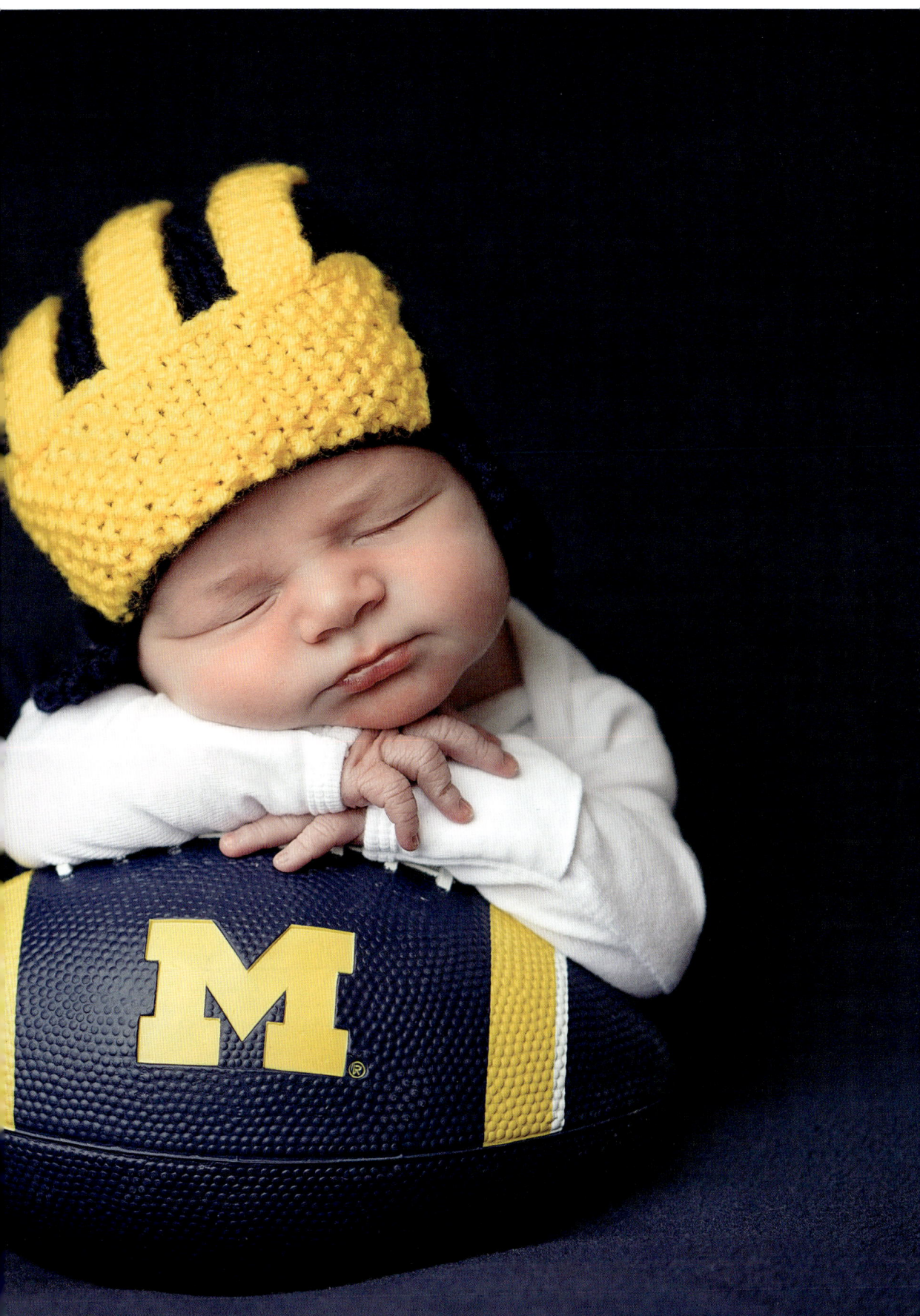

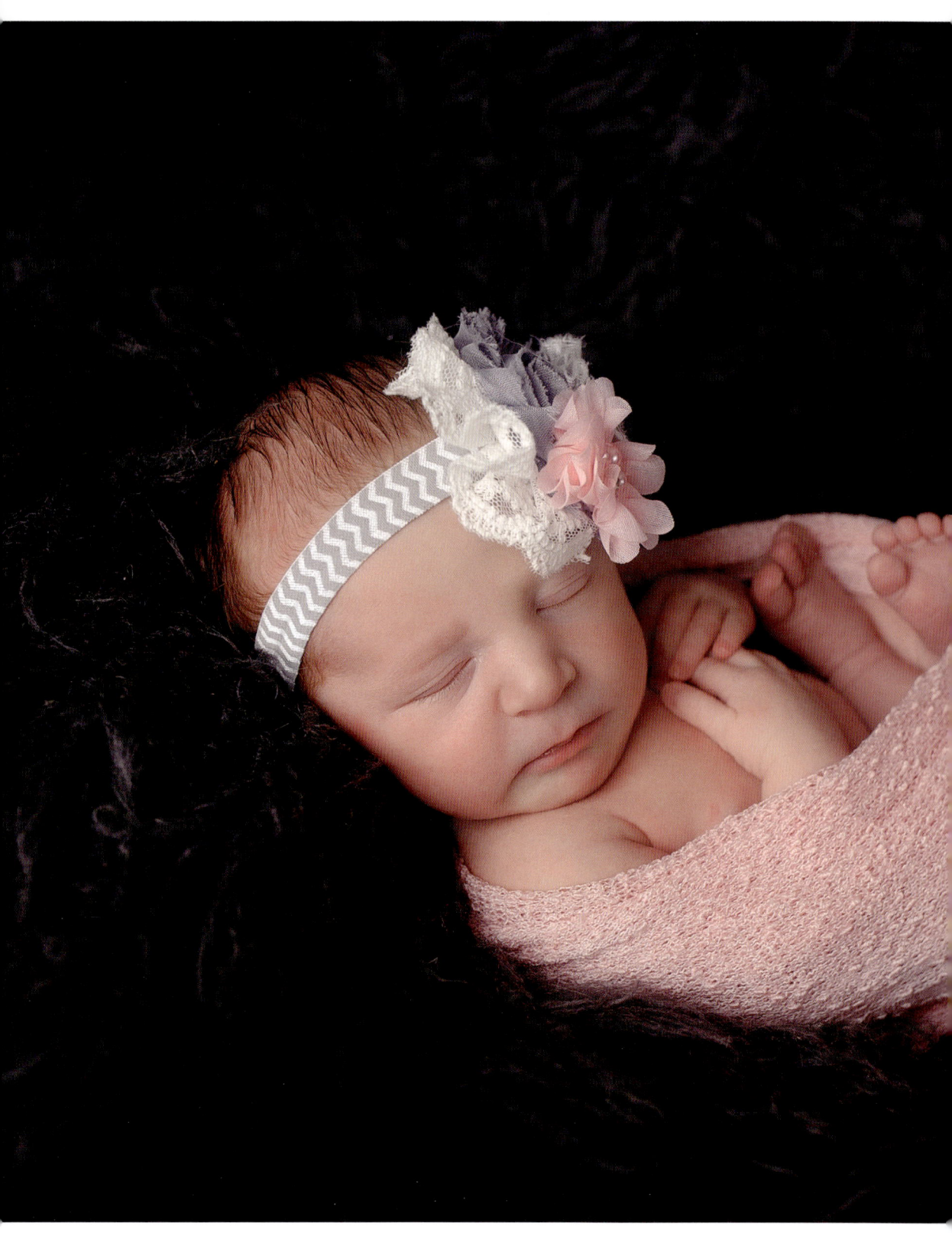

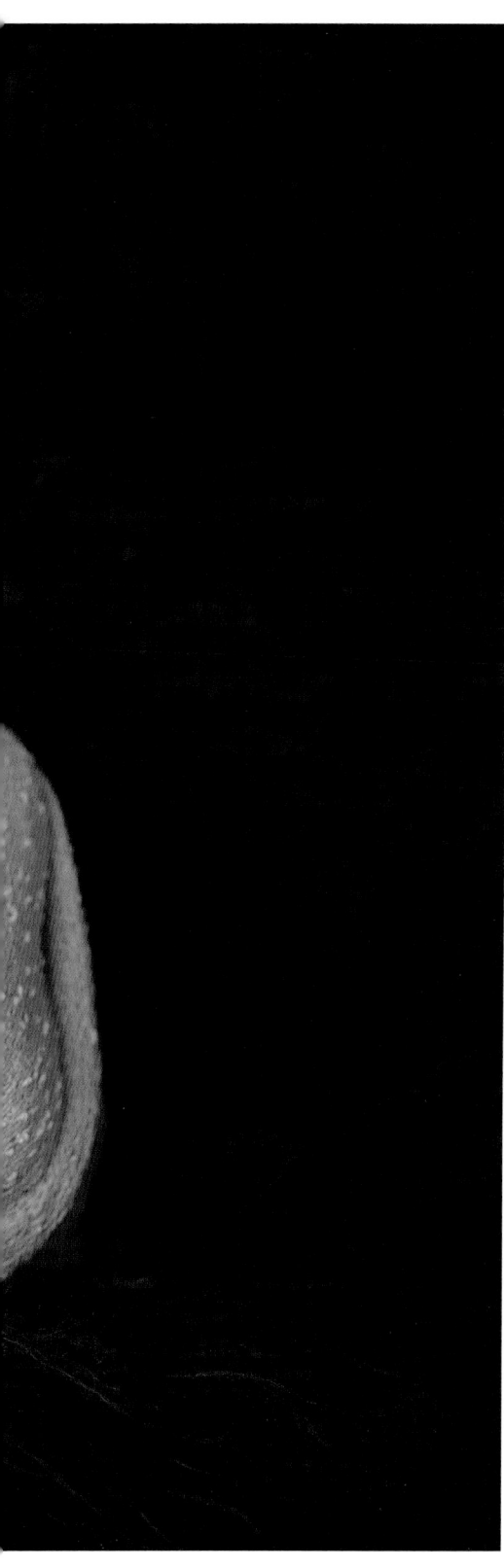

BRYNLEE

"The first time I held Brynlee, all the trials of pregnancy were immediately erased and replaced with an instant, indescribable bond. It was an experience that I'll never forget."

—Magen, mom of Brynlee,
born January 19th, 2015

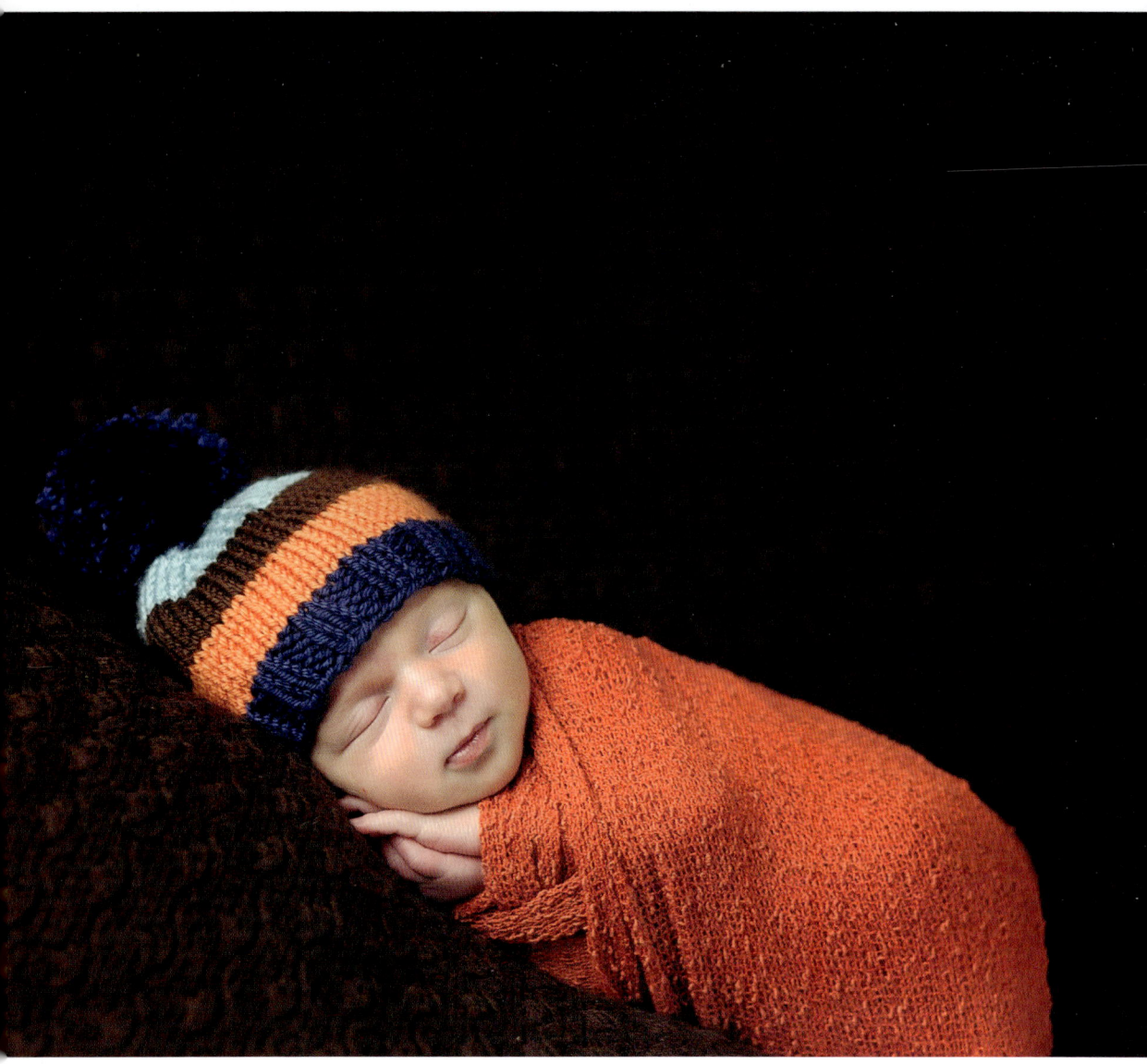

MATTHEW

"When I first found out I was pregnant, I felt like I was dreaming. We had wished and prayed for him for so long. Earlier that month, we had been told that we had a very slim chance of ever becoming pregnant. Just a few weeks later, we found out what a miracle looked like. We were expecting!"

—Alicia, mom of Matthew, born September 30th, 2015

EVELYN

"My favorite part about having a newborn was just sitting and holding her for hours. I loved watching her movements and facial expressions."

—Kimberly, mom of Evelyn, born April 25th, 2016

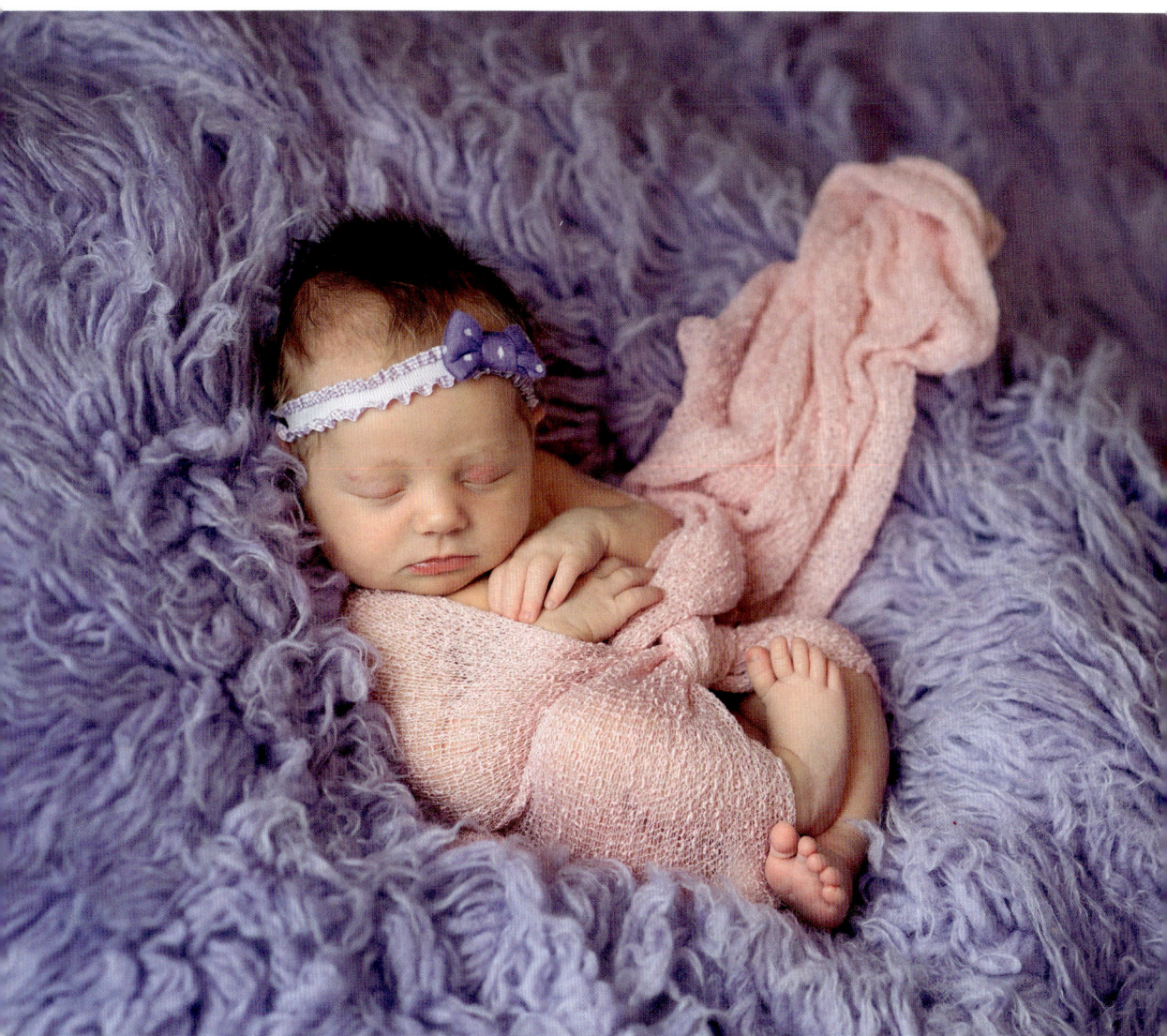

LUKE

"The first time I held Luke, I was overwhelmed with joy and gratefulness for such a precious blessing."

—Stephanie, mom of Luke, born April 22nd, 2017

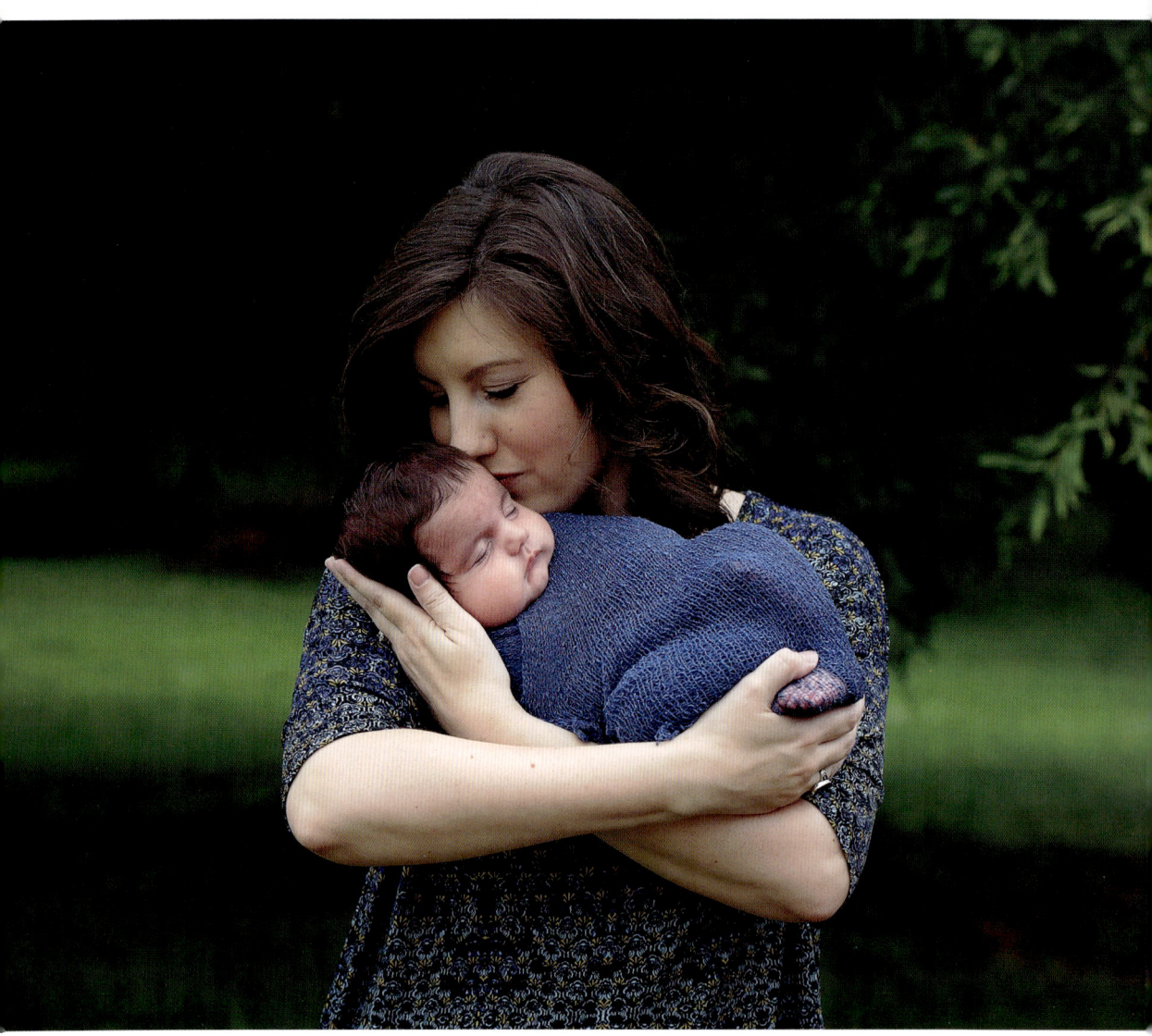

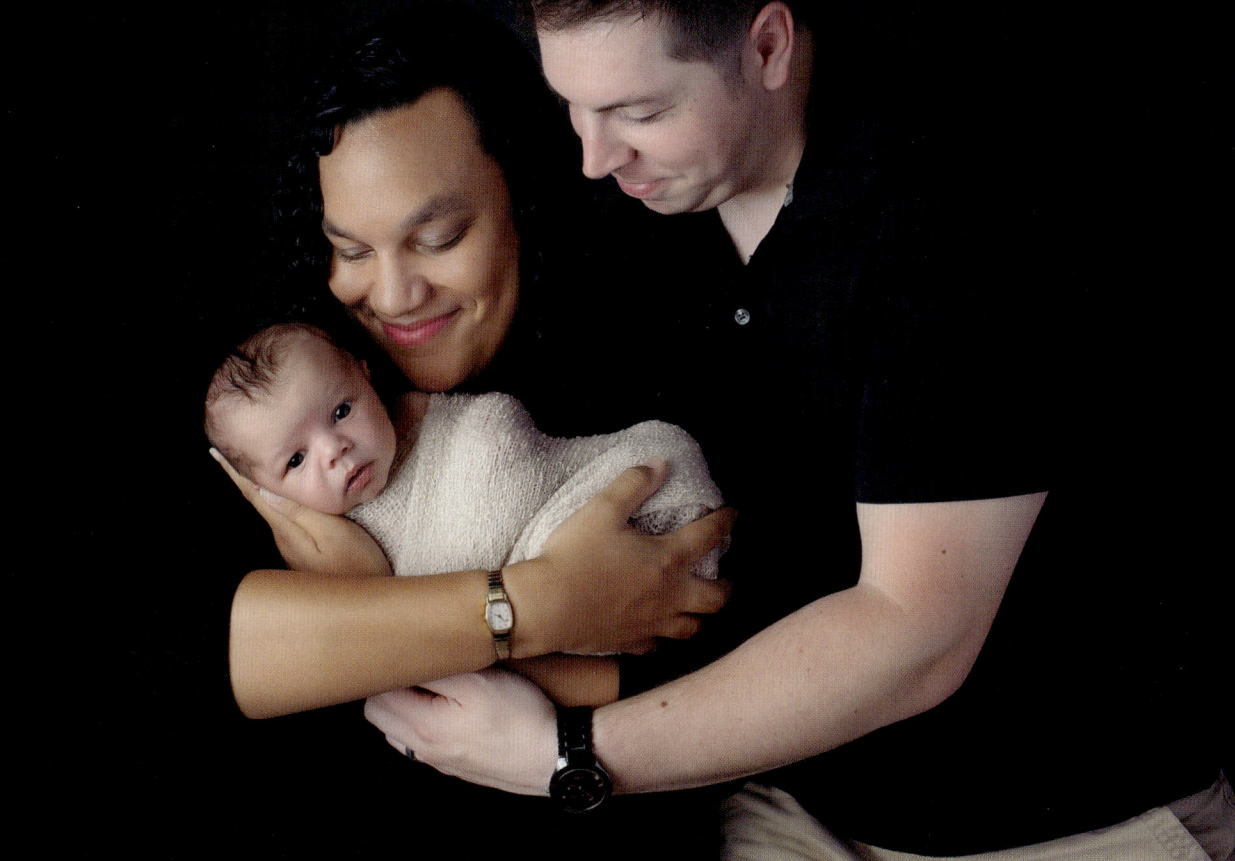

JACKSON

"I had been told since I was a teenager that it was probably going to be difficult for me to get pregnant, so when we decided we were ready to start trying, we were completely shocked when the first test we took came back positive! I remember coming out of the bathroom and telling my husband that the test must be wrong.

When we first saw Jackson on the ultrasound, I was overjoyed. I still couldn't believe I was pregnant, but when I saw him on an ultrasound for the first time and heard his heartbeat, it finally became real."

—Andrea, mom of Jackson, born June 30th, 2014

EVERETT

"Sweet little Everett! The first time I saw him, I studied every part of his face and his sweet little body. My wedding day and our boys' birthdays are without a doubt the most precious days of our lives. These are the milestones in life that pull us through the challenging seasons and remind us we've been given the most invaluable and undeserved blessings in the world!"

—Tiffany, mom of Everett, born June 12th, 2015

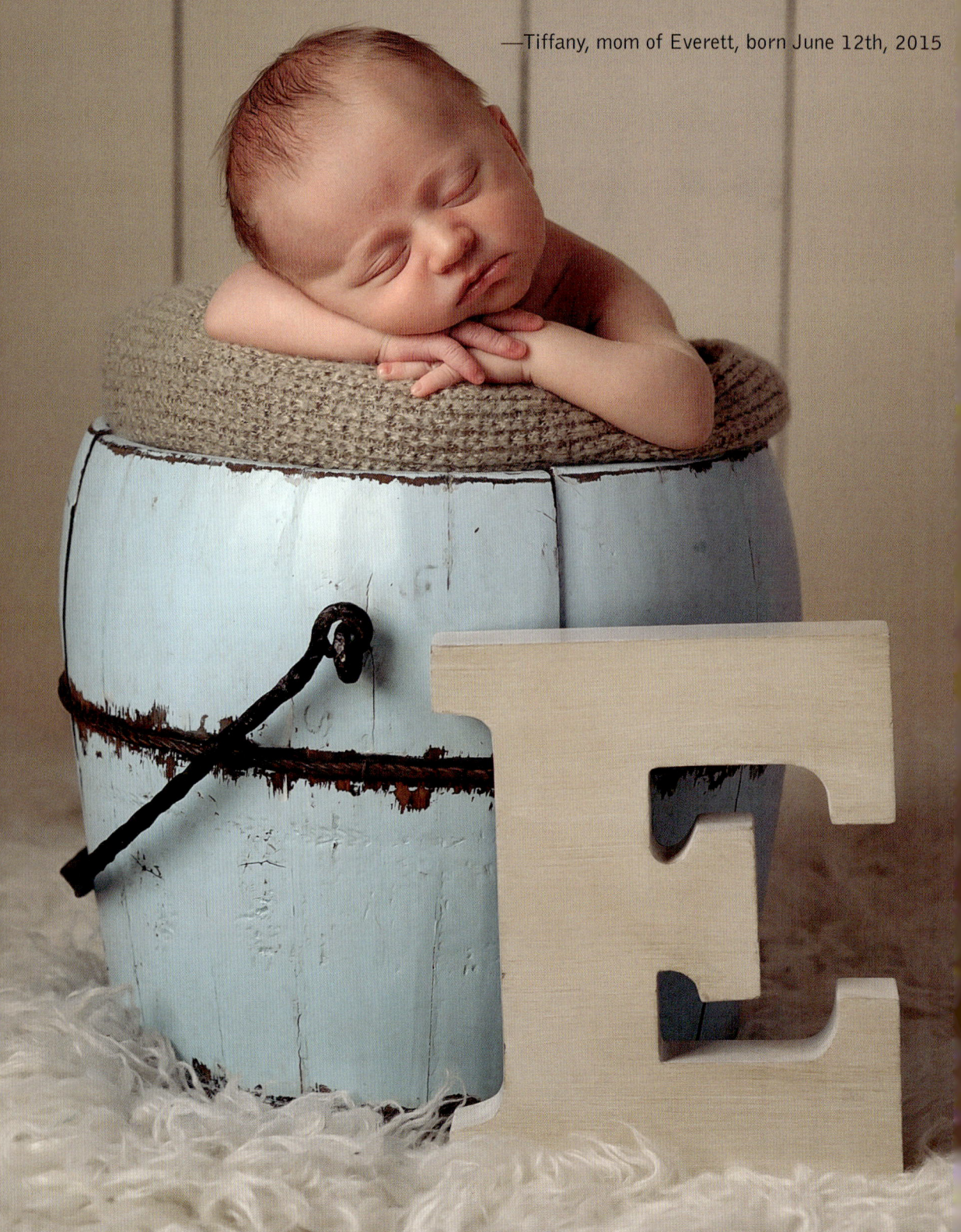

KELSIE RAY

"When I went into labor, I was ecstatic. Our family would be complete. Little did I know a prolapsed umbilical cord would result in an emergency C-section and I would end up sedated because my epidural hadn't taken effect. I woke up in recovery, and my husband brought my sweet baby girl in to me and laid her on my chest. I had lost a lot of blood, but the first thing I remember is the look on her face. When my son got to come in and was introduced to his baby sister, he climbed in the bed, and I was able to hold both of my babies. My world was complete."

—Melissa, mom of Kelsie Ray, born November 16th, 2015

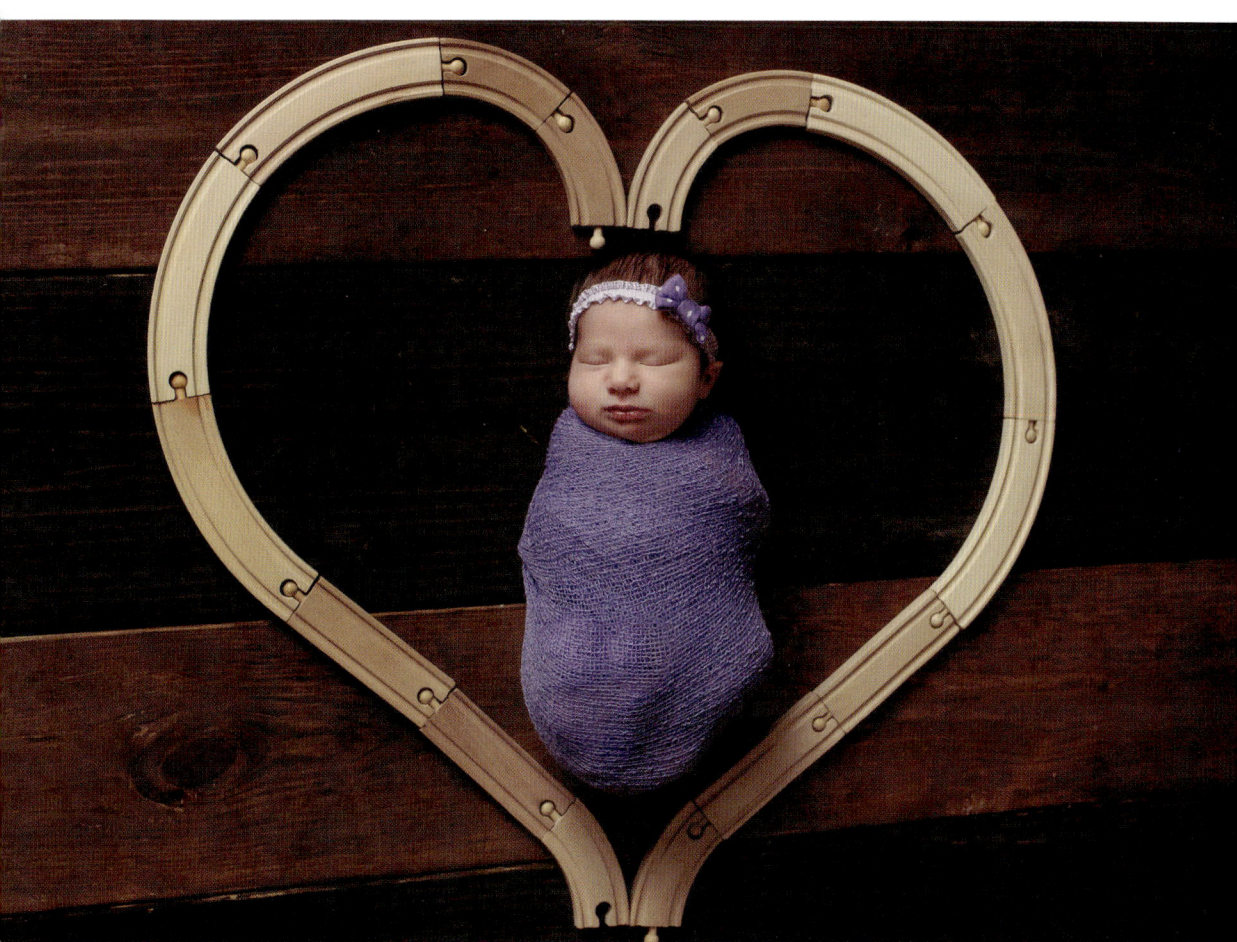

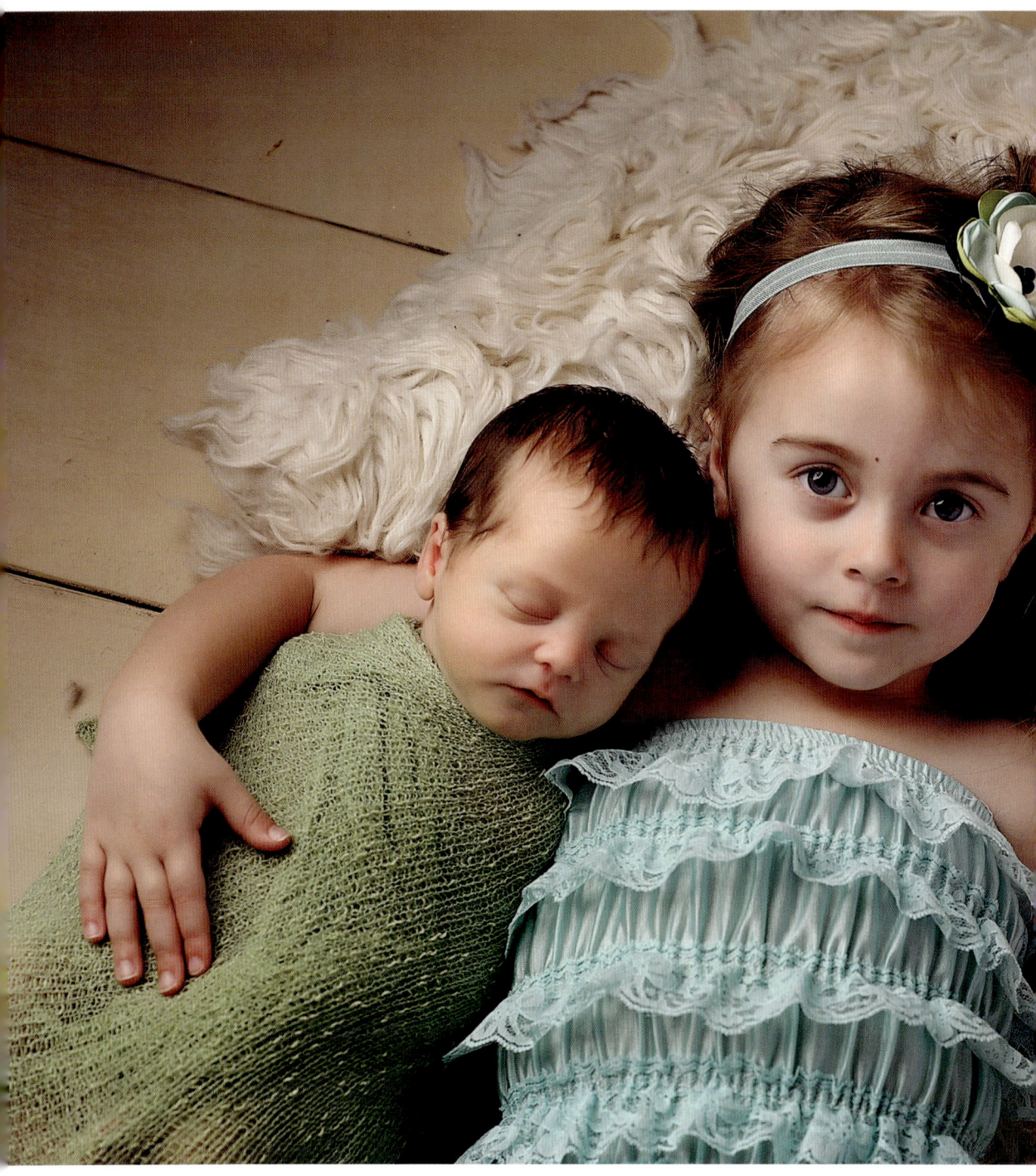

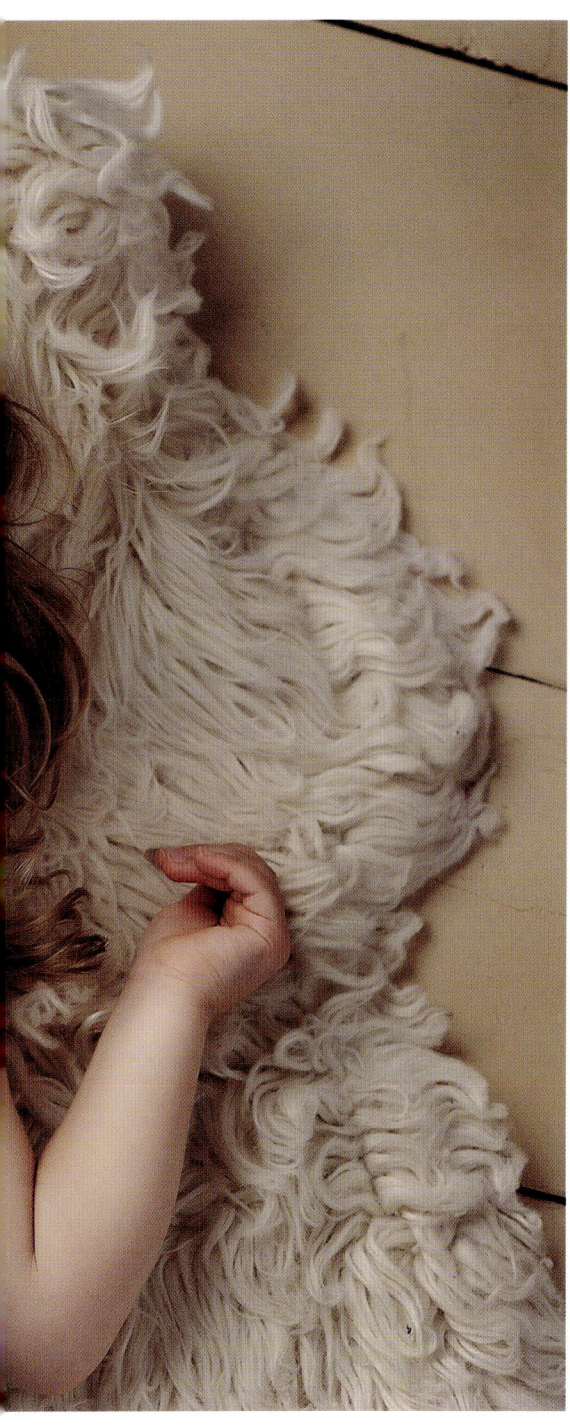

SCOUT

"Scout's big sister loved holding him. I knew they were going to be the best of buds!"

—Adrian, mom of Scout,
born June 13th, 2015

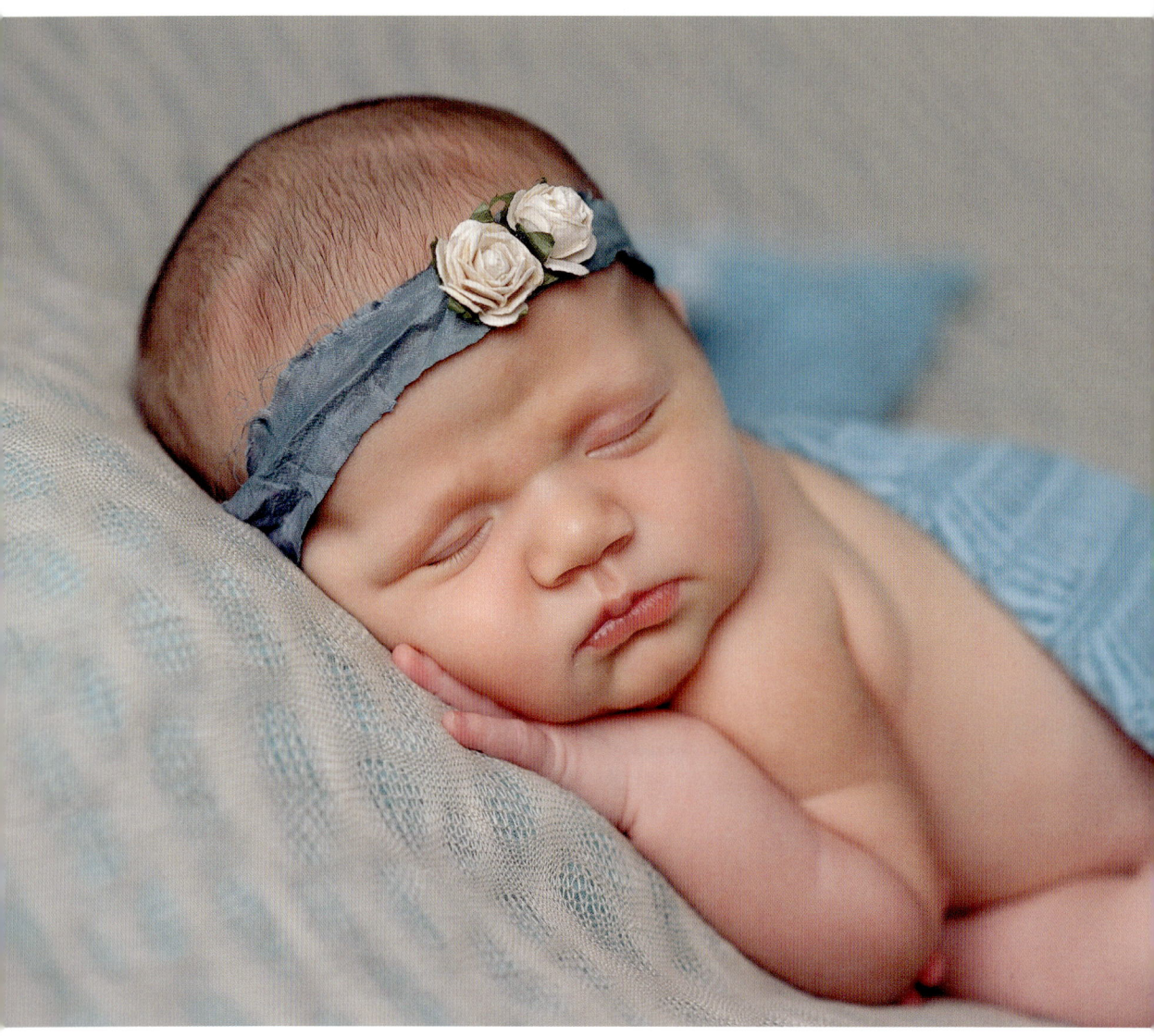

BRYNLEE

"When I felt her move for the first time, it was amazing. I had read all about the fluttering feelings, and it was the best feeling ever when I felt them myself."

—Kayla, mom of Brynlee, born August 1st, 2013

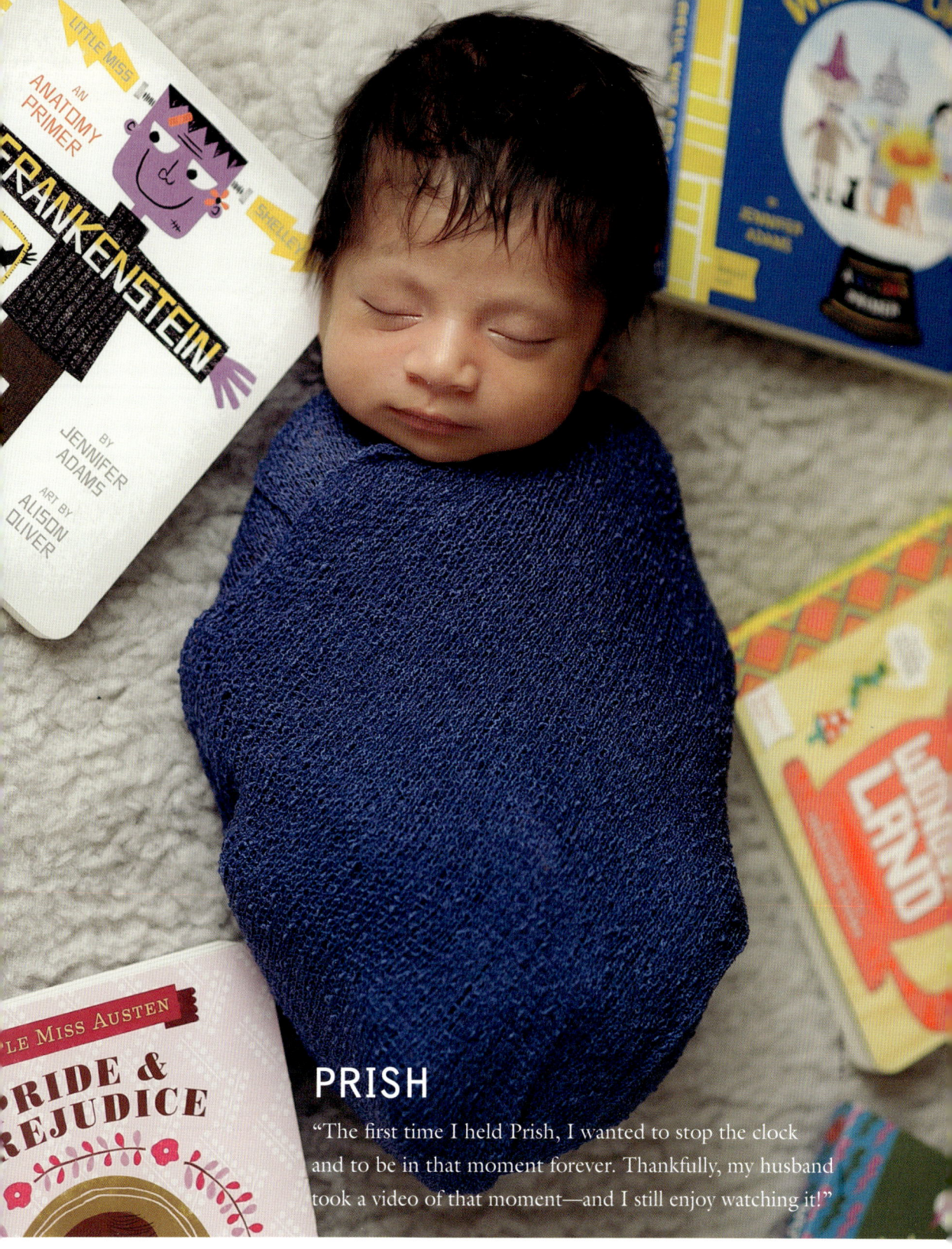

PRISH

"The first time I held Prish, I wanted to stop the clock and to be in that moment forever. Thankfully, my husband took a video of that moment—and I still enjoy watching it!"

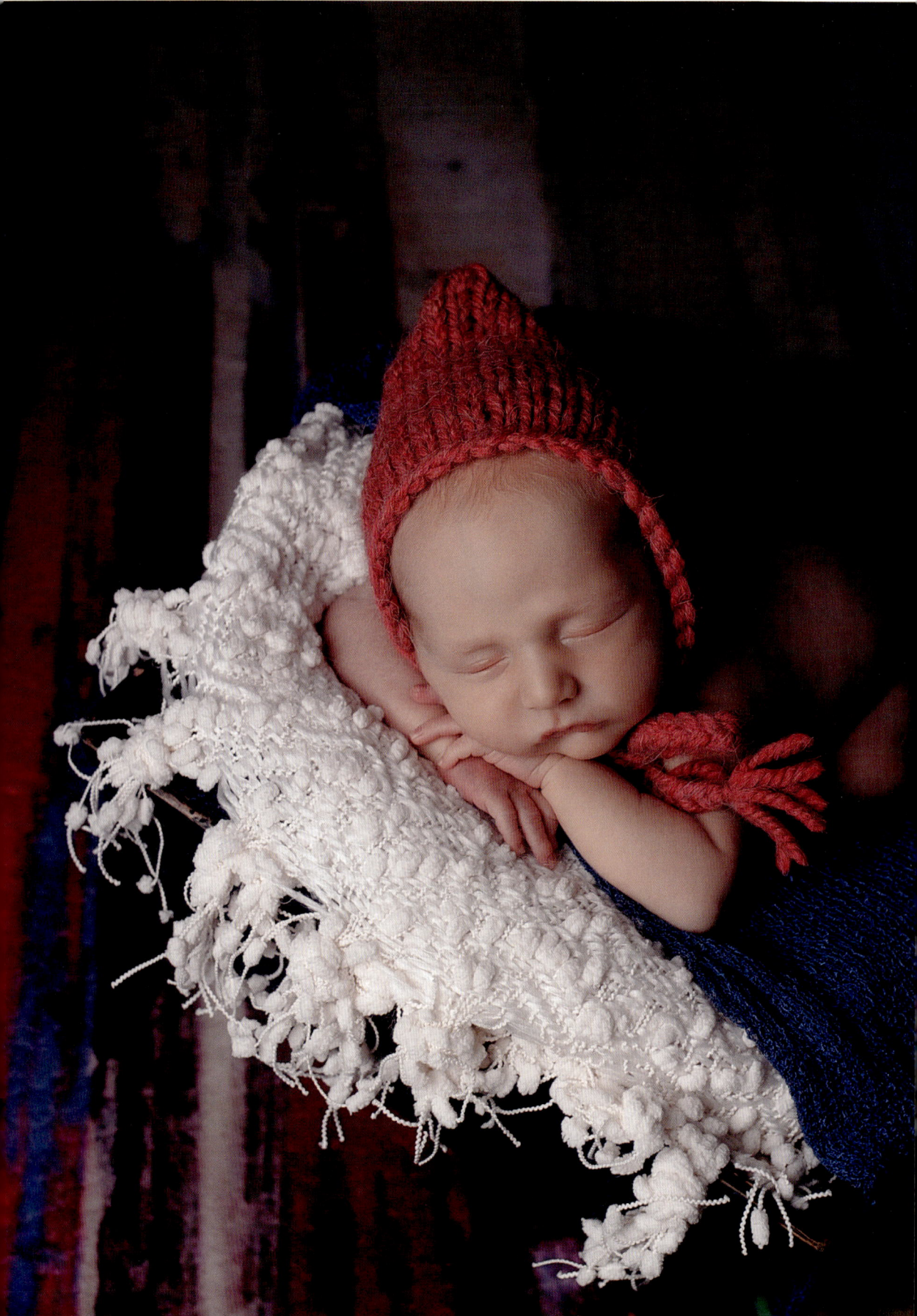

EVAN

"I was thankful that there was a heartbeat. It was rough the first couple of weeks. They couldn't find it. All they could see was a sac. The doctor asked if I wanted a D & C when they didn't find anything the first time I went in. I told them no, I wanted to wait. Two weeks later, we finally heard it. I was so thankful for that little heartbeat."

—Victoria, mom of Evan,
born February 23rd, 2015

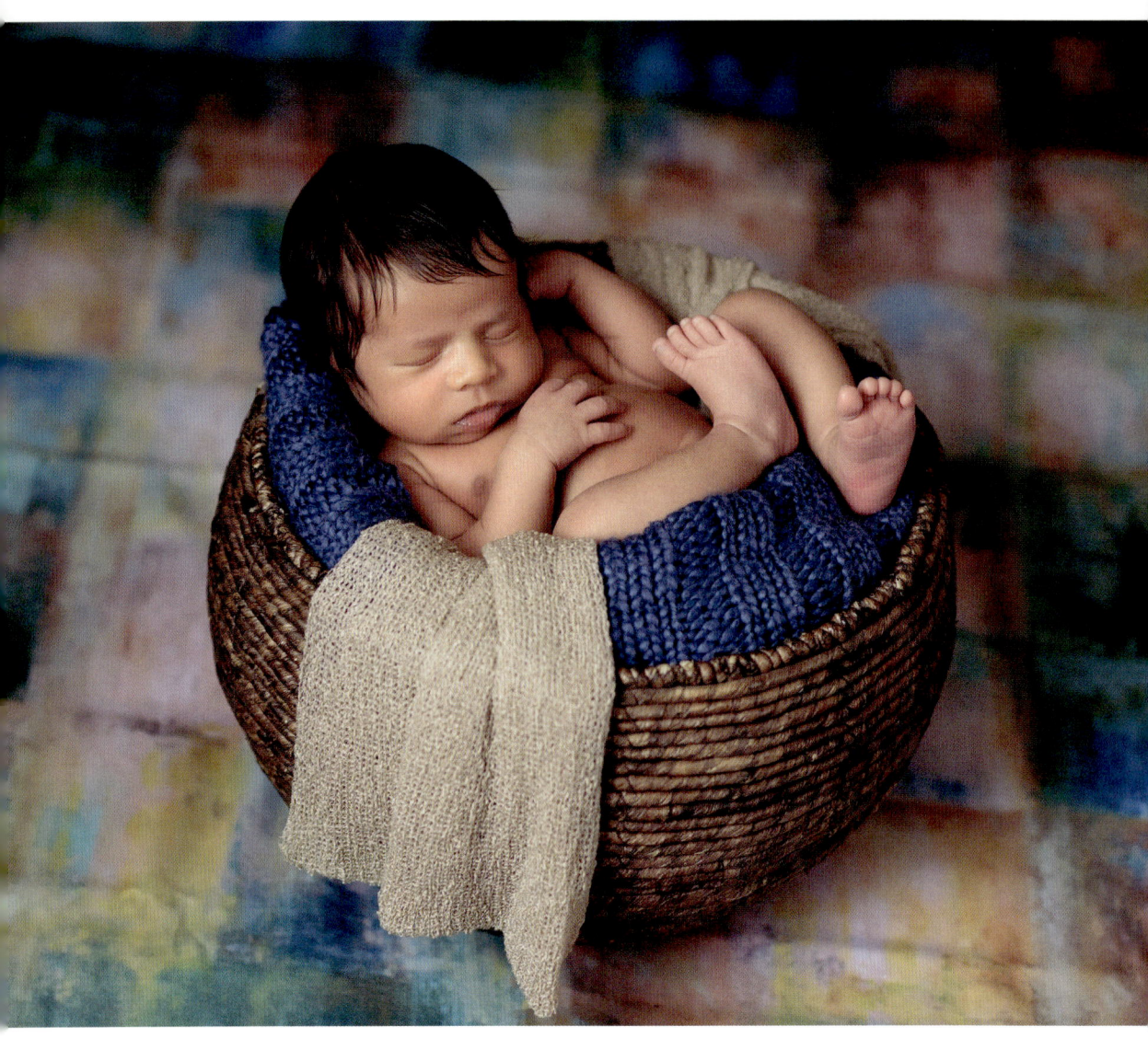

AGNEIV

"The moment I found out I was pregnant, my whole world changed. I had already started to love the tiny one growing within me."

—Susmita, mom of Agneiv, born November 13th, 2015

MASON

"When I heard his heartbeat for the first time, it didn't seem real—it all seemed like a dream. But when I saw him on ultrasound for the first time, I cried!"

—Addi, mom of Mason, born June 30th, 2013

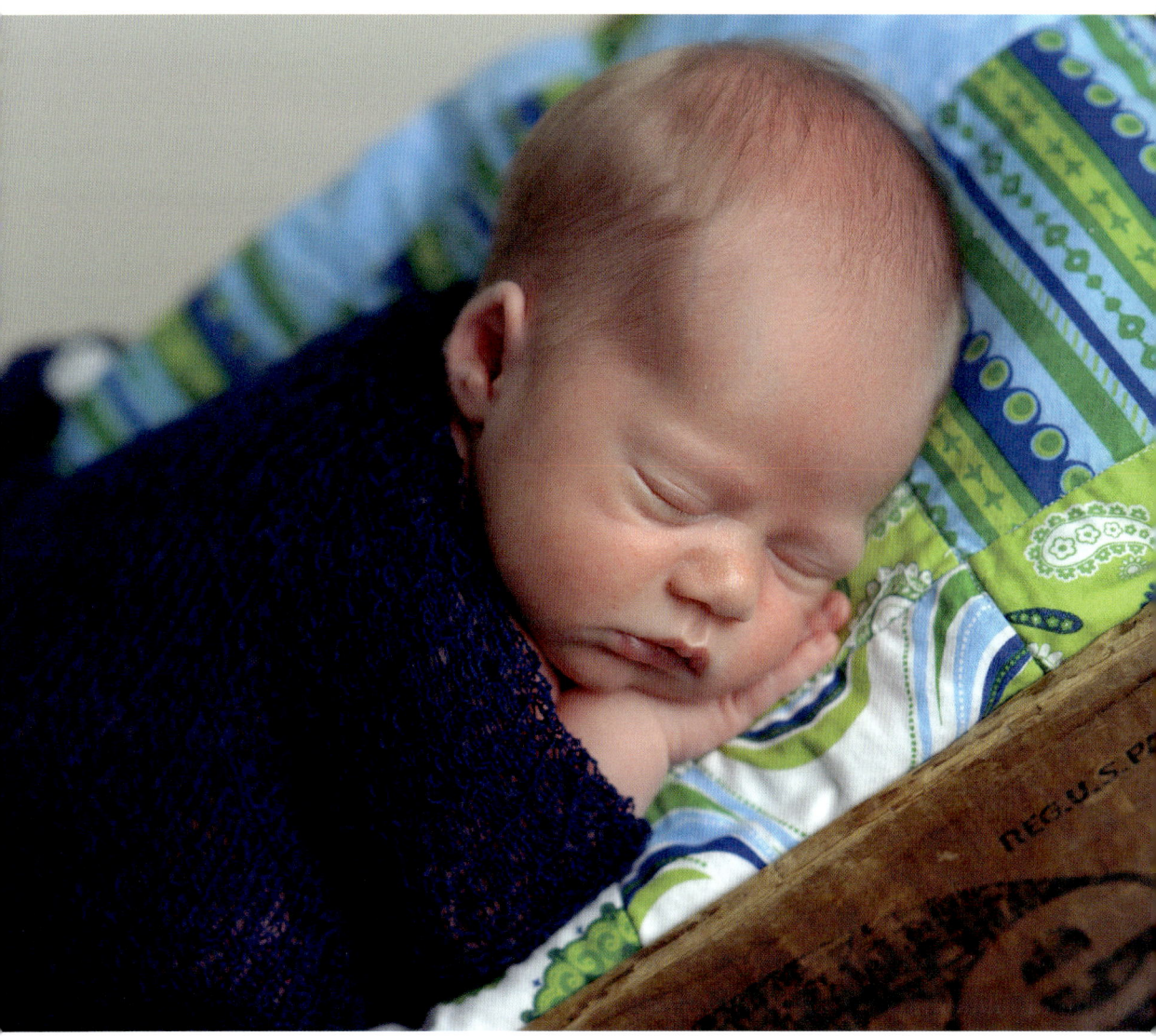

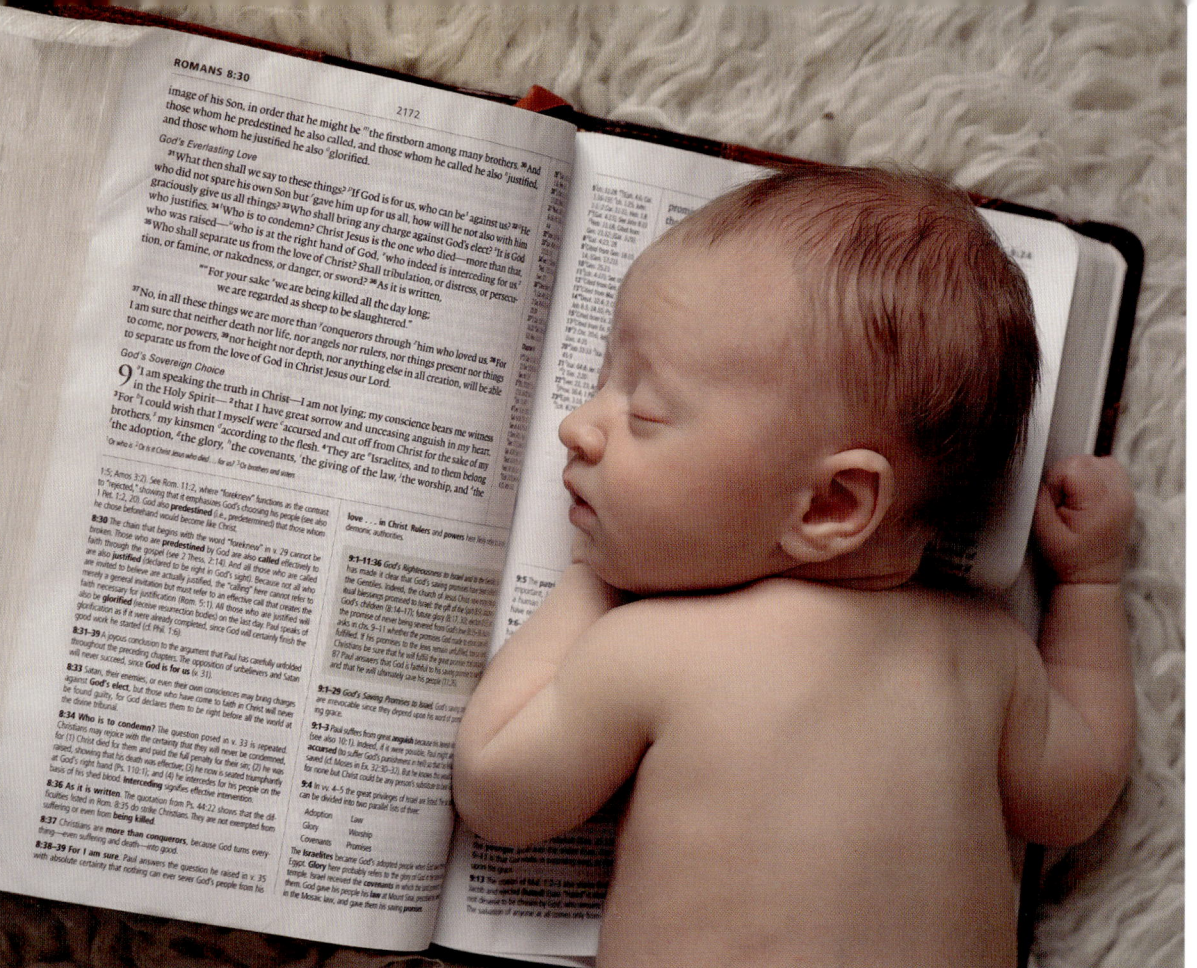

Index

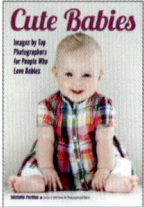

Cute Babies

Relax your mind and renew your sense of optimism by perusing this heartwarming collection of precious faces and tiny features. *$24.95 list, 7x10, 128p, 500 color images, index, order no. 2173.*

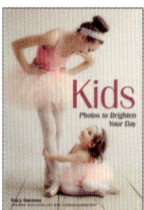

Kids
PHOTOS TO BRIGHTEN YOUR DAY

Tracy Sweeney captures the joy, moods, and relationships of childhood in this magical book. *$24.95 list, 7x10, 128p, 180 color images, index, order no. 2182.*

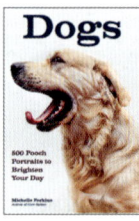

Dogs 500 POOCH PORTRAITS
TO BRIGHTEN YOUR DAY

Lighten your mood and boost your optimism with these sweet and silly images of beautiful dogs and adorable puppies. *$19.95 list, 7x10, 128p, 500 color images, index, order no. 2177.*

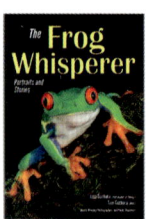

The Frog Whisperer
PORTRAITS AND STORIES

Tom and Lisa Cuchara's book features fun and captivating frog portraits that will delight amphibian lovers. *$24.95 list, 7x10, 128p, 350 color images, index, order no. 2185.*

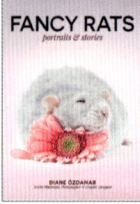

Fancy Rats
PORTRAITS & STORIES

Diane Özdamar shows you the sweet and snuggly side of rats—and stories that reveal their funny personalities. *$24.95 list, 7x10, 128p, 200 color images, index, order no. 2186.*

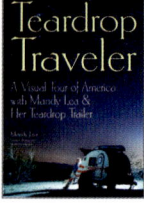

Teardrop Traveler

Photographer Mandy Lea left her job for life on the road—and along the way, captured both life lessons and incredible images of America. *$24.95 list, 7x10, 128p, 200 color images, index, order no. 2187.*

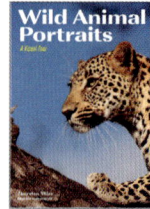

Wild Animal Portraits

Acclaimed wildlife photographer Thorsten Milse takes you on a world tour, sharing his favorite shots and the stories behind them. *$24.95 list, 7x10, 128p, 200 color images, index, order no. 2190.*

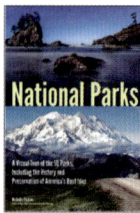

National Parks

Take a visual tour through all 59 of America's National Parks, exploring the incredible histories, habitats, and creatures these lands preserve. *$24.95 list, 7x10, 128p, 375 color images, index, order no. 2193.*

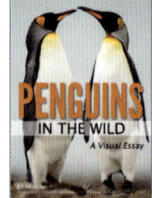

Penguins in the Wild
A VISUAL ESSAY

Joe McDonald's incredible images and stories take you inside the lives of these beloved animals. *$24.95 list, 7x10, 128p, 200 color images, index, order no. 2195.*

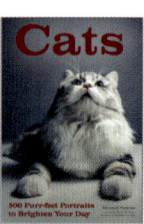

Cats 500 PURR-FECT PORTRAITS
TO BRIGHTEN YOUR DAY

Lighten your mood and boost your optimism with these sweet and fiesty images of beautiful cats and adorable kitten. *$24.95 list, 7x10, 128p, 200 color images, index, order no. 2197.*